"Have you ever wondered: 'How could she get through all that?' or 'What is schizophrenia really like?' This book answers both questions with a strong woman's experience. Writing with a rare kind of honesty, Maxene Kleier describes her life from experiencing a pleasant childhood on a Virginia dairy farm, to marrying a doctor and having his imperfect child while he was in World War II, to moving to Florida and discovering that two of her treasured daughters suffered from schizophrenia, which showed up in their teens. Kleier details the efforts made to treat schizophrenia; the discouragement and the lack of knowledge about the disease. She does not flinch from the heartbreak she experienced when she finds her daughter Jyl murdered. For all its horror, this book has poignancy and a beauty that are heightened by its authenticity. Kleier is an extraordinary woman. Her credentials include efforts to create new treatment options and to change mental health laws to protect the sufferer and society; yet in this book she shares her personal story. A must-read for health professionals as well as for the general reader."—**Elsa McKeithan, Ph.D.,** author of *Writing the Stories of your Life, How to Turn Memories into Memoir.*

"In *Possessed Mentalities*, Maxene Kleier has written with great honesty and insight about the most difficult of subjects. Her work is a tribute to the regenerative powers of the human spirit to overcome what should destroy it. Hers is an unflinching look at heartbreak and the ultimate horror a mother can face—the death of a daughter at the hands of another daughter. Hers is a fascinating story, a healing story, a triumph of the best a human being has to offer."—**Pamela Uschuk,** Director of the Salem College Center for Women Writers and author of *One-Legged Dancer* and *Scattered Risks.*

Possessed Mentalities

Possessed Mentalities

Maxene Obenschain Kleier

To
Fern County Public
Library
Maxene Obenschain Kleier

iUniverse, Inc.
New York Lincoln Shanghai

Possessed Mentalities

iUniverse books may be ordered through booksellers or by contacting:

iUniverse
2021 Pine Lake Road, Suite 100
Lincoln, NE 68512
www.iuniverse.com
1-800-Authors (1-800-288-4677)

ISBN-13: 978-0-595-34436-9 (pbk)
ISBN-13: 978-0-595-79928-2 (cloth)
ISBN-13: 978-0-595-79196-5 (ebk)
ISBN-10: 0-595-34436-4 (pbk)
ISBN-10: 0-595-79928-0 (cloth)
ISBN-10: 0-595-79196-4 (ebk)

Printed in the United States of America

Contents

INTRODUCTION

One day at the capitol in Tallahassee during the 1987 legislative session, I was lobbying for some issue or other, sitting by the desk of Laura Brock, Policy Coordinator for Health and Human Services in Governor Martinez's Office of Planning and Budgeting. Laura said to me, "Go home. You need to write down all the things you say." With that she opened her desk drawer and handed me a small tape recorder. "There; you can talk into this even while you are driving around."

I did begin to talk into the recorder, and I did feel inspired to get serious about writing a book. I had considered being a writer since I was twelve years old, but my life experiences and unexpected tasks had demanded too much of my time and energies until 2002. My topic ideas when I was twelve are not the same as those I write about in *Possessed Mentalities*. My adult life experiences have replaced childhood experiences with the facts of life. Now at last, I have time to write. I have time to take a nostalgic reverie-walk through my life—a pleasant walk that is rarely interspersed with painful recalls of traumatic, nightmarish events.

The walk is
dedicated to
Jyl Stuart Obenschain
(1947–1973) who loved
everyone, and who
wished for everyone
a fulfilling life.

For me, survival skills to manage traumatic challenges began with a less-than-traumatic sexual molestation when I was seven years old. The horrors of World War II, my son's death, my husband's cruel harassment by a few unethical politicians, mental illnesses within our family, and the ultimate nightmare, my daughter Jyl's murder, and my husband's death happened later. These later experiences were truly traumatic.

When they removed the life supports from my first husband, Jack, before he died on February 3, 1976, our youngest daughter, Jan, and I were the only survivors from our family of five remaining to live in the real world. Jack never recovered from a diabetic coma that occurred during surgery to remove a diseased kidney.

Traumatic experiences have offered me an education that has created within me a compelling conscience to share with others knowledge that I wish had been known to me many years ago.

ACKNOWLEDGMENTS

I wish I could remember every kind encouraging word or every issue that someone has asked that I write about: I cannot. But here are some whom I wish to thank for their gifts of compassionate support, faith, and sometimes an understanding, of my compulsion to write Possessed Mentalities.

Betty Adam	Pat Brown
Catherine Allen	Beverly Burnsed
Ella Rose Allen	Baldwin Bunkley
Helen and Carter Allen	Vickie Byrnes
Nancy and George Appun	Rod Cardiff
Carol and J. L. Barksdale	Dominic Calabro
Bennie Barnes	Dennis Carroccio
Tom Batchelor	Suzanne Casey
Budd and Bill Bell	Lea Chavez
Paul Belcher	Anne and Jim Ciotti
JoAnn Bernas	Jim Clark
Cynde Bostick	Dee and Lauren Corr
Anna Briggs	Gene Costlow
Jack Briggs	Neil Crispo
Laura Brock	Janet Crowe

Fely Curva

Brenda and Fred Daily

Debby Daily

Tim Daily

Helen Dann

Buzz Dawbarn

Penny Dechert

Lynn Dickson

Peter Digre

Polly and Dick Dillander

Evelyn Driver

Joyce Dunaway

Naneki Elliot

Kitty and Jerone Ellis

Wanda Evans

Joella and Don Falkingham

Ed Feaver

Sara Fincher

Kenneth Fischer

Donna Fraleigh

Cathie and Tom Herndon

Joanne Hobbs

Martha Holton

Brenda Frank

Marie and Charles French

Ginny Funkhouser

June Garber

Hayley Gardner

Bill Garvin

Chris Gilmore

Shirley Giraudo

Kathy Goltry

Philip Gould

Ted Granger

Margaret Gullette

John Hall

Kelly Hall

Mimi Hamilton

Marta Hardy

Margaret and Lacy Harwell

Virginia Hawfield

Betty and Robert Hendron

Emily Hendron

Midge Kleier

Gwenie Lawson

Shellie Levin

Jim Howell

Virginia and Tom Howze

Steve Hull

Mary Kirk Huske

Virginia Laird Jackson

Jeanne Jackson

Melissa Jacoby

Anne Kaye

Ellen Kellam

Hazel Kersch

Jane and Bob Kibler

Bettie and Jack Kleier

JoAnn and Frank Kleier

Joyce and Michael Kleier

Lacey Kleier

Karen and Dick Kleier

Melody and Steve Kleier

David Pingree

Carol and David Pedley

Larry Pedley

Larry Polifka

Mary and Jimmy Powell

Diana Ramsdell (Hull)

Val Richards

Bill Lindner

Domenick Maglio

Ron Manessa

Rosemary MacIllwaine

Wallace McAllister

Lynn and Rich McCreary

Becky McGann

Agnes Messimer

Peter Mitchell

Betty Moody

Betty Morganroth

Nancy Jeffries Obenschain

Sam Obenschain

Leanne O'Keefe

Larry Overton

Jan Owen

Bob Pierce

Mary and Donald Shank

Nancy Shank

Romaine and Ben Shank

Sid Shapiro

Rowe and Jack Sharpe

Judy and Phil Sieg

Geraldine Simpson

Gina Richardson

Emmett Roberts

Glenn Robertson

Edgar Rodgers

Barbara and Tom Rothchild

John Rothchild

Nina and Kennon Rothchild

Jill Sandler

Chris Schuh

Betty and Bob Shank

Dave Shank

Harriette and Charles Shank

John Shank

Sara Tyndall

Pamela Uschuk

Patty VanArsdale

June Vernon

Debbie Walters

Shirley Warner

Doris and Jim Sipe

Jerry Slavens

Alicia Smith

Victor Smith

Kitty and George Snead

George Snider

Nancy and Bob Storm

Bill Steed III

Martha Steed

Sue and Dan Sutherland

Jo Ann and Walt Szelogavski

William Thomas III

Fuller Torrey

Nancy and Glenn Wayland

Bob Watts

Bev Whiddon

Tamara Wilson

Bob Zigler

SPECIAL THANKS

Kenneth Kleier
for expertise and patient encouragement.

Elsa McKeithan
for invaluable editing assistance.

Thomas Powell
for professional manuscript submission assistance
and website construction.

1992-1996 CCMS staff for caring.

Education Under an Apple Tree

As an only child, I lived the first seven years of my life surrounded by beautiful rolling countryside on a one-hundred-twenty-acre farm where peacocks sometimes roamed. It was enthralling to watch the vain male birds strut while pluming their tail feathers. Mother told me that they were trying to look their best because they wanted to attract female peacocks to be their wives.

This nostalgic refuge from the world lies about five miles northeast of Edom, a hamlet in the Shenandoah Valley of Virginia. Edom, when we drove there on country roads, was about a five-mile trip, two miles not yet macadamized, from our farm. I went either in a car driven by my mother or in a horse-drawn buggy with my Mennonite neighbors. It was only about three miles from the farm as the crow flies. The best way to go was to leisurely stroll across pasture fields and by gentle creeks.

I found that farm, my earliest home place, changed when I revisited it in 2002. The white picket fences were gone. The broken window shutters had been taken down and stored. There was a new grass pasture where an apple orchard once graced the view from the house. The baby chick houses were gone. Only the rock foundation and concrete floor of the milk house, where milk and cream were separated and butter was made, remained. The old barn, bare of paint, looked ready to fall apart; it stood ready to topple into the desolate remnants of a lifeless barnyard. There was no vestige of the hen house where I loved to go with Mother to put my small hands beneath the warm bodies of cackling hens to gather eggs. The springhouse and wood house endured only in my mind's eye.

For as long as I can remember, my mind's eye has mirrored scenes and events of my life to create a wonderful stockpile of memory reels in my brain. During the seventy-nine years since I lived on that farm, I have known twenty-four other places of residence in six states and Washington, DC, but

1

the reels of memory of that first home place remain my favorite reels for pleasing reverie.

These pleasing reverie reels contrast sharply with some other reels that examine traumatic events that have occurred during my lifetime. The trauma reels include the trauma-management education that has been absolutely essential for my self-survival. When I bring to mind my comparatively stable early country life, a stage is set for studied reflection when more strident environments threaten to hinder calm reasoning.

I did not have children as playmates. I had Collie, a collie dog, bought as a puppy by Daddy on the day I was born. Collie was my constant companion, and he assigned himself to be my vigilant watchdog. Once Mother heard him barking frantically. She found him standing protectively close to her baby girl in the middle of the rarely traveled dirt road that ran through the farm. I had managed to climb over the high sides of my baby bed during naptime and toddle approximately three hundred feet to the dusty country byway. Collie, standing guard over an errant toddler, and barking as loudly as possible, dog-screamed for Mother's help.

I imagine this early escape from captivity offered a clue to Mother that she should watch over her child more closely in the future. I never have been willing to accept authority or restrictive confinement without silent or articulated protest. It was said of me as a child, "she has a mind of her own." I believe that was true.

Thankfully for me, and for most other people, we do have minds of our own. It might be stated another way. "We own our minds. We own and possess our minds today. Hopefully, we can retain possession and ownership until death." There is no guarantee. Personal ability to possess or own one's mentality is a gift to be cherished and carefully guarded.

Even as a child, I usually resisted any effort to circumvent any freedoms I desired. Even today I always question requests of myself that seem to be illogical or inappropriate. Shouldn't a request from anyone at anytime to another person have integrity? Shouldn't a request seem rational and agreeably doable in keeping with the capabilities and desires of the person from whom a request is asked?

Favorite explorations for me on the farm, always with my companion Collie, took me to the springhouse or to a large sunken area about four feet in diameter in a field adjacent to the house. Near the sunken area, I would spread-eagle face down on the ground, looking as intently as I could, as long as I could, down into a dark chasm that had no bottom that I could fathom.

Mother once laughingly told me not to go near this mysterious sinkhole because I might slip into it and fall down, down, down to a land far away. She thereby created for me an inexhaustible curiosity about an orb called Earth. My fantasy that I might see Chinese with pigtails flying as they ran about on the other side of the world was never satisfied. However, the curiosity was not enduring enough or strong enough to make me a serious geography student. By the time geography was introduced in my classrooms, I was old enough to have found boys more exciting and interesting than twirling globes.

Collie preferred another adventure. We would go to the springhouse where I stretched out on the rough rock floor to put my face just above the serenely flowing cold, clear water. Foods were kept fresh there in covered pottery crocks immersed in the chilly water. I peered into the water at the crayfish that seemed to swim aimlessly back and forth in search of something they seemed never to find. I always laughed when Collie flashed a paw toward one of these intriguing, swift-moving, little crustaceans. Their horned eyes, ever watchful for their safety, were faster than Collie's paw. The crayfish always scooted safely away.

Mother never knew about these little adventures and flights of fancy, which made them doubly exciting. Almost every day while she napped, I defied her admonitions and sneaked out to one or both forbidden sites to see whether Chinese children had shown up or whether crayfish had finally decided to move around with some kind of logical purpose or direction.

Mother never realized I was looking for Chinese people or studying crayfish because I always made certain to be busy creating outfits for my paper dolls, looking at books, or being innocently busy with some other approved activity when she woke up from her routine afternoon nap. Her nap afforded me wonderful, secret freedoms. She trusted me too much. I treasured that trust, and I never intended to violate her faith in me in any dangerous way; yet, as a child, of course, I did not understand what could be dangerous for me.

Mother kept me close by her side or within ear shot most of the time, which caused me to feel constrained. As a carefree, fun-loving child, I had secret, overpowering escape tendencies that always wanted fulfillment. A taller, stronger person towering over me and deciding what was best for me was annoying, and much of the time that heightened my inherent urge to fly free. Today I still think of the butterfly as symbolic of my inner self.

There's one adventure I don't remember—that of being carried by Daddy across the rutted, dusty dirt road that ran between the barn and house when he and Mother went to milk the cows. From tales told to me when I was older, I know that they took me with them even when it was very cold, when I was just a baby, and later when I was a toddler. They wrapped me in blankets and, while they milked, they perched me high up on an old rock wall that surrounded the milking stalls. Sometimes Daddy would playfully turn a cow's teat and squirt milk toward me to hear me laugh.

I was a child of laughter. Mother told me about my first spontaneous outburst of laughter. She even recorded it in my baby book. She was changing my diaper when I was only seven weeks old, she told me, when she stepped back in amazement as she listened enthralled to the sudden, hearty laughter being emitted, for no apparent reason, from a small bundle of infant femininity.

Perhaps there is within me some unexplained bubble of joy, announced by that seven-week-old baby's demonstration of its presence, which stands me in good stead today. I am fortunate never to have known more than moments of depression. That is not to say that global, national, state, community, and personal tragedies never deeply challenge my state of contentment and happiness, which I choose to maintain. My ability to prevent possession of my mind by anything other than myself is a daily awareness. Every day when I wake up, I note my ability to maintain possession of my mentality, and I appreciate it spiritually.

Later I will talk about some traumatic challenges. Sometimes it takes conscious, steeled determination to keep my joy bubble intact. I believe my memory reels are helpful in this. Some of them, when called upon, help protect me from pity-me despair. It is realistic to know that no one lives long enough to see all the beauties of earth, sea, and sky; to hear all of the inspirational music that exists; or to read all of the educational and entertaining literature that has been written. I have lived long enough to have heard more wonderful music, to have read more wonderful written words, and to have traveled to find more sights to see than have many others. While participating in all of these activities, I have consciously developed an automatic ability to discover beauty and joy during most of my waking hours. No matter where I am or under what circumstances, listening and learning from others and from the world around me are exciting intellectual and emotional exercises that I find stimulating and essential for self-preservation. For me such habitual searching has been crucial to survival of the minor and major traumas during my lifetime. Why should any person, whose self owns a mentality, prefer to see or to absorb the less exciting or less uplifting stimuli that exist wherever (or however) one may be?

In 1922, when I was three years old, tenants came to work on the farm, leaving my father, David Shank, free to go to Harrisonburg to work as manager and treasurer of the Valley of Virginia Cooperative Milk Producers, Inc. He helped solicit and organize dairy farmers into cooperative ownership of that company. When I was older, I asked him whether he ever regretted that he had not, when the business faltered at one time, borrowed money to buy the business. He smiled and said that he wanted the farmers up and down the Shenandoah Valley to be the benefactors. When Shenandoah's Pride was sold to a company in Texas for one hundred ten million dollars some years ago, many farmers in the Shenandoah Valley were enriched. My father's dreams had come to final fruition. He had successfully contributed to the welfare of many people by his dedicated devotion to them and by his loyalty to the dairy industry through the years. He left a valuable legacy to the cooperative farmers. He succeeded, as he had wished to, in making possible better lives for others.

He spent half of many weeks in Washington, where he brokered milk and kept himself informed about legislative issues. I doubt that he ever discussed it with many people, but he told me when I was a teenager that he did not believe that milk commissions should regulate the dairy industry or that other tax-free cooperatives should be commission regulated. Rightly or wrongly, he felt that he was capable of operating the business on the basis of supply and demand. He did not believe that the taxpayer should shoulder the fiscal responsibilities of businesses. He could see no good end in sight for that practice. He wondered aloud to me about fairness to the taxpayer, about where it would end, and about how much of that sort of thing our national economy would finally be able to tolerate.

My father's portrait is no longer on the wall in the reception area of the plant. It now hangs in the dining room of our summer home in Bloomfield, Kentucky. The milk trucks may no longer be white. The product name, Shenandoah's Pride, painted in black on those gleaming white trucks probably is no longer seen on city streets. I remember the company paying twenty-five dollars to a lady, Mrs. Gilmore, in 1926, when she won a contest for suggesting the name "Shenandoah's Pride."

The changes at the plant are credited to an accepted thing called "progress." Progress can be a painful, stifling experience to longtime employees and to their community. Loss of longtime pride of places and people can demoralize a community, in my opinion. Progress without heart contributes to dehumanization of an area and diminishes bonds between businesses and folks. I think the heart of Shenandoah's Pride may be gone. I think I may feel that way because so much of my young life was intertwined with and affected by "the plant" that absorbed so much of my Daddy's time.

Tenants and farm hands took over the farm's manual tasks. My father disliked the hard physical farm work so much that he happily left the farm to develop another career. After he began traveling to sell the plant's products, my mother became almost a single mom. When she had been a small child and teenager, her only task at home had been to make her own bed and to fill the lamps with oil every Saturday. I never heard her complain about our farm tasks until many years later when she spoke with some chagrin of being poor on our farm. I suspect she was looking ahead to an exciting life in the city when she had daringly taken that train "out west" to marry Dave in 1917.

I knew, though my father became very preoccupied with business, that I was loved and considered special by both my parents. I never doubted that. From hearing some adults speak about the parenting they received, I know that the stork was kind to me.

Christmas was the highlight of my year. Christmas seasons were enhanced with wonderful presents and trips with Mother to a small, wooden church, painted stark white, on Route 42. Edom Methodist Church's hard oak pews did not deter my rapt attention or delight as I sat through hymns and sermons feeling smugly secure amidst caring Methodists.

The farm was where, at Christmas, my loving parents first lavished secular and religious holiday spirits on me. My father was around the house more. I was the center of attention. Neighbors and family members dropped by to talk, laugh, and enjoy Christmas goodies. The big range in the kitchen and the pot-bellied stove and fireplace in the living room were warm and glowing. It was a time to celebrate peace and goodwill toward all. A gleeful little girl found everyone and everything happening around her exhilarating and intriguing.

One Christmas, after I no longer believed that St. Nick with his eight tiny reindeer really did come with presents on Christmas Eve, my doting parents told me that they had had someone dress as Santa on an earlier Christmas Eve and come to visit me personally. I had been so entranced by that visit that I forgot to ask where Donner, Blitzen, and the rest of the reindeer team were hiding. I feel certain that I took for granted that Santa's sleigh was parked in the apple orchard near the house. I feel just as confident that, as I went to sleep with sugarplums dancing in my head, I heard sleigh bells ring as the sleigh rose to the sky without Rudolph. Rudolph had not been born when

Santa Claus came down the chimney that exciting 1923 Christmas Eve. Rudolph with his red nose belongs to later generations.

For me, not to question was unusual. I remember Daddy laughing once when asking his very young daughter if she could for the rest of the day not one more time ask "why." I now know that asking why, aside from research projects, does not indicate great intelligence when there are no known answers. Research projects exist to look for unknown answers to well-formulated questions. Irrational questions are best not asked unless the usual failure to get sensible answers can be accepted with good humor.

Walking to Edom with my cousin Richard was another adventure for me. He often came to visit our grandmother who lived just about a mile down the dusty road from our farm. Going to buy candy and talk with the Edom storekeeper provided multiple treats. The store was not very large, but it was stocked full of wonderful candies, cookies, school supplies, and hardware. Interesting people loafed around the pot-bellied stove. The store aisles were almost impassable because of the open barrels filled with candies, nails, or whatever else might be needed or wanted by Rockingham County folks. The trips to Edom provided exploration and examination of my territory; they offered friendship and wholesome entertainment, and they gave me a chance to hear what folks outside my small world had to say.

Richard and I felt privileged to be allowed, at our tender years, to walk alone without adult supervision, through farm fields, alongside creeks, and, for a short distance, on a macadamized road to Edom. Once when he went to ask permission from his mother, my Aunt Maud, I heard her say to our grandmother that he seemed to think of things when with Maxene that he would never think of without her suggestions. I thought then, and I know now, that she underestimated his creative spirit. I resented the implication that I might be an unfavorable influence. She probably saw me as a threat to her grim determination that Richard would become as dedicated as she to her straitlaced Mennonite religion.

Once when Richard very cleverly managed to build and hide a radio in the attic of their home near Waynesboro, Virginia, she found it and smashed it to pieces. His broken dream was left lying there in the cold attic for him to find. He cried alone over the shattered radio parts he held cradled in his talented hands. In those days Mennonites taught that radios were instruments of the Devil to teach their children ways to stray from the narrow pathways of the Mennonite religion. I felt sad and hurt for Richard, and I deeply resented Aunt Maud for what she had done.

Aunt Maud, an only sister to three brothers, lived aloof from the ways of her worldly, sophisticated siblings. She devoutly followed the Mennonite religion that my maternal grandmother, reared in the Church of the Brethren, had embraced when she fell in love with and married John Shank, a young and handsome Mennonite. Maud's brothers, Ben, David (my father), and John, were never baptized as Mennonites. Their Anabaptist ancestors in Switzerland had become political refugees because of their insistence on adult baptism that differed from Martin Luther's belief in infant baptism. When these young American Shank men became adults, they usually took seemingly irreligious routes, though they sometimes did seek religious routes.

The three brothers were separated when mere babies. Their father, a farmer and schoolteacher, was dragged and trampled in the field by a team of runaway horses. Grandmother somehow got the bloody, wounded man to the house. She then rode a horse furiously for about three miles from their home into Broadway to get help. She did not know to leave him unmoved until help could be summoned. Telephones had only recently been invented; and they were not yet available in homes. And, of course, our taken-for-granted-911 did not exist for her to quickly summon help.

There was no relief from pain for the hideously injured man. His days of suffering and death were like pages from a book of horrors, related to me many times by different Mennonites through the years. My father seldom went to reunions of the Mennonite Shanks because of the emotions he felt when they brought up his father's tragic, early death, which they inevitably reviewed for him.

Before he died, my grandfather, John Shank, asked his brother, Lewis, who lived in Broadway and had no children, whether he would help my grandmother raise his children. My grandmother, pregnant with Maud, could see no alternative from inside her overwhelming grief but to let the two younger boys go to live with their Uncle Lewis and Aunt Mattie, his wife.

Lewis was a Mennonite preacher at that time, but by the time I came to know him, he had become a revered bishop. He was an icon of good and Godly demeanor to the Mennonites in his district. To me, he was a menacing force opposed to fun and frolic.

For the two little boys, Lewis and Mattie were in many ways the epitome of bad parenting. Lewis truly believed that to spare the rod was to spoil the child. On rainy Saturdays he would take the little boys to an outbuilding shed and spank them for an accumulation of acts he perceived as bad things they had done. From the tales I heard when the uncles came to visit from Minneapolis and got together with my father, I think some punishment was at times warranted, but not the random shed beatings. All of his life my father disliked rainy Saturdays. He might laugh about the old bishop with his adult brothers, but no one else was allowed to make fun or say anything derogatory. Daddy and his younger brother John felt great loyalty and appreciation for the moderately good life that Daddy Lewis and Mother Mattie afforded them in a relatively prosperous home.

Their mother, my real paternal grandmother, met and married C.T. Myers a few years after the death of her beloved John. C.T. was a disgrace to his good family name and a scourge to the world. His banker and veterinarian brothers were not fond of him, and relationships between him and them were practically nonexistent. Both brothers lived in Harrisonburg, and, I feel confident, shared with me an ongoing distaste when seeing C.T., rigidly astride his horse, riding down Main Street and chewing tobacco. Spittoons and tobacco chewing were commonplace, but, when he chewed, it seemed somehow more repugnant than when kinder and friendlier men did it. Tobacco chewing was acceptable to the valley population in those days. Shiny brass spittoons, antique treasures today, stood in bank lobbies, on the streets, and wherever tobacco-chewing citizens were likely to be found. Spittoons, despised by my mother, were socially acceptable everywhere when I was a child.

Once when I was walking down Harrisonburg's Main Street with one of my friends, C.T. came riding by. My friend laughed and exclaimed, "Oh, look at that funny man in the street on horseback." I replied, "He is not funny. He is not a very nice person, and he is my step-grandfather." Then we both laughed and dismissed C.T. from further consideration or discussion.

The grim-faced, unpleasant C.T. abused my grandmother emotionally in many ways. He would sit silently and stare coldly at her and at her family and friends whenever they were unfortunate enough to be near him. He loved his horse, but human beings seemed as repugnant to him as he was to them. I never see a baseball player with a tobacco lump disfiguring his face but that I remember the grossness of C.T. I also bemoan the mentor image of tobacco or snuff-using baseball players, who irresponsibly convey to millions of adoring, impressionable children, teenagers, and adults, such undesirable and unhealthy habits.

When I was taken as a little girl to visit Granddaddy Lewis in Broadway, I always made as many trips to the indoor bathroom as possible. It was such a treat. The two-hole, uncomfortable outdoor facility on our farm was hot in the summer and cold in the winter. I still remember the odor of the lime bucket and scoop for dumping lime down through the necessary openings to prevent odors and bacterial production. Indoor bathrooms with flush toilets were rarely found on farms in those days. The comparative luxury of my bathroom trips mellowed my overexposure to prayers and accusatory scripture quotes from Granddaddy Lewis. He loved the sound of his own melodious voice, and he was always ready with holy lectures for his small, then teenage, and finally adult, unrepentant step-grandchild.

My father's marriage to my Methodist mother represented a Mennonite's lost battle for a needy soul. The bishop paid my father fifty cents every time he dated a Mennonite girl. One time when Daddy was out earning date money to get a little extra cash to spend on Mother, he and a young Mennonite girl came riding down the road in a buggy toward Mother's home. When the horse got to the hitching post in front of the house, it stopped and refused to move. Mother, watching from behind curtains within the house with her sister Mary, was having a wonderfully hilarious time watching as Daddy took out the horsewhip and tried to get the horse to move along. Finally a puzzled horse and, I suspect, a puzzled young Mennonite girl, went rolling away, much to the amused sisters' dismay. They thoroughly enjoyed the complete frustration of Mother's suitor.

When I knew Granddaddy Lewis, he had a beautiful mane of flowing white hair, and he loved nothing better than to tilt his handsome head back and quote from the Holy Bible. He was a picturesque figure. He was not a stupid person; he was just narrow-minded and self-righteous. Aside from his ministerial duties, he managed a successful farm and winery while the boys were growing up. He taught himself to speak and write German. Lewis's intellect was of admirable quality, but his knowledge of child psychology was sorely lacking.

Mother, who grew up on a farm just outside Broadway, told me that my father David and his brother John were never allowed to play with other children at school. At lunchtime they had to walk up the always-rocky-and-some-times-muddy lane from the school and across a covered bridge in full view of their schoolmates to go home for lunch and to do farm chores. The farm was actually within the town limits. Other children made fun of the Mennonite brothers when they came back to school after lunch with horse manure on their shoes.

Ben, the oldest brother, who grew up with his biological mother and his sister Maud, went west when he became old enough to live independently. When his younger brothers received small inheritances left them by their father, Ben returned to Virginia to entice them to leave the valley and come with him to the West, as Horace Greeley had advised young men to do around the turn of the Twentieth Century. The three of them left Virginia with cash and thoughts of freedom in their hearts. Their first stop was at a vaudeville show in West Virginia. My father bought a pair of gold cuff links with small diamonds that he gave to me years later. They are treasures that are indicative to me of his rejection of a religion and childhood that thwarted his creative, bubbling spirits.

On Sundays Daddy dutifully took Mother and me to see the bishop and Mattie. My brothers Donald, seven years younger than I, and Charles, five years younger than Don, did time at the bishop's home also, but for fewer years. I think my brothers have fewer memories than I of the Mennonite traditions practiced there. All week Mattie cooked and prepared for the crowd of people that always came to the house for dinner after church. After Mattie died, Elva, a young Mennonite woman, who came to keep house for the bishop, continued the Sunday tradition. Some ladies brought contributions to the bountiful table, and all had a feast. There were always at least two kinds of meat, many fresh or home-canned vegetables, pickles, homemade bread, and butter, and all kinds of cakes and pies. The men ate first, with the women serving them. Then the women ate. The children ate last. The bishop always got the best piece of meat; Mattie, and later Elva, made certain of that and served him first. I always hoped, and I was never disappointed, that the Mennonites would leave some good things for my mother and me, the two outcast Methodists. Before-meal prayers were long, while the food chilled. Daddy was not in favor of mealtime blessings, but Mother persevered. We had brief blessings at our house for every meal because Daddy insisted that long blessings at mealtime reminded him of cold oatmeal.

The bishop was a true chauvinist, and Mattie was always at his beck and call. Before she went to bed every night, she laid out clean, pressed clothes and hand-polished shoes for him to wear the next day. The bishop spent his time pontificating, reading, writing sermons, visiting church members, and overseeing his farm. He was, in fact, a gentleman farmer and an intellectual in his own right. Mattie was the bishop's handmaiden. I was glad she had to work so hard because I didn't like her. She told me that my mother was a sinner and would probably go to hell because she wore gold jewelry and dressed fancy. When Mattie died as a young woman in 1932, I was not sorry. My vigilant Mennonite antagonist would never reprimand me again for wanting to be worldly like my sinful mother.

When I was about four or five years old, I used to go spend some time with Mattie and Lewis. I trotted around their house wearing a little white net sifter on my head and listened to wondrous praise about Eastern Mennonite College. Although it is an academically well-respected college, it will be forever tainted for me by the evangelistic spiels of Lewis and Mattie. A sifter is a small, white, fitted mesh cap to keep a woman's head covered as decreed, according to Mennonite doctrine, somewhere in the Holy Bible

My solo visits were abruptly discontinued when I came home wanting to wear a sifter, planning to go to Eastern Mennonite College someday, and determined to change my mother's religious philosophies. My mother was not about to allow Mennonite missionary efforts to be successful with her little fledgling. Her daughter was not going to be a Mennonite. Mother never said unkind things about Mattie and Lewis, but she was adamant that their religious beliefs were unacceptable to her. Both of my parents made it very clear that, while I was not to take the Mennonite couple's endless admonitions as to my worldly ways seriously, neither was I to show disrespect. In those days younger people were taught to respect members of the older generation. Younger people stood when their elders entered a room to offer them comfortable seating. They held open doors for their elders, and, in the South, we said, "Yes, ma'am" and "Yes, sir." Such yes and no polite answers were akin to "Amen."

Because of my Dutch haircut, I was often the bishop's Sunday target as he tilted his leonine head back and quoted scripture to affirm that long hair is a glory to woman. This dictum is found in 1 Corinthians, Chapter 11, Verse 15. He had a Scripture ready to support all points of view for anything that came up. I thought his scriptural renderings a useless waste of time, and I let them fly through my head like swift water over a dam. Some, however, are reeled in my memories, and they occasionally pop out to remind me of my heritage and the bishop. Sometimes those reels offer good advice.

The bishop and Mattie lived well. Their house had two side-by-side front doors, one for women, and one for men. It was a comfortable home with its marvelous inside bathroom, a big kitchen with an extra large wood-burning stove, a dining room, two living rooms, and four bedrooms. They had a nice car long before many people owned an automobile. When they bought it, it had a narrow red stripe, barely visible, around the body. Granddaddy Lewis took a tiny paintbrush and laboriously painted the stripe black. I found that giggle-funny. Surely such a tiny stripe would not send anyone to hell.

After they were married, Mother and Daddy lived "out west" in Saint Paul, Minnesota. They rented a one-bedroom apartment. I was conceived there. Daddy pointed the place out to me on a trip that my first husband Jack and I made with him and Mother to Minnesota in 1959.

A few months before I was born, the manager of the Swift meat packing plant where Daddy worked called him in and said, "Young man, I am going to move you here into my office beside my desk and teach you everything I know. We think you can go places with Swift."

Moving into an office after traveling northwestern states as a salesman, inspector, and monitor of far-flung Swift plants was not my father's ideal for a lifetime vocation. He came home and told Mother that he did not want to be forever desk bound, at someone else's beck and call. World War II had ended, and the wheat market was skyrocketing so he decided that he wanted to return to the Shenandoah Valley and make lots of money as an independent wheat farmer.

The company's leaders had told Daddy that they saw him as a "comer," and that his boss had been instructed to bring him into the office so that his training could begin. Daddy, though flattered, was unwilling to listen. He was flabbergasted by the generous offers from Swift. Mother told me that she, in turn, was doubly flabbergasted when he came home and announced that he wanted to go back to Virginia to farm. He informed Mother that he was simply not willing to take orders from other people for the rest of his life. He wanted to be his own boss. He ambitiously dreamed that his family would be better off if he could just get to a Virginia farm to plant and harvest wheat.

The daring young couple, unusual for their time, headed home and moved into Mother's home. Her father, who, as a teenager had lost his own father, had supported his mother, younger siblings, and finally his own family by working hard at many different vocations. He had finally climbed the ladder far enough to be able to own real estate and a general store in downtown Roanoke, Virginia. When Roanoke downtown property appreciated to a value that would allow him to sell with enough profit, he bought an old house near Broadway that he had always coveted. He moved his money and his family about a hundred miles farther north from Roanoke into the valley, just outside Broadway where he felt his heart belonged.

The old house he bought still sits by the North Fork River. Some of Mother's favorite recitations about her home life were wonderful tales of huge bonfires and ice-skating on the river in the winter. As a child and teenager, my mother lived the good life. Household help always took care of cleaning and most of the cooking. There was also outside help to maintain the farm. "Papa," as his children and grandchildren called him, started a roof-tinning business after he moved near Broadway. That business provided employment to others and made still more money for him and his family. His wife Margaret died while Mother was eighteen and away at college. After his wife's death and the departure of his daughters from home, Papa shared his home with Mother's brother John and his family for many years. I loved visiting there when I was a youngster.

So it was that I came to the valley to be born. My name is not Virginia, as my parents had planned before they decided to come back home to begin a family life. Papa bought the farm I would come to love so much; and there, Mother, Daddy, and I, lived happily-not forever after-but until 1926.

After a lifetime of supporting others, Papa now found himself with an adult daughter who was without a home, without money, and with a new baby. He stepped up to the plate as usual by providing temporary shelter for the birthing. Then he bought the farm to offer future shelter for the young family. The farm he bought for us was only about a mile from Daddy's biological Mother's place.

Daddy never really knew his biological mother until he and his pregnant wife came home from the West in 1919. The bishop and Mattie did everything possible to prevent their nephews from knowing their biological siblings Ben and Maud, and their mother. It was not until some child in elementary school blurted out to my father that the bishop was not his father that the two young brothers learned that they were not living with their parents. That cruel taunt by another child never left my father's psyche. He often sent checks to Boy's Town in December when he sat down to write checks that he and the government, Uncle Sam, gave to charities annually.

My grandmother's elderly, blind father, Michael Zigler, lived with Grandmother and her husband, C.T. Grandmother Myers and her father were very much a part of my life when I was a young child. Great-Grandfather Zigler always carried peppermint candy in his pocket for me. Grandmother always saved fresh homemade bread for me. Even now the aroma of freshly baked bread, no matter where the bakery may be, always rekindles the pleasure I knew whenever I visited Grandmother Myers and ate bread fresh from her oven, slathered with butter made from the milk the cows in their pasture had produced. Best of all were the wonderful custard pies she loved to bake. These two, Brethren and Mennonite respectively, never mentioned sin and soul salvation to me. They just unconditionally loved me, so I returned their love, and

I deeply respected them. Being around them made the bishop and Mattie seem even more critical of me than they probably were.

Great clouds of dust were raised some summers as speeding cars flying low on our dry dirt road brought Minnesota relatives to visit. Mother considered it her good luck that usually only one of Daddy's brothers, with family, showed up at a time. They never let us know when we were about to be invaded, and it frustrated Mother because she never had a warning of their arrival. They were Minneapolis city people, and they had no concept of what it was like to run a farm. Mother felt they were also contemptuous of her country role. There was no time to get beds ready, and there was no time to cook in preparation. However, all of us were glad to see them. They were a lively bunch and a happy, healthy respite from quiet country life.

These city folks, unused to, and sometimes obviously amused by our rural habits and way of life, found us just as unused to them and, sometimes just as amused by their differences from us. Those differences always melded smoothly shortly after their arrival, and everyone relaxed, told tall tales, and laughed heartily. Some of the bishop's quixotic ways always came in for hilarious review. We all respected the integrity of Mennonite doctrine and the Mennonites, but we rejected many of their beliefs and their lifestyle, which seemed inconvenient and terribly dull to us.

Three of the Minnesota children were near my age. Gwenie was six months younger, Jack (John) was one year older, and Babe (Ben, Jr.) was two years older. Gwenie was the nicest of the four of us, I think. She steered clear of our pranks and sometimes risky, rowdy pastimes. Gwenie was very fastidious, and she was quite the young lady. Regardless of that, she and I got along well, and we remain friends to this day. She warmed my heart a few years ago when she told me how all of the Minnesota cousins recognized Grandmother Myer's fondness for me. "Whenever you came into the room, Maxene, Grandmother's face would light up with pleasure." Gwenie, by sharing that observation with me, gave me hope that I may have made Grandmother's life with C.T. easier.

When my present husband Kenneth and I first visited Minneapolis in 1990, Gwenie came over to her older brother Bob's house, where we were staying, to see me and meet Kenneth. As soon as introductions were over and she was seated, she began to laugh. "Oh, Maxene, I will never forget one day when Donnie was annoying all of us by wanting to be included in our games, and you kept asking him to go away. Finally, when he persisted, you grabbed his hair and banged his head against a nearby brick wall." Everyone enjoyed her little memory blip; I did not. I hope my brother Don does not remember that unkind treatment. I am sure that the bang was justified in my childish opinion. I don't want to think the "bang" was as forceful as Gwenie represented it to my new husband. It does illuminate my early rejection and unhappiness in having an undesired sibling underfoot in my space. Kenneth, much to my chagrin, loved Gwenie's remark and my discomfiture since it flew in the face of the image of kindness and sweetness that I keep trying to sell him.

Jack Shank, Uncle John's only son, was the wildest one of the four of us. Mischief danced in every glance of his eyes and in every move he made. He was a lot of fun. He and I loved to taunt C.T. C.T. seemed to dislike children so Jack and I did everything we could to get even with him. I remember how once while we were playing in the barn, we labored to tie the reins on his horse bridles in tight knots. I remember hiding his black snake whip that snapped loudly when you whipped it around and around high above your head. The whip was kept in an upright holster on his buggy, which was garaged in the barn. We delighted in moving the whip to places where it would be difficult for C.T. to find it.

I remember Jack making tiny tight spit-balls and blowing them from a rolled up paper tube across Grandmother's living room to hit and bounce off C.T.'s bald head. None of the adults, busy with their own conversations, ever noticed our exuberance and high amusement when C.T. swatted away at what he perceived as flies landing on his shiny pate. Sticky coiled flypaper, used by everyone in those days, hung around the house to entrap the many nuisance flies that proliferated on farms without any deterrence from pesticides, but C.T. always mindlessly swatted away to our delight.

Once when we were playing in the barn and wreaking havoc, Jack jumped into the hay, which was full of barley beard. He deservedly itched and burned for hours, but he never repented for the disarray he left in the hayloft. C.T.'s displeasure was worth the itch.

Babe was the more dignified of the two boys. He and Gwenie were siblings, and they had more reserved manners than Jack and I. I remember Babe more for his participation in my Harrisonburg social life when I was a teenager. He sometimes dated some of my friends. One night he and Gwenie attended a SSS Club dance at Massanutten Caverns. The SSS Club, a formal organization, had as its core the small clique of Harrisonburg girls that had existed since third grade. I would tell you what SSS stands for, but there was sworn agreement among the members never to disclose the silly name of our snobbish little club. Six of the members are still alive, so I must keep my pledge. I have managed not to be a cast-out for more than seventy years. I hope to be alive to keep the secret for many more years. I do not wish to tarnish my golden years by breaking a promise made to life long friends.

I did not partake of any alcoholic beverages (Grandaddy Lewis's way of stating abstinence) in those teenage days. I was just naturally exuberant and happy, but I think that my actions, alone or with others, may have sometimes seemed tipsy to observers. After the Massanutten dance, some of the weary dancers stopped downtown in Harrisonburg to go to Gus's restaurant to get something to eat before going home. Babe swept me up in cradled arms and carried me across Main Street. As he dashed between two parked cars along the curb after crossing the street, my pretty yellow evening dress skirt caught on a car bumper and ripped a long tear. He put me down on the sidewalk in my tattered finery; we laughed, and went merrily into the restaurant for more laughter.

I, as usual when something amiss happened, delayed facing up to it until a more convenient time when nothing more interesting was happening. I dismissed thoughts of explaining the ripped dress to Mother and put off thinking about it until later. I think I probably put it away and never wore it again. All three of these Minneapolis cousins have lived successful and productive lives. Gwenie's and Babe's older brother Bob and his wife Betty became dear friends during the golden years after we became Florida snowbirds. All of the Minnesota Shanks are jewels of delight for me when I entertain myself with Minneapolis reels.

A haunting reel sullies those enchanted early years of my life on the farm. One sunny warm spring Saturday afternoon, I disobeyed parental instructions to stay away from workers on the farm. I sneaked out to the wood house where Jake, a sixteen-year-old, part-time farm helper, was chopping wood for fireplaces and the kitchen stove. I, an only child, was bored and wanted to talk with someone. I often schemed for ways to find someone with whom to talk. I liked to talk, I liked to listen, and I wanted to learn. However, that ill-chosen wood-house trek taken eons ago still emits shrill warning notes of caution. Take care with whom you speak. Take care to whom you listen. Take care from whom you learn.

I climbed up on the tall wood box and sat, legs swinging back and forth, chattering idly while watching Jake chop wood. I was having such a glorious time. I had escaped surveillance. I was flying free. My memory reel shows me wearing a pretty lavender dress and matching panties trimmed with lace that Mother had made for me. I loved wearing pretty clothes, and she enjoyed making them for me. When she was a child and teenager, a seamstress came to her home twice a year to make clothes, draperies, and whatever else was needed. She wanted me to have things as nice as she had as she grew up. Because during the first years of her marriage, there was not enough money for a seamstress, she had taught herself to sew, and she kept both of us well dressed.

I was feeling completely self-satisfied and carefree when Jake suddenly lifted his head. With the ax in his hand raised high above his head, looking straight into an innocent seven-year-old child's blue eyes, he lunged toward me. As he lunged, he dropped the ax before putting his hand over my mouth. I felt a fleeting moment of terror when I saw the raised ax coming toward me. There is no record on the reel of what he said to ease the fright I momentarily felt. The reel does show an acquiescing child being carried deep into the apple orchard beyond hearing distance from the house. Jake sat me down under an apple tree and gently removed my pretty lace trimmed lavender panties. I was not afraid. This was someone I knew, liked, and trusted. When he sat down and unbuttoned his pants to display an erect penis between his outspread legs, I was truly intrigued. I did not know what it was.

I never had been told that boys were different from girls between the legs. This experience was very intriguing. I was insatiably curious about everything, but here was something I had never even wondered about. I was eager to watch to find out what this strange looking thing was all about. He positioned me astride his open legs and began masturbating my genitalia with this newly discovered body part. It felt good. I enjoyed it. He made no attempt to penetrate, and I remember no wetness to indicate ejaculation. I suppose, if he ejaculated, he may have spilled his semen onto the newly green springtime grass amidst the fallen petals of blossoms under the apple tree.

Finally he put my panties back on me, stood up, smiled, and said, "Maxene, if you tell your mother, I will get you worse next time. Remember, this is our secret." I ran into the house so I would be there before my mother wakened from her afternoon nap to discover that I had been disobedient. I was very puzzled about the word *worse*. I wondered what worse could be. If what had happened was not bad, how could it get worse? If it had been good, couldn't it get better?

Jake was in high school; I was a second grader in the same consolidated school near Linville. He worked at the farm after school and on weekends. Things were going fine for me. I was a good student at school, but by the following Monday, I was feeling pensive and puzzled about my new experience. I was determined to keep the secret and not say a word about it to anyone.

In a few days some teenage students started asking, "Maxene, what did Jake do to you?" I felt hurt and confused because the teenagers teasing me seemed almost maliciously delighted with the information Jake had given them. It was extremely distressing for me that Jake had not kept our secret, but I was glad that I was now free to try and find out what worse meant.

It now was obvious to me that whatever had occurred was something quite extraordinary, and I began to consider talking with Mother about it, but I did not know what to tell her. I thought that Jake was not very smart to have told. Surely he must know that he could be risking displeasure from my adoring parents, and loss of his job if they found out about our tryst. I also believed that he didn't care much about me since, by telling our secret, he made it possible for my parents to hear about my defiance of their adamant instructions not to wander away from the house alone. Did Jake not think that I might be punished? Jake's telling was surely double jeopardy for me. I was learning to dislike and distrust Jake. The word *worse* began to ring with a more ominous sound. In a few days I came up with a plan. I decided to provide Mother with as little information as possible to make sure the now formidable Jake would have to leave the farm and be removed from my life. I hated being teased about something I did not understand, and I did not want to fret about worse anymore. Some intuitive sense was telling me that maybe what Jake and I had done was something that felt good but was really bad.

I was a conniving child, and I often entertained myself by eavesdropping on my parents' conversations when I tired of reading or playing. After sharing some of the secret with Mother, however, I didn't hear any discussion about Jake between my mother and father. I felt perplexed that whatever I had told her distracted her enough to prevent her from chastising me. Unfulfilled expectation of hearing discussion about it was a relief, but puzzling.

When Jake did not leave, I started thinking about what else I should tell Mother to make her want to get rid of him. I wanted the teasing stopped—and soon. Before I worked up courage to more graphically detail my pleasurable experience under the apple tree with Jake, I looked out the window late one afternoon and saw Jake's parents coming across the meadow toward the house.

As my parents exited the house from the front door and sat down on the front porch to talk to Jake's parents, I ran out the back door. I hurried around the house and quietly slithered under shrubs near the porch. I got close enough, just in time, to hear my father saying that Jake's behavior meant that he could no longer work at the farm. I was elated. It was hard to believe that Jake was leaving, and that I could chalk all of it away on a reel. Even at that age, I had learned to compress material on a reel when it was ready for history.

I rushed away to enter the rear of the house so that I would be found exactly where my parents had last seen me before they went out to the porch. I did not wish my sleuthing talents discovered. They came in. They never mentioned the subject to me. I was exuberant that the incident was passed over so lightly. Jake was going to leave. I no longer needed to learn what worse meant. I would never have to share the *worse* threat with Mother. My success in keeping the entire incident so minimal was wonderfully gratifying. Now my parents would surely forget all about my clandestine visit to the wood house. Everything was going well. I, with conscience clear, could get on with my life. It would be many years before I would seriously consider the effects this experience had on my life.

On Sunday, September 12, 1926, Mother sat down to fry chicken for our dinner. I did not know she was pregnant or that she did not feel like standing over a hot stove. After our noontime Sunday meal, she and Daddy told me they were going to town and were taking me down the road to Grandmother's house for a visit. I was pleased because Grandmother was part of my spoils system. I liked to go to this other household where I always got so much special attention.

It must have been about five o'clock that afternoon, while I was swinging back and forth on the big entrance gate to Grandmother's lane, when I saw our car kicking up dust as it came down the road. Daddy was alone in the car. Puzzled, I stopped the gate so that he could drive through. He drove through, then stopped the car and got out to walk over to me, wearing a broad, happy smile. He said, "Maxene, you have a little brother." This was terrible news. Where in the world was my mother? I stomped my foot and said, "I do not have a little brother. Where is Mother?" He stooped down and started to put his arm around me, but I was having none of that. I jerked away as he said, "Your mother is with your little brother at the hospital. They both are fine, and I will take you to town tomorrow evening to see your new little brother."

I was absolutely livid. I had been so happy swinging on the gate, waiting for my parents to come driving in, and now I had no Mother there. She had chosen to stay away with some little boy that I never wanted to see or have anything to do with. I felt my little world disappearing as "my own" space.

Daddy gently picked up his sulking child. He put me in the car, and we rode up the lane to Grandmother's house. To add to my utter dismay, Grandmother was happy about the little boy, too. I have no memory of how those two defectors from my camp talked me into going to see Donald Eugene at the hospital. I imagine Grandmother spent Monday convincing me that I was to go with good manners and good grace. I do remember that I did not find seeing the baby boy helpful. Seeing him just verified my worst fears. I just could not believe that my parents had gone to town to the hospital to get a baby boy without asking me if I would like to have a little brother.

He was seven years younger than I. When he and Mother came home, he really was not much bother to me; he just slept, ate, and, sometimes, cried. I thought he was rather a nuisance to have around, but he did not seem to take attention away from me. I accepted him gingerly and reluctantly since it was obvious he was there to stay. Some friends of my parents came to see the baby and talked about how cute he was. I silently wondered how they could think he was cute. I certainly did not think he was attractive.

Little Donnie did have spirit. As soon as he could sit up, I would rush my hands along the spokes of his playpen just to hear him howl in protest. I guess he thought I was invading his spot in the universe. Mother would come running, pick him up, console him, and say to me, "What in the world made him cry out so loudly?" I always just let her wonder and then waited for the next opportunity to create a repeat performance. It bothered Mother that he seemed to have temper fits for no reason; I was delighted with them. He and I had something in common; we both knew why he demonstrated a temper, but he couldn't talk so I was safe.

A few months after the baby brother-birthing event, I was surprised when Daddy told me told that we were going to move to Harrisonburg, a small city five miles from the farm. He and Mother explained that it would be better because Daddy's business was there. Springtime 1927 found me diligently adjusting to a new school and trying to make new friends in an urban environment. My little brother, who was called Donnie by my parents, slowly became an accepted fixture around the house, and he did not interfere with my life very much. I was beginning to find him more tolerable as I became preoccupied with my new city friends.

On the first day in Miss Fanny Speck's third-grade class, I raised my hand and asked if anyone lived near me who would walk home from school with me. Miss Speck identified a child and asked the little girl if I could walk with her. After school, we set out for home, but my companion did not live as far up Franklin Street as I did. When we got to her house, she asked me to come in for a treat. We entered her house, and she went to the kitchen to get the treat while I waited in the living room.

I could see a black man in the kitchen talking to her mother. I heard her mother ask the man, "Who is that child?" He, the yardman, replied, "I think her father is manager at the milk plant." I wondered why it mattered who I was. It was my first revelation of Southern snobbery. My father's position apparently put me across the winning wire because the little girl's mother encouraged her daughter's friendship with me. We became best friends. Clearly indicated, it seemed to me, was that connections mattered most; it mattered not what kind of person I might be.

I was accepted by a little "in" clique of third graders. The acknowledged leader of the pack was a truly mean-spirited little girl. She held sway by withdrawing her personal approval from any child who dared question her authority to decide what games would be played at recess or who would be on teams chosen for a game.

There was another group of children who liked to shoot baskets at recess. It looked like fun, and so I wandered off and began playing with them. None of them lived near any of the girls in the clique, and clique girls never seemed to notice the other girls. I happily shot baskets for a few days until it dawned on me that the clique was shunning me. I went to the nasty leader and asked what had happened to make clique members unfriendly. She said, "Maxene, if you play with them, you cannot play with us." Since none of the other girls lived near enough to me for after school playtime, I chose the clique.

It was a long time before I began to realize that pecking order in many small Southern towns unflinchingly maintained exclusive groups that deliberately ostracized others whom they did not consider worthy of friendship. What made members of a clique worthy seemed to have nothing to do with value systems; clearly there was no fairness in choices made for clique membership. When I became aware of some rather silly, even selfish, attitudes incorporated in Southern cliques, I chose, for self-serving reasons, to privately reject the attitudes but not to question them.

At the farm after my parents had decided to move, I had heard my father and Mother talking about buying a house in town, and I remembered him saying, "Well, we need to be careful where we buy." Now I understood that puzzling remark. As Realtors say, "The three most important things when choosing a home to buy and a place to live are location, location, and location."

Obviously my social survival in this small Southern town depended upon acceptance by the right people who lived on the right streets if I wished to have the best times and be considered OK. *I'm OK, You're OK* by Gregg Easterbrook had not yet been written. Now that the word is out, I wonder if the impact of it has truly penetrated the cold protective shells of small town cliques of children, teenagers, and adults.

One day in the schoolyard of my new school, Keister Elementary, a third-grade girl classmate mentioned something that indicated her curiosity about boys being different from girls. I was ready and eager with first hand information. I was delighted that I was free to share information that Jake had decided not to keep secret. Wide-eyed city girl children listened in wonderment as a country hayseed child, once taunted for wearing white stockings to school instead of "in" knee socks, gave them fascinating facts about a mysterious body part assigned to males only. The episode with Jake became extra special as I was encouraged by clique members to describe every detail. The pleasure that Jake and I had shared under an apple tree was spectacularly helpful in breaking the social ice for me with third grade girl children in Harrisonburg, Virginia.

Years later Mother and I were shopping in Washington, DC, where there had been some widely publicized rapes. When expressing empathy for the victims, I told Mother exactly what had happened to me in the wood house and under the apple tree. She was so startled that she stopped short on F Street in front of Garfinkel's Department Store. Turning to face me with a shocked look, she said, "Maxene, you never told me this before. We would have treated the incident quite differently had we realized the extent and seriousness of it."

Neither of us could remember exactly what I had told her. After that informative discussion, both my father and mother indicated sorrow that they had not been given all the wood-house apple-orchard facts. They felt concerned that they might have inadvertently failed to ensure safety for other little girls.

Today the molestation scenario does not seem incidental. My response at the time, I think, is key to understanding why children often remain silent when sexually molested. Sans the *worse* threat and Jake's failure to keep our secret, I believe that I might have sought continued pleasurable sensations created by contact with Jake's penis. It would have been a natural thing to do.

I have always been appreciative that my parents, either from delicacy, lack of complete information, or from inhibited reluctance, did not inform me about private body parts and sex activities in ways that some other parents did then, and sometimes do now. They never made me feel sinful, bad, or guilty. I am grateful that, from my first sexual experience, there was no fallout of unhealthy attitudes about a natural body function.

As the apple orchard reel has played back from time to time through the years, it has prompted in me firm convictions about education to prevent child molestation. It seems to me that curiosity sometimes triggers desires to learn by looking, and I wonder how many children, both boys and girls, have endured guilt from what, in some instances, was simply innocent inquisitive behavior. The hellfire and brimstone responses given to children after discovery by adults of sexual exploration or molestation seem ill advised. Such responses, when offered to children by religious zealots, naive friends, or uneducated parents, must surely be damaging factors to development of mature, healthy attitudes toward normal sexual functioning of human bodies and wisely planned-parenthood.

In my opinion, overpopulation is an almost frightening and an outstanding social, economic, and environmental issue confronting the inhabitants of our planet Earth. Education is also an extremely important issue. That these two issues must be paired for the salvation of all people seems obvious.

All education is vital, but it seems to me that it is high time, if we wish for our own survival and desire the best health possible for everyone in the world, that public demands must be made and heard for human reproduction and rational, planned parenthood to be taught in all classrooms worldwide.

We desperately need to give immediate intellectual attention to all issues surrounding population proliferation to provide for the future of humanity. For all peoples there must be deliverance from the misguided and uneducated directions that illiteracy and ignorance regarding human sexual behavior seems certain to guarantee. Leave the claptrap of emotionalized Bible thumping or other religious inhibitions to churches and parents, but let us not piously and egregiously deny youngsters the offering of scientific factual knowledge within our public school systems.

The U.S. Supreme Court judgment for Roe versus Wade gives a female the right to decide whether she will have an abortion. The U.S. Supreme Court decision determined that it is not a decision intended to be dictated by government. No one prefers abortion as opposed to delivery of healthy full term babies. That there is serious opposition to abortion without a corresponding guarantee of prenatal care proves the cruelty and hypocrisy of opponents to abortion rights. That there are few right-to-lifer promises to all children for impartial public education, health care, good nutrition, and decent housing makes their issue of opposition to the right of a woman and her doctor to decide whether an abortion is needed amoral, not moral.

Sexual behavior, sexual orientation, and religion are not governmental issues. These very personal, private considerations should be left where they belong—for private decision-making by individuals alone, or with whomever they choose to share their concerns. Politicians, beholden to conservative rightists in legislative bodies and within voting booths, want to invade women's privacy for self-serving reasons.

In 1967 I taught sex education in middle school science classes without approval from anyone. I used books published jointly by the American Medical Association and the National Education Association. I made an appointment with the assistant superintendent of schools because I had a friend who knew Dr. Mary Calderone, a pioneer in sex education for children. My friend believed that Dr. Calderone, if he asked her, would volunteer to come to Pinellas County and offer a seminar for teachers chosen to teach the subject. Such an opportunity would provide the county children with wonderful state of the art information, I believed. The deputy superintendent did not agree with me and impolitely asked me whether I was crazy. He said parents would ring the phones off the board of education office walls if anything like I suggested took place.

I decided that if I were fired for doing what seemed so right, I would happily go my merry way. Making sure that some children left behind would be sophisticated enough about their own bodies to make educated decisions about sexual activities made my decision easy. For some unknown reason, the school principal, when I told him what I wanted to do, did not raise his hands in holy horror. He did caution me that I was on my own and that, if anything hit the fan about it, I would stand alone to take the heat. It was obvious that his job was not going to be threatened, and that all complaints would be dumped on my desk.

Jack, my husband, was public health director of Pinellas County, so I did ask his opinion. He stayed in trouble with certain county commissioners because he refused to aid and abet their political goals to protect their business friends who did not measure up to health standards, so I did not wish to add to his unpopularity by providing fodder to unsavory politicians. I did not wish to offend their inflexible pseudo moralistic souls. Jack thought teaching scientific facts about human reproduction was a wonderful thing to do. We were not ones to sacrifice principles for our own protection when we believed issues of importance to us needed our support. Through the years we paid some heavy prices for our zeal to maintain integrity in the face of a few petty unethical powerful politicians and bureaucrats.

I ordered and paid for books published jointly by the National Education Association and the American Medical Association. I told the children that it was material that I was personally providing because, even though it was not in the curriculum, I felt they might benefit from the knowledge they would find in the books. I bought books all the time, so this was not a novel experience.

Never in my entire teaching career had I seen youngsters so avidly interested in class work. You could have heard a pin drop on that first day as they read. It was such a thrilling experience. It was exactly as I knew it could be in the right environment. Any question anyone wished to ask was allowed. No question was ever couched in other than respectable or academic terms used in the booklets, but the students let me know that they understood we were dealing with subjects that many adults considered taboo. I think they were pleased that I believed them to be mature enough to handle studying the human reproductive system and its functions.

I don't think one student went home with the news that there were unusual, wonderful books available in their science classroom. I never heard from one parent. I will never know whether I heard nothing because the students kept their mouths shut or because the parents decided to be grateful for a teacher who was helping them with a topic that they may have felt hesitant to discuss with their progeny.

These children were older than I was when Jake carried me to the orchard, however their lack of factual information about their reproductive organs was shocking. In class false ideas were simply put aside and replaced with education geared to the students' developing mentalities. Having access to facts made them capable of offering discerning answers when questions arose. Middle school boys and girls were being educated to understand natural sexual yearnings. When sexual desires posed serious questions for them, they would be prepared to make thoughtful decisions in accordance with knowledge of the consequences of making unwise choices.

Too many adults discredit the ability of children to make decisions. In my opinion discussions and sermons suggesting that parents and churches need to take total responsibility for sex education are very shortsighted. To teach reproduction of plants and animals in school, but to stop short when human beings are studied, is, to put it mildly, gross failure of an educational system. The students deserve opportunities to consider a triangle of impersonal, secular scientific facts in conjunction with parental opinions and religious beliefs. Thanks in part to the learning jolt I got from Jake; some junior high school students learned what they should have been taught many years earlier for their own protection.

In my opinion there are not enough parents who are qualified to home-teach anything; therefore I eschew home teaching as a political or a religious issue. Teachers need to be qualified. Anyone teaching children anywhere should be certified to teach the subject they, in essence, tell and sell to children. It is important that teachers provide intellectually informed, objective viewpoints to counterbalance misinformation and extremism.

For politicians to suggest that publicly funded vouchers given to certain children to enable them to attend schools of their choice will leave no child behind is the epitome of nonsense. It is also intellectually insulting. Here I see political responses directly tied to Christian Coalition and Moral Majority goals. Religious freedom to embrace any religion of choice or no religion should be totally unrelated politically to issues of human reproduction. If the wisest of us do not demand that politicians remain aloof and separated from our private sexual and religious lives, we may find ourselves vulnerable to the loss of many of our privacy freedoms.

It is pretty scary that there isn't massive outrage across the land about selective distribution of school vouchers. Voucher recipients are not likely to receive standardized education, as children in public schools must. It is unlikely that voucher recipients will receive consistent education in human reproduction instruction or any other topics. If vouchers are not to be given to *all* children, how can it be said that no child is left behind?

A resounding wake-up call is needed for everyone to listen with critical judgment to political jargon and empty spins. Politicians, to be respected and elected, should have to present common sense solutions for accurately identified problems.

Public-funded education with national standards should, in my opinion, be available to everyone. Politically motivated chatter about communities establishing independent school systems without consistent federal guidelines is more poppycock, and it is just another way for expenses to be shifted irresponsibly away from the federal budget to a mishmash of states and counties. Like it or not, there are counties where the intellectual level of officials is not adequate to make proper educational decisions for citizens within their jurisdiction. There are areas where there is not enough money available from taxation for provision of essential infrastructures; thus adequate funding for public schools cannot be provided. Quality educational systems are usually not affordable without federal funds. That is not to mention that multiple biases, including race, religion, sexual orientation, and abortion, comfortably exist in some communities. The need for children to understand and relate to cultural differences, as they learn that there are many ways to consider personal aspects of others, is, in my opinion, essential for a more enlightened, intellectually healthy society.

There has to be a nationally structured educational networking system for curricula to be consistent, meaningful, and enforceable. There must be especial emphasis that the public education system be free from the imposition of religious doctrines if respect for constitutional rights and freedoms are to be honored.

Shrink the Earth's population to a village of precisely one hundred people, with all existing human ratios remaining the same. Discover that it would look something like the following: There would be fifty-five Asians, twenty-one Europeans, fourteen from the Western Hemisphere, both North and South, and ten from mixed origins. Fifty-two would be female. Forty-eight would be male. Seventy would be nonwhite. Thirty would be white. Seventy would be non-Christian. Thirty would be Christian. Eighty-nine would be heterosexual. Eleven would be homosexual. Six people would possess fifty-nine percent of the entire world's wealth; those six would be from the United States. Eighty would live in substandard housing. Seventy would be unable to read. Fifty would suffer from malnutrition. One would be near death. One would be newborn. One would own a computer. Only one would be a college graduate.

When one considers our world from such a compressed perspective, when one accepts and understands these glaring frightening factors, is it not absolutely, without reservation, obvious that education offers the most responsible solutions? I have not researched these statistics. They came to me from an email buddy. It is noteworthy that there is no mention of pedophiles, rapists, or other sexual molesters since we, the public, are so preoccupied with these once-closeted activities and unknown perpetrators. Everyone now knows that pedophiles, rapists, and other sexual molesters are found in most of the compressed perspective categories.

Simplistic conclusion: Had I been aware of some very basic, very easily understood facts about human bodies and how human bodies are created to function from first grade instruction, with ongoing education at each grade level, Jake would not have been easily allowed to carry me to the orchard. But since Jake and I, because of our ignorance, did what we did, I feel compelled to speak out with concern for the benefit of children and parents everywhere.

The opportunity to become intellectually inspired in appropriate settings while learning the basic facts of life should be a right granted to every child. As I write, I know that many children are being exploited just as I was, some in ways that are much more frightening and terrible than my experience. I also know that too few adults give a damn.

I had inhibited parents who did not properly educate me about human reproduction. If they had properly educated me before my brother was born, Donald would have been spared the teasing and harassment that I showered upon him because of my resentment. My parents, like many parents today, simply did not know or realize the importance of including me in the knowledge about conception and birthing experiences. I needed to be prepared in order to appreciate the value of a wonderful little boy.

Human reproduction is a biological, scientific process. It is not a process that all parents understand well enough to know how to discuss intellectually, unemotionally, or objectively with their children. Even if one is qualified to discuss the subject, it is often difficult to talk with one's own children about sex and the complications of it as involved with human reproduction. On the other hand, it is a topic that fits naturally into educational curricula. Children with scientific facts related to human reproduction presented to them in schoolrooms by qualified teachers from an impersonal, scientific point of view, can be brought to understand and calculate the risks of sexual promiscuity. The teacher can discuss and realistically describe the attendant threats to their health from sexually transmitted diseases. The personal consequences of unplanned pregnancies can be explained, including possible horrific economic deprivation and its effects on the family.

Related social issues that are of great interest to teens must be integrated into educational experiences. Weighing the advantages and disadvantages of becoming parents with questions as to why, how, when, and where, should be challenging considerations. All children at present, or some future time, or perhaps at many times during their lifetimes, will make decisions, wisely or unwisely, related to their reproductive powers, decisions that may create babies irresponsibly. Failure to provide the knowledge necessary to enable wise decisions seriously threatens and demoralizes the welfare of individuals, their communities, and their nations. It is irresponsible to not offer common sense, quality education to all children so that they can know how to foresee and prevent undesirable, unhealthy, or unhappy difficult situations for themselves as well as for children yet unborn.

My first sex education lesson was taught under an apple tree. It was taught either by a curious teenager or by a sexual molester, whose mentality may not have been self possessed. There is an old adage, "Put a good experienced teacher with books under a tree with children, and lessons will be learned." That concept, sincerely and practically embraced by parents, legislators, and professional educators, could eliminate lessons taught without books by the Jakes of our world.

Papa owned one of the first cars in the area of Broadway, Virginia. Mary, Mother's older sister, is driving, with her fiancée beside her. Mother and Daddy, who were dating, are on the back seat. They rode with the luxury of no competing automobile traffic, but dirt roads were often rutted.

My parents, David Edgar Shank (1889-1972) and Bertha Bateman Bare (1894–1984) as they looked in 1915 when riding in the Ford.

I was conceived in Saint Paul, Minnesota in 1918. In 1959, when we were in Minneapolis to visit relatives, Daddy insisted on taking me to this address, where he proudly proclaimed his most important activity while living there.

My birthplace at Papa's home near Broadway. I was born at three o'clock in the afternoon on Saturday, May 31,1919. I never asked, but I feel confident that it was a sunny day.

This is the bed, upon which I was birthed, that was brought to the parlor on the first floor because there was no downstairs bedroom. Cora Mason, a birthing nurse, attended Dr. Armstrong with the birthing. Cora took care of me for weeks after that until Mother regained enough strength to look after a baby. Times have changed! The bed shown here is now in the guest cottage of our antebellum house in Kentucky.

The farmhouse near Edom, as it looked in 2002. Papa bought the farm in 1919 to shelter Bertha, Dave, and Maxene.

The barn at our old farm as it looked in 2002.

Grandmother Myers

Grandmother Myers's house

The infant Maxene

Maxene, age four

The Methodist church at Edom

Bertha and Maxene dressed to go to church.

Maxene, age seven

Maxene, age sixteen

Donald, age nine

Charles, age four

SSS Club at a Rawley Springs house party in the summer of 1936.

Dave and Bertha in 1938, standing by a redwood tree in California's Muir Woods

Jon's Death

I had no home and no place to go, when my husband Jack Obenschain, a doctor, was shipped overseas in 1944 during World War II. When my parents invited me to come back to Virginia's Shenandoah Valley, I decided to go and stay with them and Charles, my thirteen-year old brother, for the duration of the war. Since I was pregnant, going back home to Harrisonburg gave me a feeling of security that I needed during those frightening and unsettling wartime circumstances.

Jack had resigned from his medical residency at George Washington University Hospital in Washington, DC, to volunteer for service in the U.S. Army. His blood pressure reading was high enough to exempt him from service, but he applied again and again until he was finally given a waiver in March 1944. He was told that he would surely never see overseas service, but he received orders for Pacific duty within the year. I think no one was surprised. Doctors were desperately needed, and Jack welcomed his orders. Four of his brothers were already in service. He wanted to fulfill what he strongly believed was his duty to preserve cherished freedoms that were being threatened by the Germans, Italians, and Japanese as they fought to expand their boundaries and political philosophies to other countries.

Two of Jack's brothers, Dick and Bill, were pilots. Another brother, Sam, was a navigator. A fourth brother, Philip, had a complete "nervous breakdown," according to the family, just before he was to go overseas. Philip was hospitalized for a short time before being discharged from the Army infantry.

Philip, with a master's degree in mathematics, was considered a mathematical genius; it was easy for him to find a teaching position in a secondary school after his illness seemed to be in remission. He tried to teach school, but his problems with maintaining discipline in the classroom were continuously unsettling to him, to his students, and to everyone in the family. He had to be

40

hospitalized again after he began teaching, for what was finally correctly called a mental illness. To this day I have not heard any descriptive discussion about a diagnosis of his illness. His career as a teacher was interrupted again and again by periods of illness, and he finally had to give up teaching school. It was unfortunate that this kind and caring person never became well enough to cope with his mental illness and use his unusual and much-needed mathematical talents to educate children.

When weather permitted, Philip often sat on his front porch staring straight ahead, as he rocked his chair back and forth monotonously. He and his wife Nita raised four children in a bungalow just about two blocks down Selma Boulevard from Selma, the family home, in Staunton, Virginia. Phil usually managed to carry on a minimal conversation, but he was obviously troubled. Nita, a paragon of virtue, worked as a dental assistant to supplement a pension Philip received from the Army. Her heroic efforts managed to maintain family unity in a household with a seriously mentally ill father. Largely, I think to Nita's credit, all four of the attractive smart children are college educated and live productive lives. To the best of my knowledge, none of Nita's and Philip's children or grandchildren have been challenged by mental illness.

Before Jack left for overseas, he asked me if I would go to Selma and stay for a few weeks before our baby was due to arrive. I had grown up in a quiet household; the commotion in the Selma household made by the presence of so many people coming and going made me crave privacy many times when I was visiting there. I loved the big hearty family, but I sometimes found their lifestyle in the big old house tiresome. I was not eager to go there without Jack, but I wanted him to go off to war as worry free as possible so I agreed to go with unspoken trepidation and reluctance.

Jack's father and sister Margaret had medical offices on the first level of the antebellum three-story plantation house. Because I knew that Jack believed that his father and his sister, both doctors, would make sure that the baby and I would receive the best of care, I went cheerfully to Selma around the first of February, 1945, to await the baby's arrival. My parents were hesitant about my leaving Harrisonburg for the baby's delivery, but the son-in-law's wish as he left for overseas duty was never openly questioned by anyone. As it should have been, peace of mind for the soldier was the most important consideration.

Since it was wartime, gasoline, shoes, hosiery, and many other things were rationed. There I was, twenty-five miles away from my family and about six long-time friends who had returned to the area for the duration of the war just as I had. Four of them had toddlers or babies at the time when my baby was born. These loyal young women saved gas coupons and came to see their marooned friend whenever they could. A memory reel shows one of them, who was feeling lonely for her overseas Boston attorney husband, perched in one of the deeply recessed window seats in the library at Selma when she said, "Come on, Mac. Sneak away and come home with us." We all laughed because we knew my duty was to stay put to please Jack.

I began seeing a doctor in Staunton. When I went in for the third routine examination, he told me that he wished to induce labor, and he set a date for me to come to the hospital. I entered the hospital on Thursday morning, February 22, 1945.

I knew that the doctor had a beloved son who was overseas in combat and that he desperately wished to go to New York for a few days of rest away from his medical duties. Going about routine business and doing necessary usual activities took courage that sapped the strength of everyone who had loved ones in the midst of battles on lands or seas far away. Sometimes such sustained courage left tired and caring people unable to persevere without an occasional escape to some unfamiliar place, removed from wartime's sad and stressful local news. I understood the doctor's need for respite.

Prior to this pregnancy, I had two natural abortions. The first happened when I was staying at my parents' home during summer vacation from teaching in 1942. Jack stayed in Washington; he was busy almost around the clock with duties in medical school and at the hospital. There was no air conditioning before World War II. Washington was much hotter in the summer than the Shenandoah Valley; and the humidity, due to the proximity of the Potomac River, caused me to have uncomfortable bouts with my stuffy sinuses. That, coupled with Jack's unavailability, made Harrisonburg the best place for me under the prevailing circumstances.

Without warning the miscarriage of my first pregnancy began, with a massive gushing hemorrhage. After a fast ambulance ride to the hospital, swathed in towels and sheets that my mother had used to try to staunch the rapid bleeding, and after efforts by the doctor had failed to preserve the pregnancy, I was wheeled into an operating room for a D&C to formally finish aborting the pregnancy. It was a dramatic and unexpected finale to the promise of what I believed would be a more fulfilling life. I was very upset, but when I was told that the abortion did not indicate that I could not become pregnant again, I relaxed and appreciated the knowledge that I could, at sometime in the future, succeed with another pregnancy. The pregnancy had not been planned, so the loss may have been easier to accept than it would have been if we had been better prepared economically to have a child.

I don't remember much about the second miscarriage. It happened in our Arlington, Virginia, Colonial Village apartment early one Saturday morning. Once again Jack was at the hospital on duty. I was roused from a groggy, half-sleep state, hearing loud knocking at our apartment door. I stumbled to the door to find a neighbor, whom I had never seen before. She had heard me moaning. She asked for my husband's phone number, called him, and stayed with me, a bewildered, almost delirious stranger, until Jack got home.

An obstetrician with whom Jack worked came out to the apartment, checked me over, and gave me medicine to lower a high temperature, and, I imagine, an antibiotic. This pregnancy was not as advanced as the first, so I quickly recovered and was back in my Claude Swanson Junior High School classroom on Monday morning, still weak, but recovered from an unexpected and unpleasant experience during a hazy weekend.

I felt exhilarated as I walked down the hall of Kings Daughter's Hospital in Staunton, Virginia, to a large, high-ceilinged private room on Thursday morning, February 22, 1945. It was like gliding down a golden-carpeted pathway. Every month that had passed without any sign of anything amiss with this third pregnancy was a celebration for me. Soon, I thought, as I settled into my hospital room, the promise of nine long months of fond hopes will be fulfilled. That this pregnancy had gone full term was so gratifying that I felt almost euphoric. Finally, after two disappointing pregnancies, I was going to become a mother.

I knew that Jack, no matter where he was, was thinking of me and looking forward to hearing about the baby's birth. Knowing that he was on combat duty made the event doubly important because his circumstances on the battlefront were so grim. I believed that the birth of the baby would make the burdens of war seem lighter for him and assure him that a new beginning awaited him when his grim wartime duties were completed.

Young women across the United States and in other countries at war were in the same situation I was experiencing. I think babies born during those embattled years, in many cases made war seem less demoralizing and frightening. Thousands of pregnant women had to be left behind by men who were assigned to World War II overseas military units. Couples seemed to feel that the normal process of starting families somehow guaranteed their country's future, as well as their own. Their babies were promises for family lives to young husbands in far away places fighting to save their countries. Their fighting, most believed, assured a safe and freedom-loving world for future generations. War babies heightened the necessity for battle victories for men selflessly offering their lives. Creating new lives compensated for lives taken in battles. Men who came home from battles that had been valiantly fought were eager to begin their lives anew. A war baby was a living commemorative when a father failed to return home

The doctor started medical treatment to induce labor as soon as I was settled into my room. He told me, after examination, that the baby was in a breech position. I was repeatedly examined. Concern heightened as the days wore on, and the baby's head did not turn to a proper position for delivery. Thursday night when my parents came to visit, and I told them about the breech position, they asked me, please, to get out of bed and come home to doctors we knew. They were obviously distressed by what seemed to be precarious procedures. Of course because of Jack's wishes, I refused to leave the hospital. I was on an optimistic high. I was not fearful.

The next day, Friday, the doctor continued doing whatever he thought should be done to induce labor. He continued whatever he thought should be done on Saturday. Every time I was given anything to reduce pain, labor stopped, so it was a tiring, frightening, painful experience. The doctor ruptured the membranes on Saturday, and labor became more painful. I was instructed to walk the halls, which I somehow managed to do. I wore bright green leather scuffs, and the soles of my feet were green for weeks from dye beaten into the soles of my feet by the steady, painful pacing.

Finally, early on Sunday morning, after three days and nights of labor with little pain relief and little sleep, the baby was delivered. A jubilant young mother was rolled on a cloud back to her room. In the delivery room I was not shown the baby, but I was told that I had a son. Now, relieved and happy, I was eager to see the baby and hear more about him. I kept asking that he be brought to me.

Then the doctor walked in. He stood looking down at me for a few minutes, took my hand, and said, "I'm sorry, but the little fellow is having problems. We are working with him." Then he abruptly left the room, and I was left to lie in the bed almost frozen in shock for three hours. Then the doctor returned to say, "I am so sorry but the little fellow has been unable to make it. We were not able to save him." I screamed, "How can we tell Jack? How can we tell Jack?"

When my parents got there, they were shocked, but they remained calm and superbly supportive when I told them what had happened. Apprehensions they had felt from the time they had learned that the baby was in a breech position were now horribly justified. They insisted that I have a private nurse at night. I think they thought it would be comforting and easier for me since I would be grief stricken and alone in the darkness.

In those days even regular hospital floor nurses did wonderful helpful things like massaging patients' backs before bedtime, and they took time to be friendly and supportive. They were not hidden somewhere, out of sight and out of touch with patients, doing bureaucratic, administrative paperwork. Nurse nurturing was a basic and vital part of recovery in the hospital.

By the time Mother and Daddy arrived, I had my seething external emotions under control, but only because I had suppressed them internally. When they came into the room, my abdomen was distended enough for them to think, at first, that the baby had not yet been delivered. By not outwardly displaying the unrelenting emotional feelings I had, I spared others uneasy discomfort, but I needed some very embarrassing medical procedures to bring relief from the resultant abdominal gas retention. An oiled rubber tube was inserted to allow gases to escape into a bowl of water beneath the bed. Outside my door it must have sounded as if there were a small ship, puttering along at sea. People coming into my room must have longed for scented air sprays. Under other circumstances it would have been simply comical; in my circumstances it was a painful insult of inept medical practice.

The tube was inserted and removed so many times that massive hemorrhoids developed. I called them my secret bunch of grapes with thorns. The grapes withered to endurance size except during and immediately after the deliveries of our three daughters in 1947, 1949, and 1951. Finally, in 1953, an inch of badly damaged large intestine had to be removed, and a new rectum was created. About fifteen years later, problems developed from the poorly engineered rectum. I had another operation to give me another new rectum. After suffering lots of pain during two hemorrhoidectomies, there was finally, literally, a happy ending. Thank heavens, it is not always true that what happens twice, happens three times. Possibly I have claim to the Guinness *Book of Records* for having had the most rectums.

Need I mention that the manufactured rectum is an ongoing joy? Need I tell you that whenever I pass Preparation H on a store shelf, I feel grateful that I am not passing gas, delighted that I do not have to grab Preparation H from the shelf, and thankful not to have to pay for it quickly and dash to the nearest restroom? In the previous century, I think I might not have shared this distasteful intimate reel with you, but now, in this new millennium, nothing seems sacred or taboo. I confess to you that I feel tinges of pain when I see people squirming in their seats while Preparation H commercials blare forth distastefully from TV screens.

At first, I actually felt some guilt about the death of Jon. Strangely enough I wondered what I might have done to cause him to be imperfect. Prior to becoming pregnant, I had been a light smoker, and I did have an alcoholic drink infrequently, but I had discontinued both practices as soon as I knew I was going to have a baby. I also felt miserable that I had allowed the tiny baby to be subjected to such abuse while being delivered. I did not share these feelings with anyone until I was able to seek answers from other doctors. The death of the child and the unanswered questions quietly tortured me. Having a child die, it seemed to me, must be the severest grief.

I hastened to write Jack a letter immediately, and I sent it out for mailing as soon as possible. He would not receive it for three months. Meanwhile he wrote again and again about his excitement that we were parents. He asked many questions about the baby. He was so happy to think that a child was waiting for him to come home to.

Letters and mail moved very slowly during wartime. In those days what is now called "snail mail" not only crept slowly forward an inch at a time, it often seemed to sleep for days before getting to its final destination. Slow mail service was usually just another inconvenience, a minor one at that, which everyone accepted as part of the many ongoing sacrifices we made without complaint during the five long years of World War II.

In combat areas outgoing mail was said to be infrequently collected. Incoming mail from families and friends to those serving their country in far away, unpleasant situations was often weeks old before it finally arrived. Soldiers on depressing fields of battle needed encouraging words from home. Reassurance that they were not forgotten in their hellish isolation from home and familiar places was vital to the morale of those fighters whose lives were continuously endangered. Everyone in the armed services looked forward to hearing from loving people at home. They looked forward to news and to hearing appreciation for the difficult duties they were performing to protect the democratic interests and privileges so vital to Americans. For many letters and packages made the difference between despair and courage.

Living through World War II was a trauma of its own for all of us. Death was an ever-present threat for those overseas, but also for those of us who were fearfully, sometimes tearfully, waiting at home. Thousands of service personnel died in far-away places. It was a traumatic time for millions of people. It was a period of time—five long years of time—unlike any I have ever known or wish to know again. Regular reports of deaths kept everyone aware that the next telegram, the next phone call, might come to their house—might come for them.

It was around 11:30 one night about three nights after Jon's birth. I had just been bathed and assisted to dress in a lace-trimmed, white satin nightgown, with nails freshly manicured. I was lying in a comfortable bed, when I looked around and took inventory of my large private hospital room. Vases of flowers stood on the high shelves that rimmed the room. I reached over and touched a stack of cards, telegrams, and notes on the bedside table. I thought about the deluge of phone calls and the visitors I had after Jon's death—and was continuing to have. All of those kind things that people did mattered and helped me to be strong.

My nurse spoke only when I spoke to her, but it was comforting to wake up in the night and see that pretty, smiling face. She was very kind and easy to talk with when I wished to talk. She sat silent as she knitted contentedly. Her contentment was contagious. I turned my head away from her and closed my eyes. I had to decide how to face a reality that I knew I had to accept with fortitude. I was first an only child, and then an only daughter, and no serious need or desire had ever been denied me. I had always believed that I led a charmed life. Now I knew that was not true. I realized that no one is promised protection from harm or sadness such as I was experiencing. I knew that neither persons nor things make the difference between gladness and mourning. I considered things I had previously believed to be important in my life. I reviewed the past, and then I looked to the future. Until Jon's death, I expected nothing but the good things of life for myself.

That night, aware of secure support and surrounded by thoughtful tokens of love from my family and friends, I suddenly knew and accepted the chilling fact that I was alone. I realized that I would always be alone. No matter how many good things or how many bad things happened to me, I would be alone within the core of my being, within my own world, where no one else could enter. I was alone with the grief in my soul. No one could do for me what had to be done for me to survive this relentless, penetrating grief. The shiny, clear mirror of my life as known before Jon's death was clouding, and it was beginning to crack from misery.

I understood for the first time that all people, using whatever resources they can rally, must look for strength within themselves. The essence of realistic self-survival includes knowledge that no other person can ever penetrate the spirit of another. Thorough understanding of an individual by another would, in truth, be an invasion of one's own treasured privacy. I wondered if we were created with inspiration to maintain stamina of soul. I determined to survive Jon's death in good spirits and to try never, during my remaining lifetime, to allow myself to become depressed or distraught for any reason. I opened my eyes and smiled at the pretty nurse. I have not been the same person since those moments of experiencing what seemed to me startling revelations.

Each of us is alone, no matter how close another person may be physically or emotionally. Until the death of Jon, I had lived an immature life, happily encircled by interesting family and friends. I had lived a life of naive bliss. When Jon died I became a woman; girlish beliefs that a perfect mirror would reflect my life forever were gone.

I do not know how I would have reacted to Jon's death if I had been less generously endowed intellectually, impoverished rather than fiscally fortunate, or endowed with different genes. Perhaps all of those things have made it easier for me than for some others who have also had to withstand the trauma of life's unexpected adversities. I do not wish for deserved or undeserved gold stars for good behavior such as those I received as a small child. My mother pasted them on our farmhouse kitchen wall; Miss Anna Holsinger, my first grade teacher, pasted them on the bulletin board in our country school. Much brighter adult gold stars should go to those less privileged than I who display patience in the face of traumatic events, disasters, and wars with brave forbearance beyond my comprehension.

During my remaining days in the hospital, I gave trauma management much thought. I came to believe that perhaps traumas and the related emotional shocks might affect sensibilities beyond our physical world. I wondered whether such things might be mentally willed back to an ethereal energy, where all living things may have been conceived. I asked myself, "Is it possible to park traumas to gain respite from situations fraught with grief, anxiety, or remorse?" Going beyond lack of expectation for answers, one must wonder. One might ask "Why?" The answer is simple. Don't ask. There are no logical, intelligent reasons for questioning fate. Sudden deaths, births of impaired children, streaks of extrasensory perception, unplanned occurrences, and unexpected interruptions of careful plans may leave their victims stunned and puzzled. After thoughtful reflection, victims should realize the futility of seeking answers when they cannot be known.

It seems preferable to will by choice the ability to live freely with joy. It seems prudent to apply common sense rather than natural emotionalism to long-term traumas. If not allowed to defy courage or take precedence over normal lifestyle functions, traumas can be compartmentalized within the human brain. I compartmentalized thoughts, even as a child, whenever I simply wished to put aside consideration of anything I found uninteresting. So why not park traumas that, if left unmanaged, would be debilitating? I decided that I had to do that. I knew that I had to store Jon's death on a memory reel.

Since I had within my wonderfully complex brain an endless array of memory reels illustrating scenes ranging from current times to long ago happenings, why not include traumatic memories of Jon's death? Failure to will trauma temporarily from memory leaves one open to unwelcome consideration of all the trauma's aspects. Soul-searching questions for which there are no answers available during one's life span on earth can destroy the energy needed for productive thoughts and intentional deeds. It seems wasteful and futile to expend energy on speculations. Energy needs to be stored for use during actual traumatic or trying times; using energy to fret over imagined worries is neither smart nor productive.

Sometimes I bring forth reels for examination to seek assistance for reviewing my plans for management of new life challenges. Sometimes I bring them out to remind me of who I am or what I am. I never bring them forth to answer "why?" questions. An unexpected reel's projection into my thought processes may be considered or rejected. Unexpected reel flashing is welcomed when it seems intuitive. I quickly repress the flashing of an unwanted, unpleasant reel before more than a quick and quiet, sorrowful jab is felt.

Many professionals downgrade repression and encourage full disclosure of soul and sin to purge the brain and prevent it from harboring unpleasant memories. Not enough consideration is given to the dangers inherent in surfacing and exposing the dregs of the past. Reviewing traumatic situations is not necessarily therapeutic, in my opinion. People have a right to and a responsibility for personal privacy in some matters. Professionals might do well to help clients with developing repression skills! Perhaps that would be too difficult, or not as lucrative as long, ongoing, regularly scheduled soul-and-gut-spilling sessions.

For an emotional illness or disturbance, soul spilling does have benefits. Talking about troublesome situations with anyone, when one feels mildly or deeply concerned, is soothing. There is no proven value in psychotherapy or in frequent meetings with psychologists for the severely mentally ill. Later on in life, experiences of my two mentally ill daughters would teach me that such sessions might increase a person's hostilities and introduce new areas for inclusion into delusion patterns. Such sessions, in my opinion, are sometimes simply lucrative fiscal fountains for therapists.

Management of trauma survival sets one free to see the beauty that is waiting to be seen by willing beholders. Management to survive trauma sets one free to know the joys that are waiting to be found. Pleasure in beauty and joys found close around me, or from anywhere in the world, are choices I make to preserve my central self and to avoid personal, unpleasant mental distractions. I am grateful that I am not mentally ill and that I can make these choices. I am grateful that I own my mind. My mind is self-possessed. Some people call this "living in the moment" or "being present" in one's own life.

During the period from 1980 until 1996, when I was doing volunteer work in Florida, people sometimes contacted me to talk about their perceived problems. First, I usually advised, consider any problem as a challenge. Whenever there had been the personal loss of a loved one, I often, in essence, suggested that the self be spared from mourning woefully. I usually told them, "Never ask why. Never ask questions that have no known answers. Save your energy. Save yourself months of sorrow, and accept as joyfully as possible what fate decrees. If you can do that, you will spare yourself and those around you many hours of joy deprivation."

Tragedy is what you make of it. Tragedy, always soul searing, often creates bitterness and depression that, if allowed, shields out the essential wisdom needed for self-preservation. Such wisdom, earned from unfortunate circumstances, can be absorbed only when emotional gloom and doom are abandoned, and joys are intellectually and consciously perceived, welcomed, and internalized.

Jack and I had two traumas. The trauma of a baby's death and the ultra traumatic horrors of war combined to mature us. Basic things in our lives became more important. Our allegiance to America increased because of our personal sacrifices and because of the ghastly traumas other families we knew had nobly suffered during and after the war. We became more aware of citizen responses needed to match and commend our armed forces; and more aware of the necessity to make America prosper and function as intended by the Constitution. The democratic values for which Jack and many others fought (and for which many died) do not seem generally clear to later generations.

Those who blithely fail to vote or refuse to intelligently assess the issues of our globe that cry for remedial attention threaten freedoms for all people everywhere.

Hollow bells may toll for those who have just read or heard about World War II. Hollow bells may toll for those who do not vote. Hollow bells may toll for those who cast frivolous votes without considering vote validity. My World War II memories inspire me to vote as responsibly as possible. Many died or were maimed while fighting for the freedoms too many now take too lightly. Votes cast lightly demean the valor of dead and living members of our armed forces. Votes cast lightly threaten glorious and wonderful attributes of the United States of America. Those who reject their hard-earned right to vote, and those who do not vote accountably, may, through their irresponsibility, reap seeds of remorse that will have an impact on all of us. Those who reject their hard-earned right to vote, in fact, dishonor all who through the years of U.S. history have valiantly struggled to gain and maintain our freedom to vote.

It was three months before Jack knew that Jon had lived only a few hours. He had written regularly about a child neither of us would ever see. Until Jack learned of Jon's death, his letters had been almost impossibly painful for me to read. Every time a letter came, I hoped that he would write that he knew the baby was dead. Again and again I read how excited he was to be a father.

Dr. Clarence, his father, wrote the sad news that reached Jack first. The letter came to him at his medical collection station where he was the commanding officer of a unit that removed the dead, dying, and wounded soldiers from the battlefield. His father included with his dreadful news the further tidings that Jack's son looked just as Jack had looked as a baby. When my father-in-law stood by my hospital bed and told me what he had written, I was speechless in disbelief. I smiled as I wept internally. I realized how much such an unintended, insensitive statement might have increased Jack's sorrow. I think his father found it so difficult to write that he, for some reason, thought that line would be comforting. He must have known that he and Margaret should not have allowed labor to be induced for a breech birth.

The doctor who delivered Jon told me that the baby was very small and had no fingernails or toenails. I never asked them to perform an autopsy. I never asked whether the baby had Rh-negative blood as I do. I never asked to see him. I did not wish to carry the image of a dead, imperfect child on a memory reel. In hindsight I regret that I was so distraught that I did not request an autopsy.

I will never know what transpired in the delivery room during the delivery of my first-born child. I do believe the delivering doctor felt he could turn the baby to be delivered head first, and I think he probably convinced Dr. Clarence and Margaret of that. I still wonder whether the seventy-two hours of crushing labor were as tiring to the little fellow as they were to me. The deliveries of our three daughters in a much more professional environment poignantly heightened the tragedy of our son's birth and death.

As soon as I was able, I went to Washington to see some of the doctors I had known during Jack's medical training years at George Washington University Hospital. One of them slapped the desk with his hand and exclaimed loudly, "My God, Maxene, why didn't you get out of that bed and come to me?"

So far as I know, Jack never mentioned Jon's death to anyone except once. One day he and Margaret were having a slightly heated argument about a medical procedure. He became irritated with her for not seeming to have well-founded arguments and angrily said, "Well, I have never sanctioned inducing a breech birth."

I was sorry Jack was curt with her. When Jonnie died Margaret was so distressed that for a few days she could not come to the hospital. I thought she might have failed to protest during my labor and delivery out of respect for her father and the obstetrician. She, who was a friend and my age, sat with me many hours in my room during labor. Neither of us needed to be reminded by Jack of Jon's death. I had reeled all of it away as soon as possible. I could not afford to uselessly waste energy thinking about what might have been.

That lesson also taught me that it is wasted energy to worry about anything that may happen. I now know that I must save my energy for the times when some event demands its use. Worrying, per se, is an absolutely senseless, needless waste of precious mental and physical energies. But then, again and again, I rued the fact that I had not questioned the doctor's plan. I knew that Jack was a great believer in letting Mother Nature have her way whenever safely possible. He did not favor induced labor. I should have stayed the doctor's orders and his exploring, possibly harmful, hands until I had gotten another opinion from a doctor somewhere outside the immediate geographic area. A single opinion about any serious medical condition should not be allowed to stand-alone or be accepted without question.

During the years since Jon's birth and death, experience and consideration have raised questions that did not occur to me at the time. No longer is it possible to find answers to what went wrong. Perhaps no one could have figured it out then. Perhaps no one in a similar situation now would be able to figure out what went wrong. Failure of doctors to interfere or censure other doctors is legendary, to their discredit. That relatives of a little baby stood by silently when another doctor seemed to be practicing medicine inappropriately illustrates for me, upon retrospect, the excessive loyalty that is sometimes felt among members of the medical profession. I suspect that there are few whistle-blowers within the medical profession. There is not enough accountable internal monitoring that carries deserved consequences for deeds that damage fellow human beings. Incompetent doctors should be publicly exposed by their peers and denied licenses to practice medicine.

My mother-in-law, "Ma," as she was affectionately called, put on her hat and gloves and came to visit me when I was still in the hospital, but she never mentioned the baby. The fact that this dear, introverted little lady signaled empathy by coming to visit me was comforting and very significant. She rarely left the house, and she never seemed comfortable when she did. Once she told me that I sometimes seemed more like a child of hers than her own children. I think it was because I am an extrovert, and I enjoyed joking around with her, sometimes with fairly wild abandon.

She, and the two Drs. Obenschain insisted that I move back to Selma for the balance of my recuperation time. I knew I couldn't handle that. I definitely was not going to go to my own parents' home and inconvenience them and my young brother, so I certainly would not consider going to Jack's home. I wanted to stay right where I was for a while. I needed to be alone to heal. I needed to think and get myself in tune with the new ideas I was having about my personal inner spirit.

In 1945 young mothers were allowed needed respite from home duties after a child's delivery. At least a week of bonding time was provided between mother and baby in the hospital. I remained in the maternity ward for a week while nurses passed my door carrying babies to their mothers at feeding time. One nurse brought a baby into my room and told me that she thought it would be good for me to see the baby. That was as bad as the mother of one of my friends carrying her two-month-old grandson across the room and putting him in my arms after I had returned to Harrisonburg. Such insensitivity puzzled me then, and it puzzles me today. When the grandmother came toward me and handed me her grandchild, I thought momentarily that I could not hold the child. But I had no choice other than to take him and hold him for a few minutes. It was painful. Walking in another person's shoes, unfortunately, was not a talent given to that grandmother.

Outpatient, get-rid-of-the-patient-as-soon-as-possible, hospital processes were unknown in 1945. A comparative economic study might show that outpatient procedures themselves ultimately create more expense than in-house procedures with recuperative hospital stays. I don't know, but my longer hospital stay granted me time to be cared for with privacy in an impersonal place long enough for me to think clearly about ways to fit back into a routine life different from the one I had expected just days earlier. This was essential to my healing. Mothers and infants can bond within a week of carefree, monitored, in-hospital care, and the mother can be taught how to feed and nurture her child. The mother has an opportunity to consider how she will adapt her home life to include an additional person. Studies about preventable problems with infants might benefit from a close look at the advantages of spending the first days of their lives in a more stable environment. Such studies might illuminate important benefits for parents, babies, doctors, and all others concerned.

Once upon a time some things really were better. Nowadays discourtesies and computerized shortcuts contribute to the discontent and dissatisfaction of consumers of all services and particularly of health services. Consumers merit better treatment and comfort strokes when being served in stores, hospitals, restaurants, or anywhere else they are spending their money. Surely owners of overcharged credit cards should be treated kindly; many of them already suffer enough from living beyond their means!

My parents continued their efforts to make everything as easy as possible for me. They asked a friend, a funeral director, to come to the hospital to pick me up and take me home in an ambulance. When we arrived at my parents' house, the director, opened the ambulance door, reached in, scooped me up in his arms, and carried me into the house. He put me down gently in a bed brought downstairs for me because there were no downstairs bedrooms in the house. I remembered being told that, when I was born at my mother's home place, a bed was brought down to the parlor for my birthing and Mother's recuperation. History was repeating itself, once with a newborn baby and the father nearby, and once without a baby, and with the father thousands of miles away.

New mothers in my mother's generation and in my generation were treated with tender, loving care. No walking up steps was allowed for weeks. Was all of that totally wrong for the best of all concerned? I don't know. I do know that I am glad that I had my children during the days of pampering. I am a feminist, but I do not want to be treated as if I were as robust as men are fashioned to be. I leave that attitude to the wonderful modern women who may rightly wish to do all the things men can do. Let me add that I do think that women who aspire to compete with equality of physical strengths are wonderful. I just happen to be Virginia born and bred, naturally clumsy, spoiled, and inclined toward laziness for all physical sports and work.

I am lazy enough; whenever I am planning a project or any other activity, I start by asking myself how a lazy person would do the job. Much to my great joy, I long ago discovered that the lazy way with smart shortcuts is many times the best way to accomplish a task. This is something bureaucrats have yet to learn. One of my dearest friends, the late Bill Hawfield, a career DuPont plant manager, once told me that every unnecessary movement made in performing a task is wasted energy. I think I have saved a lot of physical energy by using lazy ways to work.

I did not wish to be idle, so within a few weeks of Jon's death I went to work as an assistant manager in a children's clothing store that was getting ready to open in Harrisonburg. I helped inventory stock, and I worked in the shop for a few weeks after it opened before Dr. Duke, President of Madison College, now James Madison University, called and asked me if I would consider coming to the college as manager of the tearoom. I was delighted to accept. Some of my institutional management training had been in the tearoom, so I welcomed the chance to return to a familiar place to work until Jack came home. I had dated two of Dr. Duke's sons when I was younger, and his wife was a friend of my mother's, so it was a relaxing situation for me. I welcomed the opportunity to be busy in a familiar place around other busy people.

Soon after I started managing the tearoom, I got permission from Dr. Duke to remodel the dreary place. I told him it looked like an ice cream parlor and should be livened up to be more cheerful. He was not overly enthusiastic, but he told me to go ahead. I used sky blue and white striped wallpaper, and I put live geraniums in recessed windows all around the dining room. Students, especially the young students I taught in institutional management training, enjoyed having snacks or the frozen fruit salad that had been a special recipe there for many years. For me the tearoom was a relief from grief.

I resigned from the tearoom when Jack came home in 1946. He came home with lupus, which was problematic for him the rest of his life. Lupus was a relatively small price for him to pay. Thousands of men and women had been killed. Some were left unburied in unknown places. Many others were buried in Flanders Field or in other places far away. People came home maimed for life. People came back to hospitals to learn to walk with manufactured legs, to be taught how to spend the rest of their lives in wheelchairs, and to be treated for all kinds of devastating mental or physical scars from war. Jack came home as handsome as ever and prepared to begin a new life. I was also eager to begin a new life. Unfortunately each of us envisioned a new life differently from the other.

Margaret, unbeknownst to me, had the Red Cross request Jack's return from Japan where he was serving in the post-war occupation forces. She and her ailing father had decided that they needed help with the medical care of their patients. The doctor father and doctor sister still maintained their offices, independent of one another, on the ground floor of the home place. That was the three-story, winged, eighteenth-century plantation house with tall white columns where I had stayed prior to Jonnie's birth. The elder doctor was having heart problems, and they needed help, so the family made a decision that it was time for the doctor son to come to the rescue. The decision was made and acted upon with malice toward none, but without consideration for the wife of the expected savior knight.

I learned of Jack's requested arrival when I called to ask what Christmas gift name had been drawn for me. Jack had nine siblings. Since it was almost ludicrous to have everyone buy everyone else a present, and since no one really needed anything, names were always drawn. They, with their progeny, offered us, and later our daughters, a second Christmas celebration every year. The large tree with its mountain of presents was always shielded by a sheet hung in the arch of the so-called music room until it was time for gift presentations after a bounteous Christmas morning buffet breakfast. It was a wonderful room for Christmas celebrations. The high ceiling was centered with a large bas-relief wreath enclosing a beautiful painting of sky and cherubs.

I think perhaps the call for Jack to come home was made, thinking that he might be able to get there in time for the Christmas jubilee and the hours-long Christmas gift exchange, exclamations, and thanking ceremonies. He did not arrive in time for Christmas Day, but when he did get home in the spring of 1946, a different kind of family gathering was arranged.

The adult family members assembled at his sister Evelyn's home in Waynesboro. The topic for discussion was when and how Jack and I would assume management of the "big house" and provide care for their aging parents, who wished to stay in the lovely, old six-bedroom home for the remaining years of their lives. It was a surreal scene. I was so happy to have Jack home safely, but I was dismayed that my life was being planned with me as a silent partner. I knew that the plans being made were not to be my fate, but I remained quiet while the family members, sitting in a circle, started discussing how much each would contribute in physical assistance and financial monthly maintenance of the home place. Jack's father practiced medicine in the days before it was an absolute that doctors be rich. When he went to medical school, there were no sarcastic references made to imply that the freshman medical class 101 was about how to buy a Mercedes within the first year of practice. Dr. Obenschain often accepted farm produce in payment, and he often received no payment at all.

As I sat through that session, I was thinking how the elegant old house simply seemed like a big rooming and boarding house to me. Without giving notice, friends and family members trooped in any old time to spend a night or to eat a meal. A standing joke was that one friend had been there for three days when my mother-in-law looked around the table and said, "Why, Herbert, how nice to see you." The cook just made do for whoever showed up at the extra-large dining table in time for a meal.

Between meals there was usually some kind of card or chess game in progress at the long dining table. I always felt that there must be a line outside the bathrooms. General confusion, as found in this lovely vestige of Colonial days, was uniquely enjoyed in this happy household. It was too different from the familiar quiet atmosphere of my parents' home for me to find long-term pleasure there. I surely was not going to be a twenty-four hour, seven-day-a-week hostess in circumstances so contrary to my lifestyle preferences. I was not going to be at the mercy of whimsical visitors dropping by, sleepy or hungry, at random times of their convenience.

Finally as the siblings were offering their assistance plans, someone turned to me and said, "What about it, Maxene?" My unusual silence had finally been noticed. I replied, "I will not be doing anything because I will not be there." Jack, utterly surprised and uncharacteristically macho, said, "I will be there, and all will be well." I just smiled.

In the car going home, I calmly told him that I was perfectly serious, and, that if he chose to practice medicine from his father's office while living at home with his parents and assuming the responsibilities that entailed, he would have to go it alone. I could not see raising a family in that stressful environment. That was the end of that conversation. He was so shocked that he made no response. The ride back to Staunton from Waynesboro seemed like a very long twelve miles. Selma must have seemed to him like a house of cards about to tumble as he contemplated this unexpected opposition to his apparently foreordained savior role to preserve life-as-usual there. I felt sorry for his discomfiture, but, at the same time, I felt very annoyed about the entrapment set for me without Jack even realizing it.

To his credit Jack recognized that coming home to an ailing father had diverted his attention away from his marriage. His finest and noblest sensitivities had risen to an occasion naturally created by the aging of parents with children concerned for their health. Practicality was not a consideration until the plan began to look like harsh reality. He came to understand his misplaced sense of mission, and he notified his siblings that we had decided to establish his medical practice and our habitat just twelve miles south in Waynesboro, which was only forty miles from Harrisonburg. We would be near but not a part of the home place and the family medical practice.

We were going to live the lives we had once dreamed of living. We were both very social service orientated. Jack had grown up in the home of an altruistic doctor. I had grown up in the shadows of altruistic Mennonite and Brethren relatives. My parents had responded empathetically to catastrophic events of the world. All my life, I had heard how these events related to one another and how people who were not directly affected were, in fact, involved and should respond.

When Jack graduated from George Washington Medical School, the dean of the school, also a White House doctor, and three other prominent doctors in Washington asked him about training to work in their respective specialist areas. The dean, some doctors told me, had said that Jack and another graduate were the two in that class most likely to become outstanding medical practitioners. I did not take those remarks very seriously, and I doubted that the dean had been so expressive. Years later, however, Jack referred a patient to the dean. When she returned she asked me if we had been aware of how disappointed the dean was that Jack had not stayed in Washington. The dean told her that he still believed Jack belonged where his abilities to offer exceptional medical care could be most fully utilized.

An army general had encouraged Jack to remain in the army during the short time he was stationed at Walter Reed Hospital between his arrival back in the States from Japan and his discharge. The general had said that he would see to it that Jack would become a colonel, but Jack had told him that he just wanted to go back to the Shenandoah Valley and practice family medicine.

Jack and I discussed his unexpected opportunities and, without hesitation or reservation, decided that being directly involved with a community and the families therein, and providing strong pillars of support within their community systems, was what we wanted to do, even though the monetary return would be less. We had no clue that the transition into specialized medicine was about to take place. During that transition, family medicine was demeaned, and medicine as we believed it should be practiced began to disappear.

We had no forewarning of the upcoming changes in the delivery of medical services to dampen our enthusiasm in looking for living quarters and office space in Waynesboro. Jack opened his office and began seeing patients in October 1946. He never knew the typical hardship of an unknown young doctor opening an office when empty waiting rooms persisted until people learned by word-of-mouth about the availability of a new doctor in town. Doctors and attorneys did not advertise in 1946. For either profession, to even seem to attempt any public notice was to invite uncomplimentary descriptions like "ambulance chaser." The Obenschain family medical reputation was in place in the area because of Margaret and Dr. Clarence. It was extremely gratifying that Jack was busy from the moment he opened his office door. We had a jump start in becoming established in a stable community where we believed that our family would have happily enriched lives ever after. All of our good fortune seemed almost too good to be true. It was.

Selma, the big house with the big heart.

Maxene in 1945 after Jon's death, looking forward to the end of World War II.

Life on Wayne Avenue

I had made an appointment at the University of Virginia with Dr. John Nokes, head of the Obstetrical Department, before Jack got home from Japan. Dr. Nokes, a wonderfully kind gentleman, examined me and was very candid. I think he spoke frankly to me because I was a doctor's wife. He was outraged about Jon's death, and he made no bones about it. He told me that he was so sorry I had been victimized. He felt that I could have more children and that it would be unlikely for me to ever again experience problems like those with Jon. Knowing this before Jack got home was important to me. Jack had suffered enough grief because of a child's death. He needed to have renewed hope that he could become a father. Dr. Nokes's opinion made Jack's homecoming more exciting.

Jack located his first-floor office space in a house on Main Street in the heart of Waynesboro. The house had been a funeral home at one time, so he had to move right along with getting it remodeled and ready for a business for the living. While we looked for a house to buy, we rented a room from Mrs. Harper, the former postmaster's widow, in her two-story brick house on Cherry Avenue.

There were no houses for sale in Waynesboro, but our brother-in-law Wallace McAllister, husband to Jack's sister Evelyn, had an option to buy a very small house on Wayne Avenue. We bought the ugly, unpainted, insignificant little concrete bungalow and painted the concrete burgundy and the rather distinctive wood trim chalk white. It now looked like an attractive cottage, the perfect starter home for a young couple. One redeeming feature of the house was a good-sized living room with a large fireplace centered on one wall. The wide fireplace, framed by bricks, was centered beneath a broad deep mantle. We painted that wall burgundy and all other walls, the mantle, and the fireplace chalk white. It made an interesting backdrop for our furnishings. We bought a sofa that was upholstered with a pretty china blue, white, and burgundy striped material. I used my childhood piggy bank money to buy a good Queen Anne china blue wingback chair. We painted the brick hearth black, and put brass andirons and an antique brass kettle for wood on it. Jack managed to get the burgundy pull draperies hung that I had made while Jackie and I were waiting in Harrisonburg for the house to be cleaned and painted. With the addition of a few other occasional furniture pieces, antique blue glass lamps, and miscellaneous accessories; the little house was ready to welcome our family.

Jack managed to get his office opened in October, but he did not have the house ready for occupancy before our first little girl was born. Jackie was born at the University of Virginia Hospital on January 28, 1947. The night before Dr. Nokes delivered her, he came in at around 1:00 in the morning and sat in a big armchair in my room for the rest of the night. When Jack thanked him, he said, "Well, I just thought Maxene might have some worries because of her history." Jack was busy that night delivering someone else's baby twenty-five miles away in the Waynesboro Community Hospital. A carefree conversation with Dr. Nokes between labor pains did make the night seem shorter and the morning less threatening when I was finally taken to the delivery room.

When our precious little five-pound girl Jacquelyn Shank Obenschain, who was destined to become paranoid schizophrenic, was born, it seemed a miracle. The rejoicing of both families upon her arrival was more than supportive. Everyone felt immense relief that this child, unlike Jon, though small, seemed perfectly formed and healthy. Not until she was in her early twenties did we learn that she had only one kidney and imperfect reproductive organs. Not until recent years has it become known that her brain scans differently from a normal brain.

Once again I was brought home in an ambulance, this time from Charlottesville. Once again I was sleeping in my parents' dining room on a bed brought down from upstairs so that I would not have to go up and down the steps. I experienced some very outlandish feelings the night or two that I was left downstairs alone with the baby. Having Jackie there alive beside me in an antique crib that had originally been given to me for Jonnie was unexpectedly stressful. That I had once been alone without my newborn child in this same room caused me such extreme anxiety that I was afraid to go to sleep. My first baby had died, and I was having trouble staving off my anxiety that this baby might also die. I was actually fearful that I might accidentally sleepwalk or do something harmful to the baby. I slept nervously for the first week that Jackie and I slept in that room.

When she was a month old, the Waynesboro house was ready for us to occupy. Like thousands of other couples, Jack and I, at long last, after living through the uncertain and frightening years of war, were going to settle down comfortably. We no longer felt our futures threatened. We were ecstatic. We had Jackie. Life was beautiful. We were eager to assume family responsibilities and enjoy the privileges of living in a stable community in a wonderful, peaceful country.

Everyone in both of our families enjoyed our bright little girl. When she was only a baby, differences about her were obvious. As soon as she was able to sit up in her playpen, she rejected toys and dolls except for a little curly-furred black lamb that contained a music box. Mother had given her the lamb, and she felt good that she had found something that Jackie liked.

Jackie often sat turning pages and looking at her rag books, giving the impression that babies are able to read. She did not have one hair on her head; and it was interesting to see this tiny little hairless human baby looking completely absorbed, as she seemed to study her books. I sometimes Scotch taped a bow on her head so that she would be recognized as a baby girl. So there she would sit, happily engrossed, looking ridiculous and intellectual at the same time.

She and I often rode around on country back roads when she became old enough to stand beside me on the car seat behind my protecting elbow. She could cackle like a chicken, gobble like a turkey, moo like a cow, baa like a lamb, or neigh like a horse. Many times I stopped the car so that when she saw an animal, she could enjoy calling out to it by doing her imitation calls. She learned the sounds easily and thoroughly. She was sometimes intentionally funny. I often talked to her as with an adult. She seemed to understand, and she responded in kind when she was as young as two years of age.

In the late forties it was not uncommon to have household help. Our first maid/cook combination refused to have surgery to remove her adenoids and said "Tursday" for Thursday, and "chuch" for church. Jackie was around Ruth so much that she used the same pronunciations. One of our friends loved to ask Jackie to say that she was going to church on Thursday. He never ever let her know how cute or comical he found her response. Most of the time, it was very entrancing to watch her serious little face as she talked about things most young children are not concerned about.

Almost as soon as she started to walk, she began running. This small individualist would clinch her little fists, put her head down, and race through the house or around the yard thinking. Sometimes she would be so deep in thought that we would have to speak twice to get her attention. She never minded stopping to look at you or discussing with you whatever was on her mind. She was not secretive. She had a tricycle as soon as her legs were almost long enough to pedal it. At first she was barely able to hit the pedals with each foot in turn, and wait for the pedals to come around to be hit again. In this manner she rode the tricycle fast and carefully while being absorbed in thought as she traveled around and around through the living room and dining room of our first Wayne Avenue house.

She had a toy bulldog named Mitey Mite that she loved, and they played delightfully together. Mitey Mite thought he was a big dog, and he loved to chase cars. One day a truck that he was chasing ran over him and killed him. Sorrowfully, we planned a funeral, and Jackie was very active in the process of choosing a burial site for Mitey Mite. She chose a place by the back steps, and for a while she frequently placed flowers or some other token there in his memory. We also had two Siamese cats, so Mitey Mite was not as sorely missed as he might have been had he been our only pet.

A busy, active, intelligent child, Jackie was always happy and it was fun to talk with her. We never did baby talk at our house anyway, but, even as a very young child, she liked to talk with adults, and she preferred their conversations to childish chatter. Later as a teenager in Florida, she complained to me that teens were too frivolous in their thinking and manner of speaking. She preferred talking with older people.

Jyl Stuart was born on April 30, 1949. Unbeknownst to us, we had another wonderful child, another small baby girl weighing about five pounds, who was destined to become mentally ill. She was a dreamer as a child, and she did not talk as early as Jackie did, but when she spoke, it was in sentences. She was curious about everything around her and, as soon as she was old enough, she opened drawers wherever and whenever she could to peek inside to discover what was not evident to the world at large. Jyl was our most naturally extroverted child. A careful observer, she sometimes called attention to details that others found uninteresting or simply did not notice. She made up stories with great imagination. She had a wonderful sense of humor and was like a ray of sunshine. Though she was not as somber as Jackie, she took life and her creative ideas very seriously without appearing to be as soulfully involved as she really was with everything around her.

When Jyl was born, Jackie was as proud of her as if she were the baby's mother. She liked to hang around and help take care of Jyl. This mothering, caring attitude lasted as long as Jyl lived. Jyl, our dreamer, was extremely creative and at times fearsomely impractical. Jackie always spoke with concern for her, and she watched warily as Jyl enjoyed her own visionary thoughts that produced poetry and paintings. Jyl loved and trusted everyone, and she always tried to make others feel good.

I remember when she was about four years old, watching her take iced lemonade on a hot summer day to men collecting trash when they stopped by our curbside. She loved to make people smile. She often articulated suffering for others when there were famines or other disasters anywhere in the world.

Jan Teaford was a bouncy, normal-sized baby when she was born on November 12, 1951. Jack, due to his heightened interest in mothers who had difficulty delivering normal babies, had given me shots that he had successfully used with some mothers who had repeated failures with pregnancies or births of abnormal children. Because I was Rh negative, had a history of two natural abortions, had given birth to Jon, who was born with deformities, and who lived only a few hours, and had also had two small five-pound girl babies, Jack suggested that I ask Dr. Nokes if he minded if he gave me the B vitamin shots. The doctor saw no harm in it. I still have the little empty vial that Jack handed me to keep as a memento. We credited the vitamins it contained with helping Jan to develop in a more healthy prenatal way than her siblings.

Jan was our only child born as strong as a baby should be and as healthy looking as a baby is wished to be. Like many other mothers to whom Jack had given these shots, I was thrilled to have this wonderfully healthy baby. That she was an unusually attractive child was a bonus. Most parents believe their babies are beautiful, but there were few who saw Jan who did not comment on her beauty. Jan, when she noticed and became part of a world larger than herself, seemed more introspective than her sisters. She could be exasperating with her inclination to remain silent while making decisions and then springing the results of those decisions upon us without much regard for other persons' feelings or opinions. We did not believe she was callous because she seemed to be unaware of any possible hurt she might inflict by her rare, seemingly thoughtless, actually harmless, behaviors.

Jan refused to take swimming lessons with the other children in our swimming pool at our larger second Wayne Avenue home. I took a picture of her wearing a bathing cap, looking ready to swim, and sitting on the steps at the shallow end of the pool. She sat there big-eyed and brooding for a few weeks, watching the other children taking lessons. Then one day she calmly took off swimming, diving, and doing all the things right that she apparently had chosen to learn by observation. After displaying her proficiency in the pool, she surfaced from a dive with a wonderful, impish grin on her face to receive applause from everyone.

We made no comments to her, either pro or con, regarding her sit-down strike. We did wonder what she thought about as she sat stock still on the steps. After she came swimming off the steps, Jack and I discussed and wondered whether this attractive little girl's lack of participation in swimming classes was an attention-getting ploy, based on a fear of competing with the other children's skills, or just negativity. Jack laughed and said, "Pretty is as pretty does. This is one time that pretty Jan was not appealing in her actions until she swam."

Jack's first seven years of practice followed the standard pattern with an office downtown, but he wanted to be with the children as much as possible, so we bought a larger home in 1953 where he could practice medicine and still be at home. This much larger house was only one block away from our first home, and it provided room for both his medical practice and our family. When we bought the medical practice and home combination, we were once again ecstatic because the scene was now set for an idyllic family medical practice as well as for an idyllic family life.

Jack bought a second-hand pickup truck to use as a moving van, and again and again the ancient vehicle was loaded with belongings from our small house. He and the children made hauling trip after hauling trip, looking like Tobacco Road's Jeeter and family, moving down Wayne Avenue from the small house to the larger house. The truck was cheap, old, and tired; its brakes exhausted long ago. Jack told everyone not to fear; the avenue was flat. Jack could get into absolutely inane do-it-yourself projects that he and the children enjoyed and that I did my best to tolerate with good humor.

Jack turned moving from one house to the other into a lark for the children. Jackie, Jyl, and Jan were six, four, and two years old respectively, and they were too young to understand that this moving methodology was really, in their mother's opinion, an exercise in idiocy. They loved seeing their belongings go onto the old rusty truck that would be driven by their father, and then piling onto the front seat for a ride. They loved helping their father and his paid helpers unload their things at their new home. The girls literally helped the family move.

Jack's handyman characteristics were sometimes irritating to me because I was raised by a father who would not have picked up a screwdriver or hammer if the house had fallen down around his family. He could afford to pay others to do those jobs, and he sincerely believed that if one was fortunate enough to be able to give others a way to earn money, it was the humane thing to do. He reiterated often that he believed that each of us should help others in as many ways as possible. Putting food on tables for families, he said, keeps the world spinning. He practiced what he preached. Jack's moving was not humorous to him. It reminded Daddy and me of the remarks made years before to my parents by their friends who lived in Staunton about Jack's father, Dr. Clarence, being a nice, eccentric man.

Being in a new house engendered lots of excited running and tricycle riding for Jackie. She had such a wonderful, lively little-girl expression when she was elated about anything. Taking the new little sister Jyl out in the baby carriage with Helen, our second housekeeper-nanny in our first small home, while helping to push the carriage, and chasing Mitey Mite around the yard were two things that transformed her often musing little face into paroxysms of obvious joy.

Jack's handyman talents were displayed again a year later, rather charmingly this time, when he took an old lawn mower tractor and used it to pull a large cart that he had made to haul things around our second Wayne Avenue home. It turned out to not be very utilitarian, and it was used mostly for fun. The cart, filled with our girls and with three or four MacIllwaine boys, rode up and down neighborhood sidewalks with Jack happily at the wheel, enjoying the bumpy trips to nowhere as much as the children. When he had time free from his practice, he loved to go out and start the lawn mower motor that brought little Obenschain girls running from the house and little MacIllwaine boys flying down the sidewalk from their house, two doors away, to jump aboard. Jackie was always relaxed, looking happy, in the middle of it all. The lawn mower trailer treks, besides providing joy rides, were another way to get Jackie's nose out of books while providing hours of pleasure for everyone on the improvised train.

Whenever possible Jack came over from the office on weekdays for the daily 5:00 o'clock Mickey Mouse and Howdy Doody shows. The girls had Mickey Mouse hats, which they always wore as they ran from wherever they were and climbed into a big overstuffed chair to chant happily as the show began, "Mickey Mouse, Mickey Mouse, Mickey Mouse." If one of them was late, Jack would call out with laughter in his voice, "It's Howdy Doody time."

Today reels from my head play Howdy Doody tunes, and I see dear little girls' heads with Mickey Mouse ears silhouetted against the TV screen. Those happy hours were the happiest of the many happy hours, non-alcoholic and alcoholic, that I have known.

Jack liked to pick up the girls and whirl them around in his arms to hear them squeal with delight. My clearest memory is of Jan being whirled because he always sang out as he swung her around and up and down like a zooming airplane, "Watch out, everybody. Here comes Jannie Wannie!" Sometimes I felt he was partial to Jan. One of my friends even remarked about it one day.

My parents often came to visit on Sunday afternoons. My father went to Washington every week to promote and broker Shenandoah's Pride milk and other dairy products. He often took the train from Staunton into the District of Columbia around nine o'clock on Sunday nights, and my mother would stay at our house for a few days. The grandparents' visits provided the children with remarkable opportunities to be with their grandparents and to get to know and love them.

Sometimes Jackie would corral her sisters and teach them lines for small theatrical productions that they then presented in the living room. Jackie was a very good and firm play director. I think the other two were less enthusiastic than she, but they played their parts well. To see children as young as six, eight, and ten finding pleasure in such an endeavor was interesting to the proud adults. It was a pleasure, which provided entertaining times for both the actors and the audience.

When Jyl entered first grade, she told me how she hated Jane and Puff, who lived in her first grade reader. She complained that Jane and Puff were "really dumb." I explained that reading about Jane and Puff was part of being educated, and that all first graders had to put up with them. I told her to remember that many children found them interesting. She reluctantly read about them to me, but she disliked what she considered dull reading.

Just before Christmas, Jyl's first grade teacher sent out "readiness" reports to parents about their children. I wish I had kept Jyl's report. It was unbelievable to us. It stated that Jyl was not ready for first grade and that she seemed unable to do the tasks expected. I went to the school, looked through a small window in the classroom entrance door, and saw Jyl looking out through the window with a fairly moronic expression. Obviously, she was not mentally in that room.

We immediately made an appointment with the pediatrician at the University of Virginia who had taken care of her at birth. Pausing as I sit here writing, I can close my eyes and visualize Jyl sitting in her panties on the examining table, looking askance at us with her big blue eyes. The doctor took one look into her face, turned, and came over to say quietly to me, "Before I touch her, before anyone does any tests, I will predict that she is smarter than her teacher, and that Jyl is bored, bored, bored."

His prediction turned out to be true. After extensive testing by university psychiatrists and other professionals, it was recommended that Jyl be transferred to another school. They actually wanted to recommend to the Waynesboro school board that the teacher be fired. We insisted that not be done because the teacher, as far as we could learn, had a good record with most children. Jyl happened to be different in both creative ability and personality, and she was indifferent to classroom work.

We learned at the university that Jyl's creativity was "off the board" and that boredom with routine life situations would probably always be problematic for her. They told us that that fussing over C grades would be a great mistake, and that she could do anything she wished, but the wishing would have to be of her own volition. In other words we should not stifle whatever talents she might develop by asking her do academic things other than of her own volition. We transferred her to a Lutheran church school that some parents had found to be excellent in working with children with many different talents.

We were lucky that a friend, Becky Tressel, was the first grade teacher. We talked with Becky, told her Jyl's history from the university, and cautioned her that making Jyl like school should probably be the primary goal for the rest of the year. We told Becky that our major concern was not that Jyl be passed to second grade. We just hoped she would learn to enjoy school. In that process we hoped that she would learn the hard way that life is not just a joy ride without demands for honest, hard work that has to be done to get ahead in a competitive world. Becky, to whom we were forever grateful, did allow Jyl, within reasonable limits and without harassment, the freedom to work as little or as much as she chose.

When Jyl came home with her final first grade report card, she ran into the den, climbed into my lap, looked up into my face, and, with those big blue eyes full of questions, said, "Mother, everyone passed but me. Why?" I smiled and asked, "Jyl, did you work hard to pass?" She looked at me as though that was a silly question and replied, "No."

I told Jyl that I was sorry she had not passed, but not surprised. I explained that everyone has to work to be rewarded, and that in school that means studying and trying to learn so that they can be passed ahead from one grade to another. I smiled and said, "No harm done. You can study next year." She laughed and said, "OK," and ran off happily to play. She probably went off to draw pictures and scribble jingles, which she did well and loved doing. That was play to her.

Every week I spent special time alone with each child. I took each little girl to the library as soon as she could walk. I let them touch the books carefully so that they would learn to enjoy and care for them in their own independent ways. At home there were books and many magazines; they were never put out of reach of the children. *Highlights* was their favorite children's magazine. Jack's medical books and periodicals were left wherever he might be reading. Our children had access to lots of interesting reading materials, and they gained knowledge on their own many times. Our read-aloud storybook became tattered and torn from being used so frequently. Best of all, they loved to hear Jack and me mimic Billy Goat Gruff as we read. All three girls learned to love books. All three liked to write and do artwork. All three of them have done creative work as adults.

Jan, always a source of great pride to her late father and me, remains that for me today. She has written books published by reputable publishers, and she has written a syndicated column about computers. She did all of that exceptionally well, even though she had no extensive formal training as a writer or in computer operations. I am grateful every day for the contributions that Jan, as an educator and writer, has made and continues to make to her community. She has been, at most times during her life, all Jack and I ever wanted or dreamed for our children.

When I ramble through my memory reels, I see exciting events. I find many happy, loving faces around Virginia Yuletide trees, and I see many happy holidays in many different places. Reels of Christmas dinners at my parents' home, Jack's home, at my own homes, and at my two brothers' homes play back to bring me renewed pleasures that rekindle courage of soul, heart, and mind. The poignancy of Christmas seasons for me, I think, can be traced to the fact that I have always saved Christmas memories, whether for elaborately or less ceremoniously observed holidays, in a special cherished segment of my treasure trove of mirrored reflections. Some of my Christmas reels reflect crossroads and turning points in my life. Some of them are free from care. Some are them are fraught with sadness. I love best those that have brightly hued, almost photographic-clarity memories, reflecting joyous family Christmases.

In 1953, for instance, Jack stood outside on our front porch steps, painting a huge spruce tree. It was ten feet tall, and it had at least a six-foot base diameter. He merrily sprayed it top to bottom, grinning through the white paint spots that were freezing on his face. He was a family doctor for fourteen years, 1946 until 1960, to many Waynesboro and Augusta County families; but he always found the time and patience to enjoy his own family and to do special things with our three little girls and me. At our house, even though we were involved with community activities, quality time for the children collectively, and individually for each little girl, was guaranteed without inspiration from Dr. Spock. At Christmas, 1953, all of us worked to decorate the house and tree in gold and white to offer a change from traditional green and red colors.

Twisted, gold-painted chicken wire encircled the front-hall newel post and the dining table centerpiece. Little gold elves climbed golden wires between large and small pink, sparkling Christmas balls. We had an adult party that year. The old house sparkled with friendly laughter from the light hearts of parents of young families freed for a few short hours from parental responsibilities. I remember one of the guests saying "Isn't it wonderful to have enough space to really enjoy everyone present? The ongoing social life in this town, with its large parties, sometimes gets tedious. This is so relaxing." I recall that I laughed and replied that I had once remarked at a huge Waynesboro Country Club private party one night, "You know, a lot of money has been wasted on beautiful clothes for this party. It is so crowded that the ladies could have worn only a blouse, and they would have gone unnoticed because of the compressed crowd." I think of that 1953 Christmas as the last one when our family had freedom from shadows—sinister shadows—cast by the forewarnings of mental illnesses, that came to be challenges for all of us to share and suffer for the rest of our lives.

In 1954 we put in a swimming pool because we thought it would bring other children to our house to create a social scene that would be comfortable for Jackie and fun for everyone. Because of Jackie's desire to read and her not wanting to play with other children, we hired a once-a-week swimming instructor and extended invitations to some of our friends' children to come and join the swimming classes. It seemed to work. Jackie became a good friend to another doctor's daughter. They spent nights with one another and did telephone chat time. We were elated when this friendship flourished. There were times, however, when everyone was around the pool when I would have to go upstairs and ask Jackie to come back out because we still had guests. She never resisted coming. Once back outside she participated wholeheartedly and seemed to like being with everyone and splashing around with whoever was in the pool.

The house was on a large corner lot on Wayne Avenue and Eleventh Street. We fenced in an area about fifty feet by sixty feet around the pool, and we put in a large patio. We set up a grill and plugged in a freezer large enough to keep frozen hamburgers and corn ready for grilling at any time. We also had frozen cherry and apple tarts that needed only to be popped into the oven in the kitchen that was just inside the back door. Ours was the only private swimming pool in Waynesboro, so we had lots of company and lots of fun in and around it. There were booths, tables, tall kerosene torches with citronella oil fuel, which made beautiful flames that kept mosquitoes at bay, lounge chairs, floats, and everything one thinks of when going poolside. All summer long the pool was open at least part of every sunny day. The pool was opened on Memorial Day when my family was invited to party. It closed on Labor Day when Jack's family members were invited to party. A latch at the top of the back door from the house ensured that no child accessed the pool from the house without an adult, so our pool, our summer-time fun center, was not an attractive hazard available to the children.

We also kept a badminton net stretched and ready for play. The McAllister children, Carol, Kirk, and Sara, often spent hours playing with whoever else happened to be available to play. The McAllisters were the nearest geographically of our extended real family, so the two three-girl families spent many happy hours together.

Jack found the pool a wonderful respite from his office. One reason we had bought the house was because of an extended wing behind the back hallway and stairs, which had possibly been an office or guest area at some earlier time. One entered from the main house through a back hall door. Another entrance, used by patients coming to Jack's office, faced Eleventh Street on the opposite side of the house from the pool. Every moment that Jack could be outside playing with the children or enjoying guests, he was there in the midst of games and chatter. With a home office like ours, patients would sometimes drop by or call when they needed to see the doctor after office hours. Often he would put on a robe and go from the pool through the back hall to the office to take care of someone.

Our next-door neighbor Mrs. Thomas Jefferson Randolph III and her maiden sister lived very quietly, with extreme dignity, in a large house next door. The story was that Thomas Jefferson Randolph III had played away any money that he might have saved to prevent his widow from having to live so frugally. A friend of ours owned the house and rented it to Mrs. Randolph and her sister for a pittance.

Mrs. Randolph provided us with nostalgia for vintage clothes whenever she appeared. She was always properly attired, and she behaved according to her own mores. She always wore a hat and gloves when she came out to walk the few blocks to shop or to attend to business downtown. Beautifully groomed and gloved, she was a picture of gentility. Our children were sometimes intrigued to the extent of seeming to wish Mrs. Randolph dead because it was said that she would be buried at Monticello. The girls loved to plan going to the funeral. I cautioned them again and again not to ask her about her Monticello future.

At Easter our lady neighbors drained the contents of eggs and painted wonderful faces on the eggshells. The eggheads always wore hats similar to the hats Mrs. Randolph donned whenever she left the house. I am sorry that I did not insist that the eggheads be carefully saved, but Jackie, Jyl, and Jan enjoyed playing with them so much that I could not deny them that pleasure. The eggshell Easter eggheads are gone, but the memories are precious.

We had a network of telephones. They were in the master bedroom, in the kitchen, in the den, in the office, and on the patio. Mrs. Randolph did a wonderful watercolor cartoon of Jack in a bathing suit standing by the pool with a small puddle of water dripping from his wet bathing suit. He was holding a phone in his hand as he talked to a patient. The caption read. "Ummmm. Yes. Well, just try giving him a little more water." We felt the pool provided Mrs. Randolph and her sister with entertainment the likes of which they had never expected to have. Sometimes we would see their curtains rippling slightly; we always laughed when that happened, knowing that they were leaning a little closer to see a little better.

One afternoon in 1954, Jackie, Jan, and a friend were playing outside. Jack, Jyl, and I were reading in the den. The front door banged open, and Jackie ran down the hall into the den and said, "Father, Father, there is a man out in the street showing us his penis!" Jyl's eyes got as big as saucers. "Where?" she exclaimed and ran out the front door. Jyl never wanted to miss anything. I called out to our housekeeper, Janet, who was in the kitchen, "Quick, go get Jan and Jyl and bring them in the house."

Jack called the police while Jackie, her friend, and I plotted how to trap the man if he drove back by the house. Jackie and her friend went into the yard to be decoys while Jack, Jyl, Jan, Janet, and I watched out for them from inside.

By the time the man rode by again, policemen were watching too, with license number in hand.

Originally the man had pulled over to the curb in front of a nearby church and asked the girls for directions. When they had gone over to the car, he had exposed himself. As Jackie turned to run to the house, she had managed to get the first half of his license number as he drove away. She told her friend to remember the last half. Jackie was quite elated about having gotten the license number and said, "I have been a good detective. I am helping solve this case." And, the case was solved. The man received a jail sentence for his drunken mistake. We all felt badly about it because he had a family. After a family discussion about it, however, we decided that it was right to let the justice process flow for the protection of other children. It was a difficult learning lesson for all of us. Precaution for little girls made sense to our girls after this experience.

Spring 1955 brought forth buds ready to burst into bloom in three small flower gardens along the inside of the backyard fence that enclosed the pool. Jackie, Jyl, and Jan each had a garden. Each one had prepared her garden space, laid flower blankets in place, and watered them. In a few months, beautiful flowers were blooming. Those gardens, I think, are one treasured memory the girls salvaged from their early lives, later so overshadowed by sad and traumatic experiences with mental illness. When I mention to Jackie or Jan some memories that I treasure, they now seem to perceive many of them differently from the way they apparently did when they occurred, and differently from the way in which I still perceive them. Mental illness, the ultimate sneak thief, I think, may have wreaked more havoc at our house in more ways than seemed obvious as it happened. During the times when we were enduring the presence of this sinister, cruel malady, we were not aware of how insidiously it may abuse other family members as well as its primary sufferer.

I think all five of us found life on Wayne Avenue as idyllic as could be envisioned. Then, suddenly, our comfortable, contented family life changed. Jack was asking more questions than he had ever asked of me; questions about whom I had seen during the day and what I had been doing all day. This was unusual and startling. Various civic activities that the two of us were involved with separately were not often discussed at length between us. Occasionally, we shared a new idea or briefly exchanged comments about my daily activities; our frequent conversations tended to concern the girls, our families, and a few mutual community activities. We were busy and I thought we were happy. Within a few days, Jack's more personal and probing interest in how I spent time away from the house exploded into an accusation that he knew I was sleeping around.

I thought that an incredibly hilarious joke; I threw back my head and laughed heartily, "Really, Jack, what a weird accusation. If I ever want to sleep with anyone else, you will be the first to know. I am not one to get into uncomfortable sex in goofy places in the woods, in car back seats, or parked somewhere in back alleys. If I were interested, I would just kindly tell you and ever so gently ask you to get lost." As soon as I had finished my lightly spoken words, Jack exploded into a litany of accusations that left me speechless. Luckily the phone rang for him, so he did not attempt to badger me anymore just then. He said "Hello" to the person calling in a perfectly calm, normal way. I knew nothing else to do but leave the room. I laughed only that first time when he asked stupid questions about my behavior. His sick questions were neither laughing matters to him then, nor, after that first rebuke, to me. Something foreign and beyond my understanding was happening.

Shocked beyond belief, I watched with dread as this solid citizen husband and competent doctor began exploding into crazy accusations and rage whenever we were alone. Though I wasn't aware of it, insanity had lunged into my life for the first time. I was briefly paralyzed from reacting with anything but shock and grief. I became very wary, and I stayed at home more during daytime school hours than I had before. Through subtle questioning of Janet, the housekeeper, I learned that he sometimes came from the office into the house looking for me. This was unnerving because he always knew my daily plans. One day, just after lunch, I left the house to walk a block down the street to a program that some friends were involved with at the Episcopal Church. As I crossed Eleventh Street, Jack threw up the den window and shouted, "Don't ever come back here!" Waynesboro was not a large city. Neighbors were not deaf. People did gossip. I kept walking, pretending not to hear. I also looked cautiously around and about to see whether neighboring house windows were open.

When I got home at the time when I usually came in from civic volunteer work or some female social thing, about the same time as the girls came in from school, there was no mention by him of his behavior, no apologies, no peace for my questioning mind. As soon as we were out of hearing range of the girls, however, he again taunted me, staring at me with wild eyes. His nasty demeanor was frightening, even threatening. I was alarmed, and I decided that I had to seek some advice. Since doctors do pledge silence for confidences given them and do know how to retain confidences, I talked to two of our doctor friends, Treacy O'Hanlan and Ed Smith. I also talked with Carter Allen, a close friend, and the Commonwealth Attorney for our county. All three of them were totally nonplused, but did believe me.

When Jack started laying a gun on his dressing chest before he went to bed, I was distressed to the point of wanting freedom from his presence forever. It was an old gun with a detachable part that I took out and hid. Jack apparently never realized that I had dismantled the gun. Obviously this firearm relic that Jack's father had brought home from World War I was supposed to intimidate and torture me. It did. The fact that he wanted to frighten me was such a startling factor that I wondered whether he loved me or cared anything about me. I could think of no explanation for his behavior, which was so contradictory to the kind and loving way he had always treated me. I did not understand that he was displaying schizophrenic characteristics.

The gun forced me to contemplate and plan on leaving him. I could not stay with this raving maniac who acted perfectly normal except when he was alone with me. Carter advised me to speak to my father about it. I had felt from the first evidence of Jack's sickness that I could not burden my parents with this horror of all situations. I thought of myself as a mature adult, capable of managing my own life, but now things were lurching out of control. I needed little prompting to ask for parental advice. When I told Daddy, he refrained from asking questions. He did not demean Jack, and he simply looked at me quite calmly and said, "Maxene, you do not have to live with Jack and endure this nonsense. It does not matter what it costs. Do whatever you feel you must for your peace of mind and for the safety of you and the girls."

At this time of my life, I reflect on the wisdom of a father who knew that to demean a daughter's choice of husbands in any way might, in fact, flash back to him as a criticism for that daughter's original choice of spouse. Thankfully he managed this decision as usual, by going directly to the core of the matter and taking the logical, necessary action with minimal to-do about it.

In most domestic situations, it is prudent to listen to the troubles of others without making any negative comment. When family wounds are finally healed after unpleasant situations, the offended family member is not likely to forget unkind remarks made by others during the heat of the disagreements. Though we may criticize our own family members, we usually vehemently resent agreement with our remarks by anyone outside of the immediate situation, even if we say nothing about it at the time. Neither my father nor I had any idea where the cause of Jack's jealousy lay. Post-traumatic syndrome had not yet been identified or defined. Although some veterans were said to suffer from "shell shock," it did not seem relevant to our situation. We really did not know what was behind Jack's behavior, but my father and mother strongly supported me in my need for safety.

I finally had to accept the fact that my marriage was on dangerously rocky shores. I did not know this stranger who had no sense of humor, and who seemed to find my very presence a cause for bizarre behavior. I secretly put clothes for the girls and me in my car trunk and waited for Jack to go out on an evening house call. At the first opportunity I asked the girls to come with me to the car, just after Jack had left to make an early night call out in the country. I explained to them that we were going to visit their grandparents, and off we went. I left Jack a note telling him that we were gone, with no intention of returning. Schools were out, so the action did not seem outrageous to the children. Jyl was the only one who seemed to sense something amiss. She cried and said that she did not want to leave her things to go away on a visit, but she was reassured when I reminded her of the good times she could have at her grandparents' house with the toys and books they kept for her and her sisters.

Driving down Route 11, the Valley Pike, to Harrisonburg was such a relief. The word safe comes to mind because we were leaving a fearful place behind us. We would be safe until I could figure out what future to plan for the girls and myself. I did not consider myself a feminist prior to this experience; but I quickly became converted and awakened to the plight of many women less fortunate than I as I pondered this god-awful situation. My father and mother were there for me. My parents had sufficient funds to take care of us if necessary. It is no wonder that all across our country havens from spouse abuse are necessary. Not all parents can do for their adult children what mine could offer; not all are willing to offer sanctuary.

Within a few days Jack began calling and apologizing. He begged me to come back. He promised that he would never act so irrationally again. Finally I told him, "Jack, I may give you another chance, but I want it clearly understood that I will not stay with you one minute longer if you ever again carry on like you have these past months. Also, you need to know that if I leave you a second time, I will do everything possible to prevent you from ever seeing the girls or me again. Don't reply now. Call me in a few days."

He called two days later to offer more profuse apologies. He said he did not understand what had come over him. I think that, by that time, he had figured out exactly what had come over him. Now, after the years of experiences I have had with so many different people and entities related to mental illness, I believe that he may have intelligently medicated himself for the rest of his life.

It was quite some time after Jackie became mentally ill in 1965 before I completely understood that Jack, like any untreated mentally ill person, was not accountable for his psychotic behavior in 1954.

The girls and I returned. The marriage continued in good faith and happily until his death in 1976. After I returned, however, without a request from Jack, I offered to work in his office. My offer seemed to please him, and I began going to work with him soon after my return and continued until we closed the office in January 1960. I was determined to guarantee the girls a stable home. I really wanted to do whatever it reasonably took to maintain a home with a secure family environment. I believed that we were more likely to maintain family stability if I spent lots of time every day in the office with Jack.

When we told my friends that I was going to become an employee in Jack's office, they laughed. "Too much familiarity breeds contempt." "Too much togetherness can become a bore." There was enough negative feedback on the idea for it to be discouraging, but I knew I had to do it. I imagine Jack was more eager for it to be successful than I. He was a clever man and a gifted doctor. It would be less than perceptive to believe that he did not understand why I was coming to work in the office with him.

We worked well together. Our relationship in the office and at home now, besides being husband and wife and father and mother, also became a best-friend thing. Waynesboro is only four miles from the Blue Ridge Parkway that runs atop the mountain range for miles and miles. We went up to the mountaintop or somewhere else for lunch almost every day. Sometimes on dark clear nights, after everything was settled around the house, and the girls were asleep, we would ride to the Parkway to watch bright, sparkling stars and constellations.

I still continued my civic duties; Jack continued his civic duties. Janet ran the house. I took over management of the home-based doctor's office and continued to manage family finances as many doctors' wives did. We worked closely together until we left for Florida in 1960.

While I was working in Jack's office, I found that patients, alone in the reception room with me, sometimes talked about whatever troubled them. They confided in me what they did not discuss with the doctor if they had an appointment for some malady other than emotional or mental concerns. I always relayed their remarks to Jack because he was dedicated to knowing as much as possible about his patients. He felt that personal involvement was a large reason for practicing medicine. I never asked about his cases, and he never discussed them with me. That, in both of our opinions, would have been unethical, but things patients told me were under a different umbrella. As I assisted the doctor, I did not hesitate to share with him my conversations with his patients.

When I listened to someone who seemed to be very seriously troubled mentally, it occurred to me that the conversations seemed totally self-centered, wholly centered on the individual with whom I spoke. Such people seemed to lack any awareness of situations external to themselves as they appeared to others. I told Jack that I believed that a basic symptom for mental illness was selfishness—selfishness with oblivious indifference to external realities. The disturbed people who talked with me in the office reception room obviously or subtly displayed a startling lack of awareness of the feelings and perceptions of other people. Jack disagreed with my insights; he felt that it was unkind to think so unkindly of others. Unkind? I believed the insights were just factual. I now know that this was an accurate, even astute, observation. Very few people, however, including those in settings where people seek help, have any real-world experience to help them in distinguishing mental illness from jealousy, anger, and other normal, if extreme, feelings and behaviors. One clue in identifying mental illness is the intense self-absorption of the sufferer.

Simultaneous with my medical office work, I was doing some volunteer work that included hospital auxiliary positions. I was chosen by the hospital auxiliary to attend a Red Cross-sponsored seminar in Washington, DC, about recruiting and training volunteers. The first speaker was the chief psychiatrist from the National Institutes of Mental Health. In describing prerequisites for good volunteers, he stated that one must ascertain during initial interviews that persons desiring to come into volunteer training are not selfish. He added that selfishness might be symptomatic of mental illness. He emphasized that selfish people are not needed in volunteer positions. He added that the first sign of good mental health returning to mentally ill persons is their sincere interest in some things or people other than themselves. He strongly believed that the first signs of mental illness might be manifested by displays of extreme selfishness.

I did crow a bit when I related to Jack the psychiatrist's comments, because I had been right in what he had declared to be a mere hunch of mine. He may have, with good reason, felt an ongoing, unspoken threat to his own mental health. In all fairness, I think he could not bring himself to agree because of the mental illnesses that stalked him and some others within his family. He was not normally a selfish person, and he might have felt that I was implying that he was. In any case, he clearly felt threatened. As I came to understand the matter better, I saw that the selfishness or interests limited to self, manifested as an expression of mental illness, has a different quality to it. It is more of an inability to perceive, understand, and relate to others in a normal way. It is almost as if the person was unaware of anything happening outside of one's self, or of the consequences to others from bizarre behaviors.

One day Schoern, our Weimaraner, gave birth to five puppies. Finding a daddy for the puppies had been a family search, and much excitement attended the presentation of the products resulting from our successful search. We fixed up a doghouse large enough to house the dog family and to give Schoern a birthing place. We were alarmed when we looked out the kitchen window on the birthing day morning to see Schoern crouched down in the swimming pool filter space. Needless to say, there was much consternation and lots of running in circles wondering what to do, because the filter space was not large enough for puppies and mama. Jack advised everyone to remain calm and let her have one pup successfully there. He said, "Stay away from her, but watch her carefully. When you see a puppy beginning to come from her body, come get me in the office; and I will come to move the puppy into the doghouse and try and get Schoern to come along with me. Perhaps if I tell her that the doghouse is the place where she is supposed to have the puppies, she will follow my advice."

It became a contest to see whether Jackie, Jyl, or Jan would spot the new baby protruding from the mother's body first and be the missionary to run and get help for the move to the doghouse. My memory reel does not show who the messenger girl was, but it does show the girls sitting on poolside furniture, watching the good doctor doing his bit for the safe delivery of the pups. We never knew what Jack might have whispered to Schoern, but she did exactly as he wished. She did not persist in using the pool filter space as her delivery room, but followed him to the doghouse.

It took all day, lunch outside, much speculation about what sex the pups would be, and many exclamations about the process of giving birth before five pups were deposited inside the doghouse. Schoern was most obliging. She came outside to have each pup, lick it clean, eat its placenta, and then carefully carry her baby by the nape of its tiny neck into its new home. The removal of the placentas by the bitch provided a biology lesson that could be learned in no better way. At dinner, we rehashed the day and decided that it had been a wonderful dog day for Schoern, the puppies, our housekeeper Janet, and everyone in our family.

Dinner at our house was a special time. Jack made particular efforts to delay any house calls or phone calls that might interfere with dinner. Janet had her instructions that no patient calls were to be brought to the doctor during the dinner hour unless it was an emergency. In that case, an extra long phone cord allowed the phone to be carried from the kitchen to Jack at the table. Dinner, promptly at six o'clock, was family prime time, and everyone was expected to be there in good humor.

Schoern and our Siamese cat sat on their haunches just beyond the arch between the front hall and the dining room and seemed to guard us through the meal. Trained never to come into the dining room, these two handsome animals, almost the same in color, were a stunning pair. The beautiful blue eyes of the cat and the magnificent yellowish eyes of the dog were so penetrating that we wondered whether they were out there being resentful of their ouster from the room or whether it was love, temporarily reserved, that their eyes reflected.

One night just before dinner, the telephone rang, and it was Agnes Coiner telling us that her farm pond was frozen thick enough for ice-skating. It was unusual for ice to form thickly there, so the Coiners were getting ready to build a big bonfire and have a skating party. We hurried to Becky and Pete McGann's Corner Hardware and bought ice skates for each of us. The girls and I had never ice-skated before. After dinner, we went to the pond and, at first hesitantly, but finally with wild abandon, skated with zest and cunning in the darkness lighted only by the bonfire. The next day when I saw encrusted leaves and some debris frozen in the ice, I marveled that we, novice skaters that we were, had not fallen with disastrous results. It was a night long discussed and enjoyed anew with each recall. I wonder whether Jackie and Jan remember it as nostalgically as I do. I fear and deeply regret that for them many happy memories are hidden behind unpleasant sad recalls.

In 1957 our housekeeper Janet left to work in New York, and Geneva replaced her. Janet had become quite disturbed about discrimination by white people against black people in our part of the country. She seemed very restless, and she was sometimes rude.

I gave Janet information from the New York Times, and suggested that she might be happier working in the North. She did not disagree. She called after she got settled there and talked to the children. She said she had work and was much happier there. I felt good that I had prodded her into going, even though she seemed to resent being asked to leave.

After Janet left, Jan began to sometimes wet her bed at night, and she took up sucking her thumb. Jolted into guilt, I said to Jack, "You know, I think that I have fired the mother figure." Janet just disappeared one night after our New York conversation, which made it more difficult for Jan, I think. After all the years she had been in our home, years when she was actually with Jan more than I was able to be, her abrupt departure had to be hurtful for Jan. After Jack's psychotic episode, the necessity of my being with him in the office, and the necessity for me to give much thought and primary consideration to him, Janet's role in Jan's life became more prominent than it would have been under more ideal family circumstances. After Janet left, we found a kitten that was to be Jan's very own. We made it a point to spend more time with her alone to try to help her adjust to Janet's leaving. Even so it was quite a while before she overcame the bed-wetting and thumb sucking, and it was a long time before I could think about the matter with anything but great sadness. I had to make the choices that seemed to be most beneficial to my marriage and the entire family, and Jan caught the brunt of my choices.

In October 1959, Jack and I were vacationing with my parents, when they bought a waterfront house in Treasure Island, Florida, to use someday when they would become retirees. They went back for about a month at Christmas that year, and we visited with the children for the Yuletide holiday. Jack fell in love with Florida during that first vacation, and he expressed a desire to live there someday, but I did not think much about it. He, however, was serious enough to ask me to contact the Florida Public Health Department in Jacksonville before we returned for Christmas. We stopped there on the way down, and Jack talked with the Florida state director of public health. The director suggested that if Jack were interested, he should go see Dr. Ballard, the public health director in Saint Petersburg, to discuss the functions of the department and to look around to see whether he liked what he learned and saw.

Unbeknownst to my parents Jack did go to see Dr. Ballard, and he was impressed by what he learned. We didn't discuss it very much until we arrived at the home of old friends Martha and Bill Steed in Camden, South Carolina, on the way home. After the children were in bed, Jack mentioned his interest to Steed, who was absolutely stunned. He asked Jack how he could possibly leave so much for what seemed to him to be so much less. Steed, in astonishment, said that it was unusual for Public Health to recruit successful practicing doctors, and that it would certainly be a plus for Florida if we actually followed through with our wacky plan.

When we got back to Virginia, Jack opened his office, and our lives resumed in routine patterns for a few days. The next Wednesday afternoon the office was closed, and I was visiting Anne Kay, a friend, when Jack phoned me. He asked me to come home because he wanted to talk. When I got home, I found him primed for Florida. He apparently had been thinking about it much more than I had realized. I was willing to go, but I had more or less put the matter aside because Jack was the career person involved, and I thought that he should initiate the move if it was to be taken. I knew and understood his angst about medicine and the direction it seemed to be taking. I also knew his fondness for his patients, so I had dismissed the idea without further thought.

When I got home he said that he had decided that he really wanted to go, and he asked me whether I was honestly serious about approval of the move. I was ready. I was relieved by his decision. I knew his lupus could flare up any-time. I knew that my chronic sinus condition was not going to improve in the Shenandoah Valley. I knew the girls had loved our Virginia pool, but in Flor-ida we could have a year-round pool or live on the water. And, it would always be warm. I knew it would only be a question of time until my parents would be there in the winter. Leaving friends and families would not be easy, but we figured that we would have a fun place for them to visit, and we could come back to Virginia on vacations. The die was cast. We tossed the dice knowing full well that our lives would have to change dramatically.

When I went visiting my friends to tell them of our decision, all of them were visibly puzzled and dismayed. It was not easy. I remember going into Helen Allen's house and running up the stairs to the bedroom where she was changing the diaper of her newborn baby, Catherine. Helen was startled and stunned. She remained a wonderful friend until her death just a few years ago. Helen was an unusually astute person as far as current events were concerned, and I always looked forward to discussions with her. She wrote to me every week for the first year we were in Florida because she feared that I would be lonesome there without good friends. I miss her and her credible responses to issues that seriously concerned us both.

Rosemary MacIllwaine was the only person who broke down into sobbing when I told her. Her New York upbringing sometimes put her privately at odds with some Southern habits and attitudes, and I think that I was pretty adaptable to her Northern differences. We understood one another, and that was a relief for both of us. In later years Rosemary remarkably made major adjustments and was "at home" in Virginia. Rosemary died just a few years ago. Helen, Anne Kay, and Rosemary are all dead, as are many of the people I bid goodbye before moving to Florida. Anne, who always remembered the date on which my second husband Kenneth and I married, always called to wish us "Happy Anniversary." Good friends are for always, and memories of them embellish my present life as well as my past.

There were other good friends that I visited for the last time before moving. There are many stories involving all of them. There will be another day, another book perhaps. My life in Virginia, expanded, could easily be another book. My life since moving away from Virginia, expanded, could also easily be another book. I have lived a wonderful, fully packed life.

Prior to World War II, most doctors saw humanitarian goals of medical practice more clearly than after the war. We watched and sadly lived with the dawn of specialization in medicine by especially trained doctors. Specializations became the "in" practices of medicine, while the family doctor became less respected. In fact sometimes the disrespect was overpowering and disheartening. I tired of being asked whether my husband was "just a family doctor." The balm offered by University of Virginia doctors telling me that Jack was the best diagnostician in the territory was not enough to salve the slurs by innuendo or outright smug remarks from newly born specialists.

When a call came at any time from Jack's patients, he already knew the families and medical histories of the callers. He already had their faith and respect. He understood how any malady being treated related to other facets of their lives, and how events within the family influenced the patient. Practicing medicine was for him a personal experience—never at arm's length. Knowing that the delivery of medical services was going in directions that Jack questioned greatly influenced our interest in going to Florida; I hated the thought of watching him become more and more frustrated. We rented the Waynesboro house, sold the medical practice, and left for Florida on February first.

When we made the decision to move to Florida during the first week of 1960, twelve-year-old Jackie was in middle school. We decided to tell her before anyone else knew about it. We did not want to proceed with our plans if the move was going to be too difficult for the girls. Jyl was ten years old, and Jan was eight. Jackie's younger sisters were not as far advanced in school, so we believed that they would be able to more easily make adjustments to new schools than Jackie could to middle school. But Jackie was absolutely thrilled. She loved being in on the secret. Later when we told Jyl and Jan, they also seemed to find excitement in planning the move.

Jan expressed no complaints about the fact that moving made it necessary for her to give her cat to a neighbor across the street whose cat had recently died. Sharp, clear reel pictures mirror her when returning home from delivering the cat to its new owner. She came through our front door with head ducked to hide her tears. To this day I feel sad for Jan because first Janet left without saying good-bye, and then she had to give her cat away. We should have taken that cat with us, I think. At the time it would have been very difficult. We did not know where we would be living in Florida. There would be many adjustments to make. It might be difficult to find living arrangements where animals were allowed. All kinds of reasons made it clear that we should give up our pets. Although it was not easy for any of us, that was a lot to ask of Jan. During all of the commotion of moving, we had many regretful moments for Jan because we could not take her cat with us. A neighbor volunteered to take Schoern; leaving her was difficult for me. Of all the pets I have known in my lifetime, I think Collie and Schoern loved me the most.

Jack decided not to tell his patients right away that he was leaving; but when the first patient he saw after making that decision said, "Well, Doc, I'll see you in two weeks," Jack hesitated a moment, and then told him that he probably would no longer be there and explained why. Jack told me later that he simply could not lie to the man. The news that we were going to fold our tent spread like wildfire and the office was soon swamped with calls and people dropping by. After we made announcements to family, patients, and friends that we were leaving Virginia, we advertised to rent the house and to sell the medical practice.

The final day that Jack saw patients in the office was the last Tuesday in January. He went to the office at 8:00 o'clock in the morning, and he left it for the last time at ten o'clock that night. After closing in the afternoon to take time out for dinner, Jack walked into the reception room and slumped into a chair. I looked at him closely and noticed that his lips were drawn with a perceptible white line around them. I said, "I am going to tell Geneva to give the girls their dinner. I think we need to get out of town and give this departure more in-depth scrutiny." Jack smiled wearily and said, "OK."

We drove twelve miles to the Triangle Restaurant in Staunton, ordered dinner, and talked about what we were doing and what was at stake. Jack made the decision that he definitely wanted to go to Florida. He admitted that he was finding the emotional wrench of leaving his patients difficult, but he thought it best to follow through with our plans to leave the next morning.

We were back in our home office by seven o'clock. When we arrived we saw cars everywhere with a line of people outside the office door.

When I opened the office door, patients filed in until all seats were filled and there was not even any standing room left. There was no cheerful conversation as there would usually be; the room was silent. I worked dutifully on records that had to be in order for the doctors who had bought the practice. Every now and then I would try to brighten the atmosphere by trying to get some patient to carry on a relaxed conversation with me, but they were mute with sadness. Tears rolled quietly down the cheeks of several women in the room.

Some patients through the years had shared products from their farms with us. One of the most remarkable things that happened that night was when a woman came through the door with tears in her eyes and dropped a frozen chicken on my desk. I thanked her and looked at that chicken with very mixed emotions. I couldn't laugh or cry. Having gotten rid of so many things from our freezer made this gift seem ludicrous, but it was such a wonderful expression of the woman's love for Jack that it almost caused me to join those in the room who were weeping.

Ed Smith, who knew about Jack's physical problems with lupus, was the strongest advocate for our move. Ed told Jack, "Get out of here. I have had a heart attack, and I will probably have a final one in the near future. Family practice can be a killer under the current stresses and changes that medicine is experiencing. It is not worth your life. With your lupus situation, why would you aggravate it?" Ed, I think, was also remembering my coming to him earlier about the amazing and frightening psychotic episode Jack had suffered, and he may have believed that Jack was more vulnerable because of that. He clearly thought that the warmer weather and public service position would be less physically and emotionally demanding for Jack.

After all the patients had left the office that last evening of Jack's medical practice, and after Jack had gone over to the house and gone to bed, I sat at the desk doing the final bookkeeping. It was after midnight when there was a light rap on the door. I switched on the outside light, and Ed was standing there looking very serious. He was a constant tease and always full of fun, but now he said with a very serious countenance, "Well, I just had to come by. I discovered that I just have to see the two of you one more time before you leave." I smiled and said, "Well, don't just stand there. Go get Louise, pick up some hamburgers, and we'll have a little farewell party." Ed and his wife Louise took the game of bridge very seriously, but they tolerated the indolent game that

Jack and I played. All four of us played for fun, but the Smiths were excellent players. I knew that in Florida we would miss their friendship and the bridge games. We had our farewell hamburgers, said good-bye, and were up, bright and early, the next morning to leave Virginia. A few years after our move, Ed had another heart attack and died, just as he had predicted.

When we left Virginia and moved to Florida, we made a firm decision not to become very involved in social situations that did not include the girls because we wanted to take special care that the girls never felt any regrets that we had taken them far away from their Virginia heritage. We wanted to provide a consistent, secure home life. I did teach school, but there was always someone in the house when the girls came in from school. I was usually there in addition to a housekeeper, who always stayed to cook dinner before she left in the evening. From the time each little girl was born, we tried to create a home life where she could grow to become a well-adjusted, educated adult. We believed that we were providing Jackie, Jyl, and Jan with springboards for successful futures. We discussed all facets of parenting, and then we carried out our decisions to the best of our abilities. We never, for any reason, foresaw or felt forewarned that two of our children's lives were not to be what we aspired for them. That the carefree, heartfelt concern we knew for all three of our daughters would become heart-wrenching sorrow involving two of them is still difficult to accept or comprehend. The comfort of Jan's presence is twice as treasured when I recall the years of struggle with awkward and unfortunate incidents, one after another, caused by the mental illnesses affecting Jackie and Jyl.

In June 1960 the girls and I returned to Virginia to auction the furniture and miscellaneous items from the house on Wayne Avenue. We were beginning a new lifestyle, and we decided to make a clean sweep of our Virginia possessions. The girls and I discussed what they would like to take to Florida, and I agreed that each of them would pack a barrel of special things to be shipped to them later. Deciding what to take did not seem upsetting. In fact, it simply seemed a part of the excitement of beginning a new life in Florida. On the day of the auction, a friend took the girls and entertained them. They liked Virginia Chew, and they went willingly with her. I knew the day would present some heart twinges as some happily used pieces of family furniture were put on the block. Jack and I wanted to prevent any traumatic reactions from the auction for the girls.

Mother came days before the sale and took her portrait off the living room wall and carted it home. I think she actually thought I had taken leave of my senses and just might sell it for a good price because of its silver and gold leaf frame. Mother described the auction as "trashy," an apt description from her point of view. She was opposed to personal property being displayed and sold in one's own front yard. She probably would be appalled by the Route 127 World's Longest Outdoor Sale held annually from Alabama up into Kentucky. Or, perhaps, she would have accepted it as most do now, as fun and interesting, just as long as her family and friends didn't do it. She liked auctions, but putting one's own things on the lawn. "Oh, my!" When a friend, thoroughly enamored with the whole idea, offered to record the auction with his movie camera, Mother retorted, "The fact that it is happening is bad enough. Let us not record it for posterity." As it turned out, I almost wish that I had defied her and let the fellow roll his cameras, because it was quite an event.

We hired a professional auctioneer, and Grace Lutheran Church set up to serve hot and cold nourishment on the pool patio. The lawn was covered with our belongings and some junk from the basement, which was already there when we bought the house. I had not planned to put such terrible-looking, damaged things on sale, but the auctioneer laughed at me and said, "Put them out there. You're not gonna believe what people will buy." He was right. What we had expected to bring good prices often went cheaper than reasonable; what we would have simply thrown away sold for good prices as missing parts for some broken thing at the home of the bidder, for its "antique" value, or for some other unfathomable reason.

To my horror Mother, who was an old hand at auctions because she loved to collect antiques, was a front row bidder. There was a ninety-inch-long antique drop leaf walnut gate leg table that was considered by the auctioneer as a leader, an object to attract attendees to the sale. He was right. One couple had driven more than a hundred miles to bid on it. I kept my distance from the auctioneer because I did not wish to make anyone feel self-conscious when bidding, and I was feeling unexpectedly a bit queasy about the whole thing. Therefore I did not hear Mother bidding away on the walnut table against the couple that was so determined to have it. Finally Mother threw in the sponge. Apparently, she really had wanted to buy it. When it got higher than she was going to pay, she remarked, "Well, at least, they did not get it cheap." To have a mother show up as the runner-up bidder at an auction from which her daughter profits could be embarrassingly reflective of a conspiracy to the detriment of buyers. I was glad I was moving to another state when someone ran over to report my mother's public display of indignation when she was unable to reasonably purchase the table. The remark just popped out without fore-thought, I know, because Mother was not a rude person. The purchaser and I, I think, were the only people that did not find the incident uproariously funny.

During the first visit home from Florida a few years later, I went up to Mother's attic treasure-trove for something, and there were many things there from the auction. I was shocked. When asked about it, she said, "Well, I thought you might be sorry later, and the things would be here for you."

There was a set of French prints in frames that I had gilded that were bought by a sister-in-law, Sue Obenschain. Charley, my youngest brother, was at the sale, and, when it was over, recognizing who she was, he went over and asked whether she needed help to put them in the car. Sue was pleased to have assistance, but she did not know who her kind helper was. As they were walking toward the car, she said to my brother, "Well, it really made me angry when Maxene's darned mother ran these up on me. If it had not been for her, I would have gotten them a lot cheaper." My brother said, "Really?" and smiled as he placed the prints he carried into the trunk of her car. Being the magnificent jokester that he can be, he came around the house and asked me to walk with him out front near the street. He said, "Watch your sister-in-law when she turns and sees us. I think she is about to have a very bad moment when she realizes that I am your brother." Sure enough, Sue looked in our direction, and a look of sheer consternation flew across her face as she wheeled around, got into her car, and drove away. When Charley explained to me what was going on, we had a wonderful laugh, releasing some of the tension of the sale. Sue could never understand how I found the whole thing very amusing and was forever apologetic about it. I told her the truth, "Please believe me. Your remark gave the whole experience the humorous touch it needed."

My father had stated firmly that he was not going to come to the auction. A few of my friends also said that they could not handle attending something that seemed so similar to a spooky wake. I was surprised when Daddy showed up near the end of the event that represented the final sundering of our Virginia roots. I appreciated that he came to be supportive, even though he was silently unhappy about our move from Virginia and hated the public sale of our personal properties. He and Mother, knowing full well that our departure would leave a vacuum in their lives, were wonderful sports about our venture. Because of that vacuum I made sure that they received a Sunday afternoon phone call from us or had a special delivery letter waiting for them after church every week that they were at home in Virginia for as long as they lived.

After the auctioneer's last call, when the yard was empty, I stood alone at the intersection of Wayne Avenue and Eleventh Street and reeled away into my brain the pictures of our things going off in four different directions. They went hanging out of car windows, protruding from tied-down trunk covers, on car rooftops, or secured to the sides of vehicles. I felt very sobered for a few moments as I watched the symbols of our Virginia dreams fade into the distance. We were walking away from everything most married couples dream of having for their families. Our lives in the big Victorian house on the corner of Wayne Avenue and Eleventh Street had been wonderful. The only blot upon our joy had been the brief, still incomprehensible, blight of Jack's paranoia. Perhaps with less stress for him, we would find an even better life in the Sunshine State. I could not help but feel a fleeting tremor of fear for our future as that flashing reel intruded once again to illustrate Jack's 1954 mental illness. In Florida if he became paranoid for the same unknown reasons as he had before, I would be among strangers.

We were leaving as strong a support system as a family can have. I was to learn later, when mental illness raised its cursed head for Jackie and Jyl, that a few people in the valley believed we should have stayed where we belonged. They ignorantly believed that because our roots were generations deep in Virginia, our girls would have felt security that would have prevented their mental illnesses. I do not wish to sound defensive, but I want to set the record straight. The girls never said or did anything to indicate that our decision to move away from the valley was anything but beneficial to their lives. They sometimes talked about how much better they liked the warmer climate. We knew that all three daughters were well endowed intellectually, which we believed would make adjustments to another state easier for them. From all vantage points the future seemed painted with joyful tints and hues. Farthest from our minds was any suspicion that insanity was already stalking our futures. We had no clues to warn us that menacing psychoses would bring rosy dreams for two of us, Jackie and Jyl, to crushing, shattering, unexpected halts.

At Christmas, 1953, Mother took care of Jackie, Janet took care of Jan, and I took care of Jyl on a pilgrimage to Richmond's Miller and Rhoads to visit Santa Claus.

The three girls and Maxene enjoy their backyard pool on Memorial Day in 1954.

The site of the Wayne Avenue home/office on the corner of Wayne Avenue and Eleventh Street as it was being demolished in 1997. The entire area is now a paved parking lot for a nearby church.

PUBLIC SALE   52

FAY O. HEWITT, Auctioneer

AUCTION SALE OF VALUABLE PERSONAL PROPERTY

Having moved to Florida, we will sell at Public Auction at 373 S. Wayne Ave., at

9:30 A.M. SAT., JUNE 25

the following:

Lot end tables, walnut dropleaf table, 90" walnut dropleaf table, walnut card table, card table top, walnut dropleaf coffee table, walnut washstand, pine bench, sofa, chair and coffee table, round oak dining room table, antique walnut chest, 6 chests, metal tables, lot stools, large pine play chest, 4 chairs, 4 ladder-back straight chairs and 2 arm chairs to match— all walnut; sofa and chair, antique sofa, piano, 3-way floor lamps, 7 pull wall lamps, lot table lamps, jug lamp, 4 antique lamps, 2 kitchen chairs, lot folding chairs, game table, chairs, lot folding chairs, game table, cobbler's bench, rolling serving cart, antique walnut bed, Samson massage bed, bed springs, foldaway bed, 2 Hollywood beds and springs, 3 antique wall mirrors, lot pictures—some with walnut shadow-box frames; lot matched French prints, set 6 framed maps, 2 fire screens; brass fireside sets and brass andirons, bookcases, wardrobe, lot hassocks, comb. radio, Helicrafter short-wave radio, 21"; Zenith TV, 21" table TV with new tube, portable TV set, rotary antenna, Westinghouse oven, lot glasses, lot dishes, Swiss mantel clock, hot plate, air conditioning unit, portable electric fan, 2 other electric fans, 2 old-fashioned table telephones, metal file, Kenmore double-oven electric stove, Gibson refrigerator, Frigidaire upright freezer, Gen. Elec. washer and dryer, Easy Ironer, ironing board, Bissel sweeper, vacuum, thermos jugs, picnic baskets, redwood picnic table with benches, umbrella table, 4 Scran lawn chaises, 4 lawn stands, lot alum. lawn chairs, alum. lawn glider, grill with electric rotissary, lot yard booths and tables, lawn feeder, Simplicity riding mower with snow plow, lot garden hose, lot garden tools, lot shutters, sled, 2 pair shoe iceskates, lot paint, lilly pond, old skillet, mantel piece, 20' extension ladder, 2 each, 6' stepladders, power bench saw, lot pine lumber and other articles too numerous to mention.

TERMS: CASH.
Clerk: DON SNYDER.
DR. and MRS. JOHN T. OBENSCHAIN
Lunch will be served.

Jack

Jackie

Jyl

Jan

Maxene

The family migrates to Florida in 1960

Jackie's empathy for another person is illustrated in this cartoon. She drew it during the drive to Virginia with her mother and sisters to prepare for the auction in June 1960.

Treatments and Despair

"Every morning I ask God to please let me own my mind for the day," Jackie said one morning in 1966. "I ask for just one day at a time." Jackie, because of her paranoid schizophrenia, has not owned her mind for the last forty of her fifty-eight years of life. Madness is her state of mind.

My mind belongs to me. I own it. It is not ruthlessly tormented. It is sane, controlled, contented, and comfortable. It contains a special collection of reeled memories that enable me, by using their reflections, to make rational daily decisions. My mind is not hindered by madness. That is true for me today, but there is no guarantee that it will be true for me tomorrow. Madness is not by choice.

Schizophrenia is an indescribable disease inflicted without warning or promise for a cure. The best description that I have found, which offers an understanding for all people, is in *Eden Express* written by Dr. Mark Vonnegut in 1975. He asks, "What is Schizophrenia?" The definition that he gives says, "Most diseases can be separated from one's self and seen as foreign intruding entities. Schizophrenia is very poorly behaved in this respect. Colds, ulcers, flu, cancer, are things we get. Schizophrenic is something we are. It affects the things we most identify with as making us what we are. If this weren't problem enough, schiz comes on slow and comes on fast, stays a minute or days or years, can be heaven one moment, hell the next, enhances abilities and destroys them, back and forth several times a day and always weaving itself inextricably into what we call ourselves. It can transform only a small corner of our lives or turn the whole show upside down, always giving few if any clues as to when it came or when it left or what was us and what was schiz."

Schizophrenia has truly been the bane of my existence for forty years. I wish delusions had not raped the minds of Jackie and Jyl. I wish delusions had not prompted their bizarre behaviors, early death for Jyl, and probable lifetime incarceration for Jackie. Though it is tremendously repugnant to me, I am violating and exploiting the privacy of family members in this book. Dire and devastating events are described, which might have been emotionally splintering and self-destructive for me had I chosen for them to be. Because of unwelcome experiences, I plead for cessation of crazy care for mentally ill individuals. Because of unwelcome experiences, I examine traumas in my life. Despite unwelcome experiences in my life, I explain how I live joyfully. Understanding indignities inflicted by mental illness is needed. Only then will safer streets be demanded. Only then will safe sanctuary for severely mentally ill people be found. Only then will justice prevail. I would like to stand on the highest mountain peak with the loudest megaphone to proclaim what I believe must be known. Since there is no mountain tall enough, since there is no megaphone powerful enough to explore madness, I write with fervent hope and firm resolve to be heard.

For weeks Jack and I had looked forward to going across Tampa Bay on the escort boat for the 1965 Queen of the Gasparilla. Gasparilla is an annual traditional celebration in Tampa, which depicts pirates sailing into Tampa Bay centuries ago with intent to plunder. The boat trip was by invitation, with the list of guests to include mostly politicians and a few other people of some prominence in the Tampa Bay area. I had rushed home from Madeira Beach Junior High School to dress for an unusual forecast of chilly breezes. I dug out a black and white hounds tooth wool cape and a black hat for warmth in hopes that they would reflect some sense of a dress-up party mood.

Jack was supposed to be in a meeting in Jacksonville early the next morning, so planning to participate in the festivities of the entire evening was not possible. On the trip into port at Tampa, we enjoyed good drinks, hors d'oeuvres, and pleasurable company. It was a novel experience to be on the large boat surrounded by many smaller boats bobbing around us in all directions. Folks aboard the smaller boats waved to those of us on the queen's boat. Those of us on the queen's boat waved back; everyone was having fun.

We did not get off the boat in Tampa, but stayed aboard for an immediate return trip. It was disappointing that we could not stay with the queen and entourage for the Gasparilla frolicking. The day was dreary and damp, however, which made it easier to go home to a warm house. When we disembarked from the boat in Saint Petersburg, not only had it gotten cooler, it was drizzling chilly rain. We decided that we had actually lucked out by not being caught in Tampa in such messy weather.

Both of us had worked all day and rushed around to make the evening connections on time, so when we finally arrived back at home in Lakewood Country Club in Saint Petersburg around ten o'clock, we were in a mixed mood of exuberance and fatigue. Jack started getting ready to leave for his drive to Jacksonville.

I lazily began to settle in for the night and nonchalantly began to check to see what the girls were doing. When I walked into Jyl's room, she said, "Mom, Jackie has said some strange things tonight."

I walked on into the kitchen where a long table sat at the end of the large room that overlooked the patio and pool. We all liked to sit there to talk or sometimes use it as a study or writing table when it was not being used for dining. Jackie was sitting there writing. As I walked by, she looked up and said, "Mother, it's about time somebody around here tells me what's going on." When I said, "I don't know what you mean," she told me not to pretend I didn't know. I was completely puzzled and, since Jyl had prompted me, doubly bothered by her remark.

I went to the master bedroom and said, "Jack, Jackie has just said something most unusual to me. Maybe you should wait until morning so we can talk with her." When I told him about the comments that Jyl and Jackie had made, he, too, was puzzled and said, "Of course, I'll get up and leave early in the morning."

I went back to the kitchen, and before I said anything to Jackie, she looked up at me with an impish look, laughed, and said, "I really freaked you out, didn't I?" I laughed, too, and said, "Yes, you really did." Since all of us sometimes joked around in nonsensical ways, I dismissed my concerns, went back into the bedroom, and, after an explanation, said to Jack, "False alarm. Go on and go tonight. It will be an easier trip."

After he left I finished getting ready for bed. The girls were in their rooms for the night. It was getting late. I was surprised when Jackie came into my room and sat down. She didn't look particularly concerned as she said, "Mother, I am a paranoid schizophrenic." I calmly asked what made her think that, but she did not tell me any reasons. She continued to insist that she was paranoid schizophrenic. This was the second time in one evening that I had to put myself on guard and not look as alarmed as I was feeling.

We talked long into the early morning. I explained to her that many teenagers need counseling when trying to understand the world around them. I tried to make it clear that her father and I were there for her anytime and that, if she wished, we would be happy to pay for her to go talk with someone else.

Our talk seemed to end on a happy note with an understanding between us for future talks about her concerns whenever she wished. She continued to flatly refuse to give concrete reasons for diagnosing herself as being a paranoid schizophrenic. When she stated concerns about her classmates not liking her, I persuaded myself that she had somehow picked up enough information about the disease to apply it to herself. After all, I thought, most adolescents believe themselves unpopular at one time or another without becoming paranoid.

In the summer of 1965, I went to Virginia for a short visit. Jack did not go. He and Rose, a wonderful housekeeper and cook, were there for the girls, and I thought I had no worries. Jackie had never again made reference to our late night talk when we got home from the Gasparilla boat ride. Jack and I had decided not to bring it up again unless some behavior made it necessary or Jackie introduced the topic. The girls provided so many pleasures and were so special to both of us that I now realize we had naturally gone into denial. I simply could not imagine that one of them could be mentally impaired.

Jack discovered while I was away that Jackie's paranoia was real and active. We were both alarmed. She was having classmates and teachers investigated by a detective. Jack told me as soon as I returned home. "You need to know that Jackie hired a detective last spring to investigate her classmates, whom she suspected of spying on her and making fun of her behind her back.

"The detective came to my office and told me, because she knew something was wrong. She felt she had to violate Jackie's confidence for Jackie's sake. I told her that you would be home in a few days and would call her. At first, I thought that the detective was just looking for money, and I told her that we would not pay her one-cent for services that certainly were not needed. The detective said that was not expected and that Jackie had been paying her out of her allowance."

I called the detective right away and set up an appointment for the next day. The detective was extremely upset to see this attractive girl in such a confused, paranoid state of mind. She said she took the case because she felt such urgency for Jackie's needing help. She actually had made a few calls, without involving Jackie's name, to ask about a few students that Jackie had named. She reported to Jackie that she could not find any evidence to justify Jackie's fears, but Jackie would not accept her reassurance and insisted that more time be spent watching the students to find what harm they were planning for her.

The detective and I decided to play it out while we all watched Jackie carefully to see whether she would become noticeably depressed or hostile. The

detective agreed to see Jackie if she called again, and she agreed to be very adamant about the money that Jackie owed her.

In a few weeks, Jackie and I were chatting, when she laughed and said, "I
have done something really stupid." I smiled and said, "Really. What?" She
said, "Mother, you are not going to believe what I have to tell you." "Give it a
whirl." I said. She told me. "I got some silly ideas that my classmates at school
hated me and planned to do something unkind to me. I got so carried away
that I hired a detective. I was really mixed up, and I am so sorry."

I asked how she happened to tell me and how she had paid the detective.
She laughed, "I think you have the picture. I ran out of allowance money, and
I owe the detective for some hours of useless work. She did not find anything.
I am glad about that, but I was very mixed up, and I am really sorry."

We discussed the implausibility of the entire situation, and I told her not to
worry. "Everyone does something silly sometime. You have joined the crowd.
I am just glad you recognize that it was a mistake for you to get carried away.
I'll talk with your father. I think we can raise the money needed." We laughed.
I tried to believe that the paranoia had evaporated with the relieved laughter
that both of us offered the topic.

Jack and I did not laugh when talking about it. He and I asked her to be
sure and come talk to us if she ever had such thoughts again. As far as I know,
she never spoke to her sisters about it, and things within the family continued
to hum along in seemingly good order.

Whenever I read of violent acts committed by mentally ill people when
families, friends, and neighbors come forward in shocked disbelief, I know
they speak sincerely. Only someone who has been through the sorrows resulting from mental illnesses can truly empathize. It is hideously cruel, and without any semblance of civility or fairness, for outsiders, including the media, to
respond as they do to acts of violence committed by mentally ill individuals
who are driven by uncontrollable forces.

I wonder how the general public can be so unthinking and thoughtless as to
tolerate court cases, and, worse, death penalties for mentally ill people, who,
when deranged, when not in possession of their minds, commit crimes. That
we have laws that allow medication to be given to a sick individual so he or she
can appear in court as a different person from the one who committed violence
is not the result of rational legislation or judicial compassion.

Lawyers in legislative bodies know what they are doing when they create
laws to bring money into their personal coffers. Attorneys want court cases,
and some ridiculous statues on the books give them the cases and the tainted

money desired. There is no mercy shown for defenseless sick people or the families who are equally defenseless in the face of such discrimination—discrimination that is stoutly defended by our inhumane judicial system. Judicial systems and legislative bodies should be held accountable by citizens demanding safety for the untreated severely mentally ill and for themselves when they are where untreated severely mentally ill people may be found.

Excuses made by judges, politicians, and the general public say that nothing can be done to change things because of the lack of understanding of serious mental illness. No one understands severe mental illnesses. Does lack of understanding excuse wholesale crass cruelty? Earning money from cruel judgments of fellow human beings is hell-based without question. Families who shelter and try to provide solace for their mentally damaged relatives get no comfort from judicial systems that prefer to waste taxpayers' money with frivolous court cases. Judges say that the laws hamper fairness. I say that judges are derelict when hearing cases when acknowledged temporarily medicated mental patients are testifying. Legislative bodies and governors, who allow self-serving lawyers in their midst to vilify these people by statute for personal monetary gain, should themselves be taken to task for abuses and discrimination against their severely mentally ill constituents and their families.

I notice that it sometimes seems embarrassing for people to discuss mental illness. It is easier to ignore and turn aside from issues that require sincere compassion or special knowledge for understanding. Those who could lighten the woes of those less fortunate mentally are unjustly endangering ill citizens for greedy self-self serving purposes.

Jackie's high school senior year was uneventful until she came home in tears about an F on a paper she had written about cancer research. Jack read the paper and broke out laughing. He said, "Jackie, the problem is that your teacher, through no fault of his own, does not have the medical background to read this paper."

We had visited a sick friend during the previous summer at a center where cancer research was being done. Jackie, with her usual interest in all things, asked her father to get an appointment for her with a research doctor while we visited our friend. Jack did so. When asked about her interview with the doctor, she replied that she was still organizing her thoughts. She was unready to say more than that what the doctor had to say was interesting.

I went to see her teacher, smiled a lot, and explained to him that Jackie's father felt the paper, from a medical viewpoint, was exceptionally well done. The teacher insisted that he felt the paper deserved the grade it got. Next I visited the principal who sighed and took the paper, as I suggested, and said he would have a disinterested doctor read it. The principal called in a few days, apologized for the teacher's behavior, and said that the teacher had reconsidered, and the paper would be awarded an A. Later, when Jackie's illness became pronounced, we wondered if that F experience might have been damaging for her. We worried that it might have been delusion fodder. It does not take much imagination to feel paranoid over an A paper being labeled with an F.

The next spring Jack came home from the office looking very downcast. He called me into our room and said, "Today a well-known, highly respected attorney called me. He said he was violating his oath of confidence, but, knowing our family and the outrageousness of what Jackie made an appointment with him to ask about, made him feel he had to call." Jack said the lawyer told him that he certainly hoped someone would call him if his daughter pulled such a caper. Jackie had gone to the attorney with a thieving parent story. She said we were stealing money given to her by her grandparents and that she needed help to retrieve her funds. The attorney expressed grave concerns about the fact that Jackie seemed ill.

Once again our hands were tied. Because of breach of confidentiality by a professional, we could not tell Jackie that the attorney had called her father. All we could do was sit and watch and wait for what we greatly feared would be more evidence of a very troubled mind. But we built up reassurance once again when nothing untoward happened.

She had been accepted at Florida Presbyterian College for the 1965–1966 school year. We were glad she was going there because she could live at home while making adjustments to a new environment. FPC is now Eckerd College. This school is known for its desire to attract creative students and high academic achievers. We were glad that Jackie qualified.

Early in the fall Jackie's economics professor called Jack at the office to talk to him about the quality of Jackie's work. The professor told Jack that this freshman student was turning in graduate level papers. He wondered if we would have any objections to his putting her into his senior seminar group. Without hesitancy and with a feeling of joy that she was doing so well, Jack thanked the professor and told him that he was pleased about his plan.

In the spring Jackie's grades began to be disappointing, but we said nothing. We had never hounded the children to excel. Her eyes began to look dull, and her grooming began to deteriorate. We wondered and worried that rough times were coming for Jackie and for the family. Our worst fears were realized when the economics professor called Jack and asked him if he was aware that Jackie had grown careless about herself and her work. Jack told him that we had noticed and were closely watching her behavior.

On May 9, 1966, Jack was out of town, and the other two girls and I decided to go to Munch's, a longtime popular neighborhood restaurant for dinner. We were sitting in the den waiting for Jackie to get home from school so she could come with us. We heard her drive into the garage. As she walked by us, seemingly intent in getting to her room, I said, "Jackie, we are going to Munch's. Do you want to come along?" She wheeled, leaned down with her face within a foot from mine, and said in a defiant, snarling tone of voice, "Mother, I want my money back. I know you have stolen it." Her sisters looked at her in total disbelief, and there was apprehension in their eyes. In a vain effort to calm everyone and deflect the insult, I said, "Now Jackie, surely you jest. We are off to Munch's. Are you coming with us or not?" Her demeanor changed, she smiled and, in her normal tone of voice, said, "No thank you." I said, "OK, do you want us to bring you something?" She said, "No thank you." It seemed the dust had settled, but I reeled the entire scene away for discussion with Jack as soon as he got home.

At Munch's we were enjoying dinner with diminished pleasure due to Jackie's scene when the entrance door to Munch's flew open. Jackie descended on our table with obvious displeasure written on her face. The displeasure was emphasized by agitated body language. Hands on hips, she said in a strident voice, "Mother, you lied to me, and I know it. When you get home, I expect a full explanation." Then she flounced back out of the door and slammed it. Our dinner was no longer tempting. We and other diners were stunned.

My parents gave the grandchildren money at Christmas to be saved for their education. The girls always opened the gift envelopes and deposited the money into their accounts at the bank. Of course since they were minors, we had our names on the accounts with their names, and they were unable to access the funds without one of our signatures. I never asked or tried to find out whether Jackie had tried to withdraw the money. Not until this very moment has it ever occurred to me that her paranoia, paired with her inability to withdraw her funds, might have triggered her visit to the attorney's office in early spring 1965 and the lamentable May 9, 1966, incident.

The outburst was so internally devastating that reason was not well applied. Being called a liar anywhere by anyone anytime is unsettling, but when this beloved child so damned me, it spoke to me of tragedy entrenched or in the making. I downplayed the incident as much as I could. Jackie's sisters naturally wondered what could have caused her to utter such nonsense. I stayed away from their conversation, and, before we arrived home, the subject seemed moot between the three of us. It hurt so much that none of us wanted to think about it, much less talk a lot about it.

I did consider that Jackie might continue her tirade when we returned home, and I told Jan and Jyl, "I don't know why Jackie is acting like this, but, if she is still angry when we get home, I think we need to be sure she isn't able to drive off in a state of fury." I asked Jan, who was basically more practical and was more relaxed than Jyl, to go into the garage, open the hood of the Renault convertible that Jackie drove, and pull any wires loose that she saw.

I went to my room to give some quiet thought about Jackie's obvious display of paranoid thinking. Almost as soon as I sat down to try and gain enough composure to decide what to tell Jyl and Jan, and to decide what I should say to Jackie, Jackie came into the room. Again, she displayed bizarre behavior and repeated her accusations. "Jackie" I said, slowly and kindly, "I do not want to hear anymore about this tonight. Let's both give what you have said some serious thought and discuss it tomorrow, please." My attempt to defer the discussion only seemed to make her more agitated. She scowled and left the room. I heard the entrance door to the garage from the house open. I held my breath. I hoped that finding a seemingly dead battery would cause her to pause for thought, and send her feelings in a new direction.

My hopes were dashed when she returned to my room, snatched my car keys off the chest, and ran through the front door to the station wagon in the driveway. I literally ran after her. I got to the car just as she turned on the ignition and said, "Jackie, please don't take my car. I may need it." I took hold of the car door latch with the intention of opening the door to talk with her further. She accelerated and drove away. I managed to free my hand, but I felt that she was so into her delusions that she would have dragged me, had I not been able to release my hold on the door. Had I been dragged, I could have been injured. She was doing what she had to do to satisfy the uncontrollable, demanding dictation by the demons within her head.

Dejected, I went back into the house and told Jyl and Jan that I was going to call the health department outpatient psychiatric team. I think they were relieved. They were just sitting there, staring into space with distressed expressions. The whole thing was immediately magnified for me. I had to do whatever I could to get Jackie into a safe situation for herself and for some peace of mind for all of us before something fateful happened. Jackie's implausible behavior had forced my hand. At long last there seemed to be an opportunity to get help for her. If she did not come home soon, however, I knew I would have to call the police.

Jackie later told me that she drove to the Saint Petersburg downtown police station that evening to use a pay telephone. She tried unsuccessfully to call an attorney to help her retrieve the funds she believed to have been stolen from her by her parents.

Long before we had any realization of serious mental illness with Jackie, Jack, as public health director, had put a team of psychiatric nurses in place. Their major purpose was to be on call and go out whenever an emergency call came in from anywhere from anyone when there were problems dealing with someone in a psychotic state of mind. I called the psychiatric nurse station and explained my plight to them. We decided to give Jackie a little time to return home before alerting any law enforcement personnel. I was to call back within a short time or call when she returned, and they would immediately come to the house.

My next step considered Jack, Jyl, and Jan. I surely was not going to call Jack. He was out of town and too far away to get home quickly. There was nothing he could do. Evening or night calls are often made that do nothing more than destroy a night's rest for the recipient of the call. It is much better to wait until morning when the mind is refreshed after a good night's sleep and better able to cope with the unexpected bad news. I called our minister, Bob Shirer, who lived nearby, and explained what was going on as best I could. He was quick to offer assurance that he would be on call for whatever help was needed. He asked me to call him as soon as I knew what had to be done.

Then Jyl, Jan, and I waited and listened for the car to roll up in the circular driveway, which could be seen through a large plate glass living room window that enabled a lovely view of Lakewood Country Club golf course. We were all uptight. We were all puzzled and dismayed. At least, I thought to myself, at this juncture, Jyl and Jan probably do not realize that this episode may be representative of something more than a trick to extract money from parents. How I wished that might be the case, but a dreadful cloud of gloom and doom was encompassing my space as we waited for Jackie to come home.

Then the car appeared in the driveway. Jackie got out and slowly entered the house, strolled back to her room, and stretched out on her bed with her schoolbooks. She already seemed to be studying when I walked in. I held out my hand for the car keys. She handed them to me and smiled. I wanted to make certain that she would be unable to go off in the car when the nurses came.

I went to the back of the house into the kitchen and called the nurses. I simply said, "Jackie is home." The nurse replied, "We are on the way." They were surprised, I am sure, that they had been summoned to the house of their employer. Many times, I imagine, they had seen Jackie when she dropped by her father's office for some reason when she was downtown.

When they walked through an intentionally unlocked front door, I simply indicated where Jackie was. A short distance from the entrance there was a hall leading to Jackie's room. Standing in the living room, I heard one of the nurses say, "Hello, Jackie. We are from the health department and have come to see you in hopes that we can help you." Jackie replied in soft, well-regulated tones, "I have wondered when you were going to get here."

Soon, one of the nurses came out to tell me that Jackie had agreed to be hospitalized, that they would take her, and that I could come with them if I wished. They thought it a good idea that I do that, and I certainly would not have wanted it otherwise. Bob, our minister, had also arrived on the scene. Jackie did ask for me to come in and talk to her, but I did not wish a confrontation at that time. Bob told Jackie that she could not speak to me just then. After years of utter frustration with Jackie's absolute refusals to seek help, I was not going to give her another opportunity to try to avoid the care she so desperately needed. I did not wish to be positioned so that she could perceive me as the heartless mother, forcing her to leave home to enter the hospital.

Jackie got ready and put some things together to take with her. She went quietly with no protest. We had decided to take her to Tampa because no public official welcomes the kind of publicity generated from public knowledge that his daughter is in a mental facility. Jack and I understood the prevalent, unkind, and uneducated views held by the general public about mental illness. If possible I wanted to avoid the potential backlash for all of us.

I sat on the back seat and held Jackie's hand during the silent, somber drive across Howard Franklin causeway from Pinellas County to Hillsborough County, and on to Tampa General Hospital. I remember no word spoken by anyone as we rode along. I think the nurses felt that, if Jackie wanted to talk, she would. Certainly it was no time for small talk between the nurses and me. And certainly no one felt light-hearted enough for idle chatter.

The ominous whirring of car wheels, the darkness of the night, and my sorrow for Jackie's insanity made tears sting the backs of my eyes as I affectionately remembered other times not blighted by mysterious unexplainable behaviors. Reels from places we had lived, Waynesboro, Treasure Island, and Pittsburgh were brought out for reflection while, in the darkness, tears streamed. The reels eased the frightening burden of pain threatening Jack's and my dreams and our hopes for this child beside me. I needed distraction on this night.

Family life as we had dreamed it would be was finally, admittedly, deeply flawed, and probably forever mirrored by madness. I put aside this intruding nightmarish thought by remembering that Jackie had never been anything but a model child as far as her behavior was concerned. This night was indelibly stamping a new identity for her. This child, so cherished from birth, so long awaited, was mentally leaving our family behind as she entered a world where we could not follow and that we could never fathom. Reels rolled as we rode through the dark and troubled night. Pleasant visions of Jackie's past hurtled through my mind even as I looked into what seemed to be a distorted mirror of her life. It was becoming difficult to retrieve the reflections of lost dreams.

The reflections stopped as we drove into the grounds of the hospital. Time to dry my tears and face bleak truths. It was almost midnight, eerily still, and disheartening. The nurses had been to the hospital many times, and they knew exactly what to do, which made everything as easy and pleasant as it could be under such grievous circumstances. I, like a robot, followed all directions given for filling out paperwork. I was mentally exhausted and distracted; part of my mind kept searching as I tried to put the pieces of Jackie's life together in vain efforts to find answers to explain her behavior.

Entering the psychiatric floor of the Tampa hospital, with doors being unlocked to open for entrance and then locked after entry, was woefully chilling. Being locked up was becoming literal reality for this wonderful, smart person that I knew so well and loved so much. Her inability to control her actions or thoughts, and her inability to be in possession of her mind, had forced us into "putting her away." "People in white coats" coming to get people is the frivolous, descriptive jargon too often used in a humorous vein. When I hear these commonplace references made with a laugh, I feel an internal shudder. I have put two of my children away, and people in white coats came and took both of them away. Light-headed and cold-hearted attitudes toward "crazy" people are easily identified when such casual references are callously made. When such remarks are no longer accepted as humor, there will be mature and enlightened understanding of how horrendous it is to be mentally ill. It is no joke. For families and victims of the sickness, the jokes are cruel.

Jackie later told me that the moment the psychiatric ward door slammed, her delusions stopped. I think she felt safe there. For me it was a relief to believe that some action to help her might finally be found. The psychiatric team nurses assured me that there was good medical help in the hospital and that Jackie would get prompt attention. I kept telling myself to be thankful that she was as safe physically as she could possibly be. From that first confinement, the keyword for me became safe. That word safe is foreign to legislators, lawyers, and judges who deal with severe psychiatric problems with maximum inefficiency. Persistently and consistently for purposes of political expediency, situations are established by the judicial system that are physically and mentally unsafe for seriously mentally ill individuals.

Jack came home to a new set of circumstances. He now had a daughter who would not be able to finish her first year of college, and two other daughters experiencing stress and feeling less secure than they had felt only days before when he had left on his business trip.

We went to see Jackie as soon as they allowed her to have company. Jack, being a doctor, asked to see her chart. She had been medicated, and she was very glad to see us. She asked her father a question, which set off an alarm that would continue to knell as we tried to understand and work with psychiatrists. When she asked, "Father, they tell me they know I think the food is poisoning me. I do not think that. Why would they ask that?" A precursor to the future was introduced.

It seemed to us that almost every doctor Jackie talked with suggested the possibilities of new delusions. Professional treatment personnel should be very careful not to inadvertently plant bizarre ideas into the mentalities of severely mentally ill people. Mentally ill people use many reasons to validate delusions. Mere suggestions by professionals might become as gospel to those clinging weakly to a world of reality.

Jackie always was clever. When Jack and I left the hospital after that first visit, he commented, "I think they may be careless with their charts." He felt confident that it was Jackie's handwriting on the chart that said, "Jacquelyn may have visitors anytime." That was not true, so no nurse would have written that on the chart.

Jack was not surprised to see Jackie's original diagnosis of her illness verified by the doctor. Because of mental illness within his own family, his expectations and beliefs about her mental health problems were now firmly fixed. I feel that he had feared the worst from her first display of irrationality.

He was very kind and gentle, telling me some things to expect. He said, "Maxene, you must be ready to live life like a rider on a carnival merry-go-round. We are off on a lifetime carousel that will be like a cruel ride on hobby-horses going from high to low with no median stop. When Jackie seems better, she will get worse; when she seems worse, she will get better. And we will never know at any time where the disease may take us tomorrow. You need to understand this now." I now know how right that analogy was.

The doctor conferred with us in about ten days, and he said that Jackie needed long-term hospitalization. He mentioned some facilities and asked us where we would like to send her. She had requested, and we had hoped, that the doctor would spend time trying psychotherapy. He was a gentle, honest, kind person, as opposed to some psychiatrists we later encountered, and he immediately made it clear that, in his opinion, psychotherapy is never helpful for paranoid schizophrenics. Today that is an established factor in considerations for the treatment of schizophrenics.

A retired doctor came to Jack seeking something productive to do with his time. Jack was delighted to have Ross Cameron working at the health department. He was a remarkable person. He had been sent to Taiwan by the U.S. Government to assist Chiang Kai Chek in setting up a system of public health. While there he learned to understand the Chinese language, and he could write Chinese. It amazed me to sit by him somewhere and watch his hands fly as he took notes in Chinese. Ross was experienced in the field of mental health. We asked his advice.

Ross had been involved with various mental facilities during his public health career. He told us that the diagnosis was indeed unfortunate. He said that he knew of many families who were stripped of all fiscal resources as they took their ill family member from one psychiatrist to another and paid high fees. He told us that hospitalization in private facilities usually incurs unending, prohibitive expenses for those who are not extremely wealthy. Too often, he said, homes are mortgaged or other family members' needs are sacrificed. His advise was to use all the public facilities that we could, because he had not found private facilities to be any more beneficial to schizophrenics than public entities.

With heavy hearts, we followed Ross's advice. Jackie was transferred to Northeast State Hospital in McClenny, Florida. At that time it was considered the best state hospital. Later on when we did use private facilities, we realized that the advice Ross had given us had been good advice. *Safe* is the watchword when trying to find a place where a mentally ill family member can live to the best of whatever ability the curse of mental illness will allow.

It was weeks before we saw Jackie. Whenever there was a hospitalization, a period of time for study of the patient's symptoms and time for patient adjustment to the environment and medication was mandatory. We never questioned that requirement. It seemed to make sense. Everyone is tired and emotionally drained when hospitalization becomes necessary. Families as well as patients need respite, it seemed to us. It was a relief for days to once again be predictable. It was a relief, with accompanying grief, to know that, of necessity, Jackie was in a place where there was protection so that she could not be a danger to herself or to others.

We were intelligent enough to know that any person, when hostile or angry for any reason, sane or insane, may perform an act of violence in the passion of a moment. Everyone, admittedly or not, during fun times, from forgetfulness, perhaps inadvertently, or from delusions of madness, sometimes does crazy things. For advocates to insist on no reference to craziness when discussing those of us who unfortunately suffer from the diseases of mental illness, in my opinion, skirts the truths of madness.

I question the determination of advocates for mentally ill individuals that the mentally ill never be called crazy. It seems to me that, no matter what the provocation, if an action is crazy, it is crazy. Just as a rose is never other than a rose, crazy actions are never other than crazy actions. I think mentally ill people should not be led to believe that some of their behavior is anything other than crazy when they are psychotic. The reality of madness is that crazy actions reflect the disease when it is untreated. If a diabetic flips out and does nutty things, no one pretends that the behavior is other than crazy.

Crazy is defined in the dictionary as being affected with or suggestive of madness; insane, not sensible; impractical. Unfortunately my precious, diseased daughter Jackie is crazy. Her disease cannot be gentled or moderated by insisting that she is just mentally ill. Because of her mental illness, she does and thinks crazy things as opposed to the comparatively rational thinking that is being done by the majority of the world's population.

Families, often totally unreasonable with their denial of the true nature of the illness, find reasons for denial and avoidance of actualities of the disease from some advocacy platforms. There is no way to gentle the cruelty or brutality of madness.

Between our last visit with Jackie in Tampa and the first time we saw her in Northeast Florida State Hospital in McClenny in July 1966, I had time to consider many things. I realized that I had mistakenly hoped, from the beginning of Jackie's illness, that because Jack had somehow put a leash on his 1954 short-term mental problems, that Jackie would also be able to snap out of it. I finally realized that our only hope was to find a medication to allow her to function without the bedevilment of mental illness. I had not yet learned that, even when a medicine helps the patient, the patient might be dilatory or might refuse to take the medicine for a variety of reasons.

At Northeast Florida State Hospital, Jackie was fortunate to be assigned to Dr. Elefthery. Dr. Elefthery, an Austrian psychiatrist, was working at the state hospital while he studied and waited to be licensed to practice in Florida. He was an attractive person with a contagious, good-natured personality. He also was an educated intellectual realist. He seemed to be an extremely well-adjusted person. That is not always true of psychiatrists.

Years later I would understand what Dr. Elefthery meant when he told me that I should never refer to mental illnesses in Jack's family when speaking with Jack. Dr. Elefthery said, "He is possibly carrying a heavy burden of guilt for having possibly brought bad seeds to his marriage." Dr. Elefthery did not know about Jack's personal single episode. I expect that he would have clued me in that Jack was probably self-medicating if I had told him about the episode. As I struggled with acceptance for Jackie's dilemma, I silently empathized with her father. He, I imagined, as well as I, must be having some playback to his episode of paranoid behavior in 1954.

Dr Elefthery told me that whenever Jackie did anything that was, in fact, abnormal, I should not accept it. He said that he was firmly convinced that mentally ill patients know when they are not acting like people in the real world. He said he believed that it is terribly confusing and upsetting to them deep inside their psyche. "It is not kind for anyone associated with a mentally ill person to accept behaviors that are socially unacceptable," he told me. He emphasized his remarks when he said, "I think that family members and others inadvertently enable their loved one's illness when they tolerate inappropriate actions without comment or by inappropriate reactions."

Tiptoe reactions are not my forte anyway, so Dr. Elefthery's words were welcome. Usually when Jackie says something that simply differs from my reality, I do not argue. I simply tell her that my reality does not include what she is talking about. We try to compare our worlds with respect for one another.

I made it as clear as possible during the years of living with Jackie, and then with Jyl, when she became ill, that they were functioning in spaces unfamiliar and unreal to me. If they said or did anything inconsiderate, I usually tried to make them understand in a few simple sentences how it seemed to me. I never belabored or referred back later to any bizarre statements or actions they demonstrated. I did not wish to instill guilt feelings to add to their confused internal miseries.

It was obvious that the disease somehow caused distortion of perceptions. I sometimes said, "My perception seems to be different from yours. May I tell you what I thought I heard or saw?" I can remember Jackie once telling me when I differed with her in hearing some sound, "Mother, you are crazy." And we both laughed.

Once when talking with Jackie about plans being made for me to visit with her at the hospital, she suggested that arrangements needed to be made. I said, "Jackie, I have already spoken to someone, and a meeting place has been set up for us" She said, "With whom did you speak?" When I told her who the person was, she said that she wished I had let her arrange the meeting room because she did not like the person to whom I had spoken. I replied, "Jackie, I hope you do not do anything to let others there know if you dislike them." She replied to my advice, "Look, I may be crazy, but I am not stupid." This exchange took place when she was properly medicated and able to separate delusions perceived by mentally ill people as opposed to realities as perceived by mentally well people. Even when medicated, she quickly reacts negatively whenever her wishes are thwarted, and suggestions may become twisted into criticisms. Jackie says that she has not been free from delusions since 1965.

One night she and I were sitting in the living room at the beach house when she said, "Listen to the crickets." I smiled and thought the crickets were a hallucination. She insisted she heard them. I don't know how far away they were but, with intense attention, I finally did hear weak and distant cricket sounds. Here was an illustration of heightened hearing perception. Here was an example of the "normal" person taking for granted that the "crazy" person is hearing things in her head that do not exist in the real world.

Keeping rooms neat, keeping themselves neat, and being congenial around the house were things Jack and I expected from all three girls. Our household functioned as well as any household, though with the malaise of madness ever present, it was sometimes difficult to keep things on an even keel. Many people visited our home and never realized that two of our daughters had mental problems. When Jyl was murdered, the disclosure was news to most people. When functioning became impossible for Jackie or Jyl for any reason, Jack and

I turned, when no other resort was possible, to hospitalization, with hopes always revived for recouping better mental health.

We had read that approximately one-third of severely mentally ill individuals recover for no known reason; one-third respond to medication so that they are not psychotic; and one-third never recover sufficiently to function within what is considered a "normal" range. The latter are the severely mentally ill. Many of them live without safety in the streets, under bridges, or in other sanctuaries quietly and lawlessly obtained. They live in their own special hells, sanctioned by those who fear hell after death, but care little about hell on earth for others who are less fortunate mentally than most of us.

Psychological sages introduced the term dysfunctional family while we were necessarily struggling within one. This new "in" term is still used for any family perceived as not "normal." Differentiation between dysfunctional and functional is a mystery to me. I have never known a family that was not dysfunctional at some times, and I have never known a person that has not been dysfunctional at some times, if dysfunctional refers to failure to have smooth sailing through all adversities without departure from another vagary, "normalcy."

Diagnostic jargon often supplants the sufferer and becomes the center of discussion and action within supposedly helping or healing sessions among patients, families, and treatment professionals. Family members are sometimes pacified with meaningless jargon. When there is inability to help or heal a serious mental illness, diagnostic jargon may be used as a diversion to fill some void, or mercenarily to secure income.

I think our family was most dysfunctional for our youngest daughter Jan. The family did not conform to a pattern that Jack and I would have maintained had we been granted more ideal circumstances. For Jan and Jyl, if one wishes to consider dysfunctional as being less than best for the well-being of all concerned, had to feel some adverse effects from Jackie's illness. Never articulated, but surely felt, were their senses of uncertainty, even insecurity, as concerns for the future necessarily permeated our home. Jyl and Jan were determined survivors, and actually, by their resilience, provided stamina for Jack and me. There was laughter. There was retention of normalcy as often as possible. All of us tried not to let sad thoughts deter us from or dominate our way of life.

Jan and Jyl were impressionable youngsters when Jack and I stepped with trepidation into difficult parental roles, wretchedly different from anything we had ever expected, wanted, or chosen. The clear promising mirror I had viewed as a child and young adult was becoming increasingly cracked as mental illness took its toll in our family. Jackie demanded and received attention and time that was needed for the entire family. I feared then, and I believe now, that Jackie exhibited attitudes or may have shared some thoughts originating from her delusions and tortures with her younger sisters that may have influenced some of their ideas and belief patterns. Jackie's onset of mental illness, and its endurance, marked the end of consistent "normal" functioning for the family, and it continuously fostered seeds of dysfunction. When there is a severely mentally ill individual in a household, whether desired or not, everything rotates around the needs and desires of the ill person. Mentally ill individuals may display cantankerous behavior that results from unfulfilled, imagined needs. That easily causes disruptions in normal family or individual functioning. Balanced level fields for healthy family interactions are adversely affected.

On September 23, 1966, Dr. Elefthery considered Jackie's condition stabilized enough for her to come home for a trial visit. When sent there from Tampa General Hospital on June 7, 1966, she was adjudged mentally incompetent by reason of schizophrenic reactions, paranoid type. She came home with prescribed medication, and she had been firmly instructed to continue taking her medication on schedule with no lapses. It was distressing for her when the official revocation of her driving license was delivered by mail on October ninth. She was unable to drive until restoration of her sanity was court decreed, but she once again passed all testing originally taken by all applicants for driver's licenses.

To the best of our knowledge, Jackie took her medicine as prescribed. She did see a psychiatrist regularly and, as far as we could tell, he was not doing any damage. Jackie did not like him very much, and I found him rather inept in his personal ability to relate to other people. But, if he was harmless, we believed we were giant steps ahead. I now believe that he collected fees without any clinical justification.

Immediately, in my initial interview with him, he asked me the question I had come to expect from psychiatrists, "What about your home life?" I smiled and asked him what he would like to know. He did not smile, and he asked what difficulties we had in our home. It began to be obvious after a while that this man was determined to uncover some home life customs or events that were conducive to causing Jackie's mental illness. Had the circumstances not been so serious, the questions would have been humorous. I finally said, "Look, Jack and I have not done anything to cause Jackie's insanity. I wish we had because, if other parents and we could be found guilty of poor parenting, causative factors could be identified. We could all get together and figure out how to change our behaviors, tell the world, and wipe out the scourge of schizophrenia. Wouldn't that be wonderful?" Needless to say he found my logic as repugnant as I found his asinine questions.

Jack and I never believed we were perfect in any way, shape, or form, but we knew that we had not been poor parents. We never felt guilty or responsible for mental illness within our family. The ongoing, insulting questions from almost every psychiatrist I saw were boring. They were exercises in futility for the doctor because I had no morsels of rotten parenting to present.

Jack refused to talk to them from the beginning. He told me that they did not know what caused the illness, and, in his opinion, could do nothing except try and find the right medicines for Jackie. He said, "If you don't mind too much, I would appreciate it if you would do the talking with them. I have to admit that I do not think I can do it and contain my distaste for their methodologies. They will probably never stop digging at us as parents. That is the way they put food on their family tables, and we need to flow with some of the flak.

You have to remember that some of them are quite sincere in their Freudian beliefs, and until something comes along, as it will, to wipe out all of their false premises, we have nowhere else to go. We are going to have to be patient and tolerant of the way psychiatry is usually practiced if we wish to get attention for Jackie. They are supposed to know what medicines to prescribe for specific mental illnesses, and she will probably have to be medicated forever, barring a miracle." Then he paused, smiled, and said, "The psychiatrists would much rather talk with you anyway. Mothers are their favorite red meat."

And so I played their game, though I oft times suspected that some of them had their own mental challenges, which might have helped propel them into psychiatric practice. I also knew that Jackie was feeding them lots of things from her delusions and tortures in keeping with their own beliefs. She said things to me that simply were not true about her father. She still does. Paranoia does not shed kindly lights on mothers and fathers of sufferers of delusions. Victims, whether they are the ill persons, family members, friends, or associates, come alike to trapping into nonfactual fantasies.

The "it's-the-some-significant-other's-fault" theory has been forcibly driven from psychiatric jargon today largely by findings in psychobiology and other areas that support genetic and biochemical explanations for severe mental disorders. The fact that talking never helped my daughters seemed irrelevant to the number of times most of their doctors would have seen them if we had been compliant. However, there are other distracting "hold-on-to-the-patient" techniques used today for the fiscal advantage of doctors who suggest too much counsel with schizophrenics. Schizophrenics will often talk with excessive repetition to anyone who will listen about things that have no curative benefit. The primary value of the employment of psychiatrists today, in my opinion, and as Jack believed, is their ability to diagnose specific mental illnesses and suggest prescriptions that might be beneficial to the patient's ability to adjust or adapt to sane lifestyles. As in any serious illness, two opinions are not a bad idea.

Even though some well-educated people understand that dominant theories prevalent in the sixties have been replaced by scientific assertions that biological-chemical imbalances greatly influence mental illnesses, outmoded theories persist in a world where most people seem to have no solid understanding of the difference between serious mental illness and general dysfunctions of human beings. They seem to have no clue to the difference between neurosis and psychosis. Mid-twentieth-century theorists, and those for eons before, rendered major disservice by not differentiating between severe and "garden variety" cases of mental illness, and also by failing to differentiate between emotional disturbances and mental illness.

Jackie attended William and Mary College in Williamsburg, Virginia, during the 1967 summer term. She has since told me that "they" tortured her there. She says the program and the torture stopped when she came home. For a while the whirling hobbyhorses gave us some reprieve. That fall she enrolled at Saint Petersburg Junior College. Almost six months rolled by without extraordinary happenings in our household. There was a respite from the wondering alertness that we had needed since the spring of 1965. Jackie seemed interested in us again. She seemed interested in activities that were of general concern rather than just those immediately concerning her self. Such relief seemed too good to be true. It was.

When I walked into the beach house the afternoon of February 15, 1968, Jyl, Jan, and Rose were standing at the bottom of the steps going upstairs. They just stood there looking at me, and no one said anything until I asked, "Is something wrong?" Rose said, very quietly, still in disbelief, "Jackie jumped out of her bedroom window, and her father has taken her to the emergency room." Stunned, I asked, "How badly was she hurt?" Jan said, "Well, no one realized anything was wrong at first when Jackie came through the door and started walking over to Father. Then we all saw that her leg was cut, and she was bleeding. Father jumped up to begin taking care of the wound, when Jackie said she had jumped from her upstairs window and had cut her leg on a cinder block on the ground." It sounded like Jack had done what he could and then noticed a red line on her neck. He went upstairs and unlocked her room to find that she had put cords around her neck and attached them to the bed-post before she jumped. Her weight had broken the cords.

When he came back downstairs, he helped her to the car and took her to the emergency room at South Pasadena Hospital. He, as a known doctor at the hospital, could ask them to suture the leg, and he knew no questions would be asked. He recoiled from a suicide attempt report being made, for her sake and for the sake of all of us. We certainly did not wish the two younger girls to have the impossible job of explaining the mental illness of a sister to their classmates at school.

We did not need the publicity. As public health director, Jack attempted to run an honest operation in Pinellas and Pasco counties. He was an employee of the county commissioners. Some Pinellas commissioners felt it only proper that the health department be used to further their political ambitions. Unfortunately the ongoing skirmishes between Jack and the commissioners kept our name before the public. Jack's differences with the commissioners became public knowledge when he resisted some dishonest, unsavory suggestions. He was an irritating thorn in the flesh to a few commissioners who wanted their kickback schemes enabled by the health department.

Jackie knew about her father's ongoing hassles with local politicians, and her normal intelligence would have told her that it was unkind to try to make her action a public event. He mentioned to her on the way to the hospital that it might be best if she did not elaborate on the details of how she cut her leg. He knew that it would not be easy for Jan and Jyl if their peers were asking about it. He knew it would not be great for me to have my students curious about it. A suicide attempt by the daughter of a public figure could be part of the eleven o'clock news. We lucked out. No public note was made of it.

Jack realized that Jackie was responding to delusional commands when she was unkind to him. He expected the worst. He told me later, "Nothing would have kept her from going into detail to try to make me look bad. Nothing." There in a nutshell is an example of what mental illness does to good people who are victimized by it. Serious mental illness makes them irresponsibly unaccountable for their thoughts and actions. Their behavior may in effect come to be in total conflict with behavior they have been known to demonstrate when enjoying good mental health.

When Jack and Jackie returned from the hospital, Jackie seemed dazed and was not communicative. She seemed depressed, and I suppose she was devastated that the cords had broken, and she was still alive. She has since told me that when she jumped, she had the most wonderful feelings of freedom and happiness that she had ever experienced in her life. She had been given medication for pain, and that, along with her usual medication that we gave her, caused her to sleep.

All through the night as she lay there, so still, without moving, I thought that had she had her way, she would be lying in a morgue or funeral home, still and quiet. She would not be breathing. That she still lived, I mused, was perhaps an omen that she might again become the person we had known when she owned her mind. The shock of the day paired with her peaceful sleep gave me sustenance to stay awake. I sat beside her bed all night and never closed my eyes. I could not chance that she repeat her suicide attempt. Over and over I considered what the next day should be for her sake. Jack and I agreed to wait until morning to decide what we could do to try to help her.

Before she wakened the next morning, Jack and I talked and called her psychiatrist. He agreed with us that she should come into the hospital for observation. She stayed in the hospital a month until the doctor decided that she was stable enough to be discharged. When she came home, she got a job at the Redington Beach Howard Johnson's Restaurant and worked for six months. She became discontented with her waitress job, so she went with the family to Virginia that summer.

She was not a willing participant in our vacation activities. She reverted to her habit of going off alone and ignoring everyone. She later told me that her mental torture was extremely difficult that summer. However, she attended a party we gave at my parents' Rawley Springs cabin, about eleven miles from Harrisonburg. The party was for a friend, Buzz Dawbarn, who was campaigning for a Virginia Senate seat. The intent of the party was to introduce Buzz, who lived in Waynesboro, to people from the Harrisonburg area. Jackie seemed interested in what Buzz had to say, and she mixed well with the people present. In other words, she displayed no symptoms of her mental illness. Buzz commented to me that she seemed to be an unusually intelligent young lady. This intermittent "normal" behavior is characteristic of schizophrenia, and it may cause a lapse of attention of family members from the welfare of the sick person.

Often when one reads of murders seemingly without motivation, symptoms have been successfully masked. Or worse, people surrounding the individual are incapable of recognizing symptoms. Law enforcement people are notoriously unsympathetic to warning signals from unfortunate, confused, untreated mentally ill homeless people. Some schizophrenics are dead because of police ignorance.

Jackie returned to junior college that fall to continue her education. On August 2, 1969, she completed the equivalent of two years of work and received a Saint Petersburg Junior College certification in general education.

During Jackie's sophomore year at SPJC, at Christmas 1968, Jyl came home for the holidays from Utah University. When we met the plane in Tampa, someone resembling Jyl came through the gate. Something was obviously terribly wrong. What had happened to our child so full of spontaneity and humor? This dull-eyed, slow-of-gait person barely responded to our greetings. We pretended that all was well, and we carried on fairly inane chatter while driving home. Our chatter curtained intense reactions from seeing her in this condition, and amazement that she seemed so despondent. When we got home, she did eat something, and then Jack suggested that she get undressed and go to bed to rest because she looked tired. She made no comment, simply went upstairs, crawled into bed, turned her face toward the wall, and slept until late the next morning. Once again I was sitting bedside, watching and wondering what the next day's plans should be for another daughter. Once again, before a daughter wakened, we sat and pondered puzzling conditions involving a beloved child. We decided to contact the college and talk to her counselor to ask whether he had noticed anything unusual in Jyl's behavior while she was there. Jack had appointments at the office, so I made the call.

The counselor was not surprised to hear from me. I asked him, "How long will you keep a student's body if parents continue to send money?" Right away he told me that Jyl's life at the school had been miserable. He said that when he came to the school years ago to work, he had experienced some of the same kinds of harassment she endured, but he was older and able to resist the evangelistic Mormon zeal to convert him.

Jyl smoked, wore lipstick, and was not prejudiced toward black people. Those three things, plus a fairly casual attitude toward religion, made her a prime target for young people with the souls of zealots, determined that everyone should believe what they believed and be what they saw themselves as being. Anyone else was deemed to be hell bound. The counselor said he had begged Jyl to let us know what was going on, but she saw that as a failure on her part. She did not want to give up. She simply could not believe that the Mormon young people had no tolerance because she smoked and wore lipstick. She really believed that they would finally accept her or try to help her enjoy Utah. She came home for Christmas, knowing that the Mormon young people thought she was going to hell, and she found that extremely depressing. She also bemoaned their intolerance for black people. It was not until years later that the Mormons decided to change their policy regarding black people. Had we understood the fanaticism of the Mormons, we would never have let Jyl go near Logan, Utah. I called Jack at the office, and he was as appalled as I was and as shocked. We asked the counselor to please have her things packed and shipped home because she surely would never return. Jack and I discussed how to tell Jyl that she couldn't go back, and we decided to put the ball in our family doctor's court. Jyl was so rundown that Jack told her she needed to have a physical examination. Jack had started her on a vitamin regime. Dr. Charles Bramlit, our wonderful, compassionate family doctor, approved the vitamin regime, and he told Jyl that her health simply was not good enough for her to return to Utah. He convinced her that she needed to stay at home and perhaps go to school in an environment where she could get a lot of rest until her health improved. Jyl cried and cried and said she wanted to go back. She had no idea that we had talked to the counselor.

We were amazed that she, even though the Mormon students had affected her so negatively, was grimly determined to go back and face their zealot music. Her acceptance at Utah had been a very special thing. She had fooled around, played and dreamed away her years in elementary and high school, while getting lots of Cs on her report cards. We followed the advice given us at the University of Virginia and never made academic demands of her. Just before the opening of school her senior year, she and I were sitting at the dining table talking, when she suddenly slapped the table and said, rather vehemently, "Mother, I hate school!" I burst out laughing, and she said, "What is funny about that?" "Well, Jyl," I responded, "we have always known you hated school and I expected the remark you have just made to be a recurrent complaint all through your elementary and secondary school years. Why have you waited so long to say it?" She said, "I enjoyed lots of things about school, but most of it has been a drag. Now I realize that I have truly screwed up. I want to go to college, and my grades stink." I told her that I was sorry she realized so late that she should have hit the books harder. I suggested that all was not lost and suggested she consider going to SPJC to get her act together enough to get a transfer somewhere for her last two years. I told her then about the test results from the University of Virginia when she was in first grade. "Jyl, we know that you are smart enough and creative enough to do anything you wish.

However, it will take discipline. I understand because I, too, had lots of fun and other interests than school homework. I didn't give schoolbooks the attention that I now wish I had. I, too, did just enough to get by. You and I share a free-spirited attitude that has not served us well academically."

In January Jyl, with a broad smile, handed me an acceptance letter from Utah State University in Logan, Utah. She had made good grades the first semester of her senior year and was into being a good student. I said, "Jyl, I am so pleased for you and so surprised." She said, "I wanted to do it on my own to prove to myself I could." We had lots of fun buying clothes and packing. As I write, a reel reflecting pathos for me shows her standing dressed, ready to go to the airport to fly to Logan. She had bought a nifty hat to wear, but, as she looked at herself, she took it off and tossed it across the room to me and said, "Here. You keep it. I think it is a bit too much for me." I said, "Thank you. It will be around if you change your mind and want to take it later. You do look sharp enough without it. You look ready for Utah." We had a great trip going to the airport and jauntily waved good-bye. All parents know the feeling when a child leaves the nest for the first time. We made her promise to call as soon as the plane landed in Salt Lake City. She was to connect with a bus to take her to Logan, and she made a second promise to call when she arrived at school.

We went home, and the wait began. When the time came that we knew she should be in Salt Lake City, and there was no call, we began to be concerned. Then the phone rang, and there was Jyl, laughter in her voice, "Hi, the plane was late. The bus has gone, but there is a pilot here that is flying his plane home to Logan in just a few minutes. He says he will take me. Got to run. Love you." And she was gone. We laughed, but we also fretted. Jyl believed that there was not one bad person in the entire world. She really loved people, and she was so gullible. There was nothing to do but have faith that all was well.

We sat and envisioned her hundreds of miles away, alone with some stranger, flying through the dark night, having a wonderful time. Then another call came. She was still in high spirits. She was in the dormitory, tired, but so happy and excited. She said the pilot was a regular ferry pilot of chartered planes, who lived in Logan, and he had flown her for free. He also had flown her around over Salt Lake City and shown her the bright lights. Her wings were not clipped. She was flying free. We shared her exuberance. It was a vicarious thrill for me. Such a happy beginning to have such a shattering conclusion left Jack and me with the only bias I think either of us ever knew.

Mormons had not done right by our child. Any respect we might have ever had for them was damaged forever.

The extent of our knowledge of the church was an in-house story from Jack's home. The Mormons showed up every summer in the valley, relentlessly ringing doorbells. We considered their fervent, evangelistic visits nuisances, but, when you read of their successes, you knew that there were people all over the world seeking something that they seemed to offer. I suppose we just didn't know anyone looking for religion offered by strangers packing holy books from house to house. Once when they came to Jack's home, his older brother answered the door. They started their evangelistic spiel and held out a book for him to look at. He looked at the book, handed it back, and said, "Oh, it's like the Holly Bibel, I think we have one of those." Chuckling over the evangelists' horror at his intentional mispronunciation of Holy Bible, he politely closed the door.

So now, we had two daughters needing special care. The year 1969 was to be a very sad and trying time for the entire family. Jan, a senior in high school, was living in the downstairs apartment in the guesthouse. It was near the house, and she came to the house for meals and whenever she wished. She was not living an entirely independent life from the family, but Jack and I thought it best if she could have her friends visit her without the presence of two sisters whose actions might sometimes be socially embarrassing for her.

We had a friend, Tom Howze, a professor at the SPJC in Clearwater, who was also a counselor. He suggested that he pick up Jyl on his way to work and bring her home in the evening so he could work with her in adjusting to a new educational environment. He said she could come to his department whenever she wished to study or talk with him whenever he was free. He had a staff that could also be helpful. This was a wonderfully kind offer, and we gratefully accepted. Jyl, smarting from her rejection in Utah, was fighting depression and cried easily. She went off with Tom though, and she took some classes, but she simply could not seem to overcome her sadness.

Jyl was seeing a psychiatrist, but that was a bummer for her too. She came to me after a few visits and said, "Mother, why are you and Father paying this man to see me? I go in. He sits there looking at me with a you-are-a-worm look as if I am a true dud. I discovered on my first visit that he just wants to find out anything he can about any negative feelings I have about you and Father. Believe me, he practically salivates if I say anything uncomplimentary about either of you. He lights up so much that I am getting kicks out of the boring visits by making up stuff about you and Father that no one else would ever believe. Why waste money for these ridiculous visits?" I reminded Jyl that the doctor was a fellow physician of her father's, and it was not a good idea to make the man think less well of us than we deserved. She laughed and said, "He certainly doesn't act like a friend to Father. I will stop making up things, but why can't I just stay away from him? I feel terrible after being around him." When I spoke to Jack, who was adamantly opposed to the way psychiatry was practiced and understood psychiatric pitches, he agreed with Jyl. She happily stopped going to see that psychiatrist on a regular basis.

Jackie had made us feel so encouraged in August 1969 when she received a certificate from the junior college, but our relief was not to be for long. By October 9, the hobbyhorses reached another low, and Jackie was once again too ill to function as an outpatient. Commitment papers were drawn up stating that she had relatively fixed delusions, felt that she was being experimented on by doctors, denied illness or problems, refused medication as an outpatient, could not be reached by psychotherapy, and wanted isolation by hospitalization if there were no plots. Her psychiatrist was quite adamant that she be "put away" again. He actually told me that we, the family, would be better off if we just sent Jackie away and forgot about her.

We had heard about some successes for treatment of schizophrenia by Dr. Abram Hoffer in Saskatoon, Canada. We got in touch with Dr. Hoffer's office and explained that we wanted to give Jackie every opportunity possible to regain her mental health, and he agreed that he and his staff would see her if we brought her to Saskatoon. Dr. Hoffer believed that vitamin therapy intervened in some cases of schizophrenia. Vitamins, combined with his recommended hypoglycemic diet, sometimes offered opportunities for schizophrenics to function normally. Jackie's doctor was not in agreement with our plan, but Jack, being a doctor, was able to check her out of the hospital.

We had to get a court order to take her to Canada because commitment papers were being processed. I spoke to Dr. Hoffer about Jyl's illness, and he agreed to work with her or to schedule her with a fellow psychiatrist. Jackie's reaction is best stated in her words when we picked her up at Bayfront. As she got into the car to drive to Canada, she angrily remarked, "This is a wild goose chase." Jackie rode on the front seat beside Jack. I rode on the back seat with Jyl. Both girls, now twenty-two and twenty years old respectively, rode along quietly without much response to scenery never seen before. Jackie continued to be outspoken in her opinion that this trip was not a good idea. Jyl seemed resigned to this fate, and she even offered a few comments about things she noticed on the plains and in the Badlands.

We crossed the border from North Dakota through a small rural town where we stopped for refreshment at a place that looked like an ancient outpost to us. We finally rode into Saskatoon and found it, too, was not as developed as our American cities, but it was charming. The hotel where Jack and I stayed was comfortable. One thing was rather impressive. Here in this foreign place, where we saw lots of mud in the streets carried in by farm equipment, good-looking local men coming into the hotel for lunch were extremely well groomed and dressed in handsome clothes. Everyone we met was friendly and welcomed us with warmth. One couple in town, when they heard about our being there, came to see us and invited us to their house. After we left, they went to see Jackie and stayed in touch with her and with us. Our Canadian trip was made as enjoyable as it could be, given the reasons we were there.

Jackie and Jyl were admitted into the general hospital rather than to the psychiatric ward. Both of them were pleased about that. It was an entirely different environment from that which they had formerly associated with hospitalization for mental illness. They were both receptive to the doctors and hospital staff, and Jackie acted more normal and relaxed than expected. Tests were run to see whether the Hoffer treatment might be effective. In a few days, it was determined that Jyl would not respond to vitamin therapy, but test results did not rule out hope for Jackie. Jackie maintains that her delusions hauntingly stayed active while she was in Canada, but, if that is true, she did not display any resultant unusual behaviors that might be attributed to prompting by delusions. Being around people who were not mentally ill seemed to make a difference in her attitudes and moods.

One nurse took Jackie's laundry home every week and brought it back to her. Jackie continued to hear from this friendly nurse after she came home. The Canadian experience for Jackie was exemplary. It was very disappointing when we heard from Dr. O'Reagan, who also was seeing Jackie, that the vitamin regime that many of Dr. Hoffer's patients had found so helpful was not helpful for Jackie. The staff believed that she might benefit from electroconvulsive therapy, ECT, but Jackie refused to give consent for the shock treatments. Dr. Hoffer got involved with the effort to encourage Jackie to have ECT, but she still refused. Plans were being made for her to fly home when she suddenly announced that she wanted to try ECT after all. Everyone was delighted. Every effort was being made to make it possible for Jackie to function in society with comfort and good health. Jack and I congratulated one another for having taken her to Canada. The ECT treatments were administered.

Jackie, with Halodol and Prolixin prescriptions, flew home to Florida. We picked her up at Tampa International Airport. Imagine any member of your family being uncommunicative, with eyes often dimmed by unfathomable thoughts for most of four long years. Imagine someone you have lived in the same house with since birth, obviously miserably unhappy, leaving you mentally behind, and actually rejecting you in many ways, then suddenly coming toward you through an airport gate with a sunny happy smile. An attractive twenty-two-year-old, well-dressed, well-groomed person ran toward us to hug and be hugged. It seemed an incredible miracle. Jackie had been given a new lease on life.

The family had also been given a new lease on life. Christmas was like times remembered before Jackie became ill. She and I walked the beach together She told me again and again that she could not understand how she had been so confused before going to Canada. She said that she believed the paranoid fantasies had been truly ridiculous. Walking with her on the white sand beside sea gulls and looking for dolphins to surface was a giddy uplifting experience. Only other mothers who have lived with the ultra sadness of having a mentally ill child can fully empathize with my ecstasy that Christmas 1968 season. Perhaps hopes and dreams for this unusually bright person were not going to be savagely denied. It was the supreme Christmas gift.

Freedom from fears for Jackie's future came as Christmas joy, and all New Year's wishes that we had for her seemed answered. Since I had been told that Jack had limited lifetime left due to his brittle diabetic condition, the fact that he could relax for the holiday season and enjoy a wholesome family was especially wonderful. Jackie's illness had been a factor of concern that he found dreadfully difficult. His experiences within his own family with mentally troubled loved ones made Jackie's illness doubly threatening for him. He, more than Jyl, Jan, or I realized that Jackie was better for this Christmas, but that she would probably be worse at another time. He knew from his own family history that the carousel had only paused. However, his educated judgment was overcome with holiday good spirits.

After the New Year's celebration, in 1969, both Jackie and Jyl attended college classes. Jyl returned to SPJC. Jackie went off to the University of West Florida and, when we drove out to visit, she brought attractive classmates along to dinner. Our hopes for her education still persisted. West Florida University seemed a good idea because it was smaller, but Jackie wished to try for a degree from Florida State University in Tallahassee. She enrolled in Florida State University for the fall semester. We felt some apprehension about it.

Our past experiences with Jackie's illness made us wish to prepare for any kind of situation that might arise at the university. I wrote and telephoned a psychiatrist at the university and gave him extensive information about Jackie's medical history. She had promised to go to him if she ever needed to talk with anyone there. He seemed responsible on the phone and eager to help if it became necessary.

I was teaching at Bay Point Middle School in Saint Petersburg that year. I was walking through the school office on the way to the parking lot after school one afternoon when the school secretary said, "Maxene, there is a telephone call for you from the house-mother at Jackie's dormitory." I stepped aside to take the call to hear Jackie's housemother say, "First, let me assure you that Jackie is all right. She attempted suicide this afternoon, but her wound is not life threatening. She is being well taken care of in the hospital." I told her that I was leaving for home and would call her back as soon as I got there. I did not wish to continue the conversation within hearing range of school personnel and have them disturbed. I had all I could handle without explaining such a tragic situation to them. Of course I also wanted to hurry home to my own privacy to decide what to do to help Jackie. When I arrived home, I found my niece, Carol Barksdale from Virginia with her husband, J.L., waiting to surprise me. I greeted them as enthusiastically as possible and told them I had a promised phone call to make. I said, "Just give me time to catch up and freshen up, and we can go to dinner and relax." Knowing Jack's combination health condition of lupus and diabetes made it abundantly clear that he should not be disturbed with bad news in the evening when he was powerless to do anything. I would not call him this evening. He needed all the rest he could get. There was nothing either of us could do before the next day. After speaking with the housemother and receiving assurance that Jackie was sedated, sleeping soundly, and someone was watching over her, I put this new sadness on a reel to open later.

I determinedly turned my mind to an evening that my guests could enjoy as part of their vacation. We went out to dinner, and I did not burden them with Jackie's tragedy. They were very fond of Jackie, and knowledge of her unfortunate current situation would have ruined their vacation. They could do nothing to help. Why burden them? The next morning I called Jack, I told him the sad news, but I also reassured him that I would go to Tallahassee and explore our options in this new crisis. He was expected in Jacksonville for a state meeting, and the diversion of that would be better for his health than a trip with me to try to put the pieces of Jackie's life back together.

It was not easy to take a single lead role in our family. I missed Jack's former strong hand and logical head. He was quite honest with himself and with me. He simply no longer had the stamina or the will to do things he formerly had done with ease. He was always there for wise counsel and steadfast love, but his battering by the Pinellas commissioners, his diabetes, and the girls' illnesses had duly drained from him many of his former strengths.

I checked into a motel in Tallahassee and hurried to the hospital. I found Jackie in her bed, looking pale and wan. She had stabbed herself in the chest, just missed her heart, and had been patched together by a competent physician. She said, "Hello. I did what you told me to do when I thought things were getting out of control. I went to see the psychiatrist. He told me to go back to my room and pack to go home. I felt totally defeated, so I stabbed myself." I was appalled that any human being with any kind of judgment at all had so advised an obviously ill student. I questioned Jackie closely about it, but she insisted that the doctor gave her no options as far as she could reason at the time. I found it hard to believe her until I met the psychiatrist later.

That night after leaving the hospital, the housemother came to talk with me. She told me that the students were dismayed and distressed that Jackie had been so miserable. They wanted to make it up to her. One of the most attractive girls in the dormitory offered to be Jackie's roommate if she would come back to give them another chance. This offer was made with an agreement by her roommate to make different arrangements for herself to accommodate Jackie. Teenagers get bashed and tarred as thoughtless and uncaring, but I have never felt that to be generally true or fair. These young people at Florida State University renewed my faith in young people. They went to see Jackie in the hospital. They brought flowers and silly gifts. They demonstrated love in its finest form. All their pleas went unheard by Jackie, however. She had stopped taking her medication. She was being tortured. Her delusions were rampant. She said she wanted to go back to McClenny where she felt safe. I asked the housemother if she knew of any place or any person I could turn to for help. She told me about an Episcopal lay minister, who was also a psychology professor at the university, and who had worked with a few mentally ill students in the past. I telephoned him at home and left a message asking him to call me no matter what time in the evening he returned home.

The professor returned my call after midnight. He said that he had graduate students who helped him work with troubled students and that he would be happy to talk with Jackie and then decide whether to offer her an opportunity to become part of his program. The next day he talked with Jackie. After almost an hour, he came out to tell me that he thought Jackie a wonderful candidate for his program that would enable her to complete her education. "I am pleased that you have called me, and I look forward to getting to know Jackie. I know she will be welcomed by the graduate students, who will want to get to know her, and that, in itself, will provide Jackie with some social activity." It looked like a disaster was about to turn into good fortune, but the hobbyhorses still rode.

The next morning when I woke up, Jackie was awake and looking at me. "Mother," she said, "I cannot stay here. I want to go back to the hospital." The nightmare was back, and back to stay. I gently tried reasoning to no avail. I said, "Jackie, You promised the professor that you would stay." She said, "I know, but now I have thought more about it, and I know I cannot stay in school this year. I need to go back to the hospital." I said, "I have the professor's phone number. Here it is. Please pick up the phone and thank him and tell him you cannot stay if that is what you wish to do." I thought she would hesitate, but, with composed, firm determination, she picked up the phone and dialed his number. She explained that she was sorry, she thanked him, and she put down the phone with a sigh of relief.

For Jackie to return to the hospital meant that commitment papers had to be prepared and signed by two psychiatrists and a judge. I called Pinellas County, her home county, to find out whether, if I headed for home, the papers could be drawn. I was informed, without any room offered for pleading, that it would be two weeks before anyone would help out with papers in Pinellas. I called Jack at his meeting in Jacksonville and asked him to call McClenny to see whether she could be admitted to Northeast State Hospital if I could get the papers in Tallahassee. He spoke to the hospital administrator and was told there were absolutely no openings at the hospital. Jack and I despondently discussed what to do next, and we decided that the only thing to do was for me to go to the judge's office in Tallahassee to see whether there would be help or suggestions forthcoming from that office. The judge's wife happened to be filling in that day, and I talked to her and explained my plight. She said she felt the judge would put forth extra effort to have the papers prepared, but there had to be a place to send Jackie.

I looked at the judge's wife, sighed, and said, "Well, I do know some influential people." She said, "If you ever needed them, it is now. It sounds like you are not going to find a place for Jackie without special help." I asked to use a phone in a private room. Jackie was waiting in the reception room, and I was feeling very concerned that in her weakened physical condition and her obvious mental distress that she might try to flee or do something else detrimental to herself. I did not like leaving her alone for one minute.

I opened my telephone number reference book and dialed a number. When the gentleman with whom I wished to speak came on the line, I explained Jack's and my situation with trying to help Jackie. He said, "I am so sorry that Jackie is having more problems. You do understand that I cannot become involved. In twenty minutes, I suggest you ask to speak with the judge." I thanked him for his time and concern and put the phone in its cradle, feeling flooded with gratitude. I also felt furious that the call was needed. I returned to the judge's office and related the message I had been given. The lady smiled and said, "I will go in and tell the judge that he may receive a call. Why don't you go out and sit with your daughter for a while? I will call you back when we have some information about what to do." She never asked, and I never told her with whom I had spoken. In about twenty minutes I was called back into the office. The papers were being prepared. Papers would be signed by the judge for Jackie to be admitted to McClenny as soon as I could return them to the judge with two psychiatrists' signatures on them. By that time it was mid-afternoon.

I gave serious and sad thoughts to the preferential treatment being given Jackie. I knew that some other person needing hospitalization had been put on hold so that Jackie could be admitted. I thanked the judge's wife and said, "It is so unfair that I, as a mother, must shove someone aside for my child. This is too unjust. The entire system of care reeks as far as processes are concerned. If I ever have the time to do it, I will do everything in my power to bring equal justice to the delivery of human resources to all citizens needing them, the mentally ill in particular." My advocacy was born that day.

I am fairly intelligent. I have resources many don't have. My emotions were frayed and torn between my desire to help Jackie, the difficulty of doing that, and the overwhelming recognition of dreadful obstacles existing for those with no clout or resources to get their fair share of attention and care. In those few moments a mission was identified for someday finding ways to make a difference for those mentally less fortunate and their families who lack the knowledge and monetary ability to pursue and find desperately needed help.

I went to the office of the university psychiatrist and asked the receptionist to have him come out to speak with me as soon as possible. After I had waited for a short time, he walked into the reception room, and I explained why I was there. As he leaned down to sign the papers, he looked up at me over his shoulder. He said, "I understand she stuck herself pretty good." The room was full of people waiting to see this hair-brained doctor. The urgency of the tasks at hand was the only thing that saved him from being properly chastised for telling Jackie to pack to go home. That he belittled her desperate reaction to his discouraging advice displayed an illness within himself as debilitating as Jackie's illness. "She did," I replied, in a chilling tone from a screaming heart. "Thank you for signing the papers." And I walked out of his life as coldly as he had turned away from trying to save my child's life. Jackie was waiting in the car looking stoic. I was inwardly pleading that she would remain quiet and calm until the papers were in hand to admit her to McClenny.

The day she was admitted to the hospital with her chest wound, a county psychiatrist had been called. I headed for his office because he would be familiar with the situation, and I knew of nowhere else to turn. Leaving Jackie in the car again, I went into the county office. The doctor was in. He came out and sat down behind a desk, and after hearing me explain my need for his signature said, "What if I won't sign? I think she should be made to stay in school." I sat shocked into silence. How could this man not understand mental illness any better than his remark implied? Before I could gather my thoughts enough to respond to his ridiculous query, he leaned forward across the desk and asked me to come back into his private office. He stood up and walked through a door behind him. I followed in bewilderment. Once again he sat down behind a desk and said, "I want to hear you scream." I became so infuriated that I found it difficult to speak. In measured tones, I leaned across the desk and said, "Doctor, external screams are not permissible. I am quite serious. I want you to sign that paper immediately. Jackie is waiting in the car and I cannot leave her alone any longer. Please sign and allow me to hurry back to the judge who is waiting to sign these papers." He did pick up a pen and sign. I did stalk out of the office. I felt that I had talked with two doctors that afternoon that might do well to try to help each other because both of them, in my opinion, were in dire need of learning human compassion. Neither of them came through to me as being well balanced mentally.

Jackie and I hurried back to the judge's office. The papers were taken into the judge, signed, and quickly returned to me. After the papers were handed to me, I called Jack and told him to please meet Jackie and me in the lobby of a motel west of Jacksonville at the intersection of I-95 and I-10 at ten o'clock that night. He gave me the name of a motel, said that he would make adjoining room reservations and would be waiting. He would be able to go with me to McClenny the next morning to admit Jackie. I was exhausted from my mixed emotions of sadness for Jackie and anger for uncaring doctors. I needed help and support.

Jackie and I headed east on I-10 from Tallahassee to Jacksonville at around five o'clock in the evening. She remained quiet and seemed contented to be going to the hospital. I was very alert to every move she made. I was prepared to slam on the brakes and stop the car if she moved to undo her seat belt. I was afraid. I knew that "program" suicide suggestions for her to attempt throwing herself out of the speeding car were possible. After it got dark, I was doubly wary. I decided to stop and take her in somewhere to use a restroom and get something to eat. When we stopped, I gave my whole attention to entering the restaurant quietly. Once we were seated, she sat quietly and was not communicative. I had gotten enough medicine from the hospital to last for several days, so she was medicated. We ate and had an uneventful meal. My fears that she might become agitated or display hostility toward me were not realized. To my great relief when I told her it was time to go, she came to the car with me without comment.

It was a long, almost lonely trip in the darkness of night across the eastern half of the Florida panhandle. I thought that if Jackie fell asleep, I would exceed the speed limit with the hope of a pullover by a Florida Highway Patrolman who might escort us into Jacksonville. She never fell asleep. The entire trip was one of hushed desperation to safely reach sanctuary for her. Finally the intersection loomed, and the motel sign was visible. It was like reaching an oasis in a desert. Jack was waiting. The relief of seeing him flooded through me; a heavy burden was being lifted from my shoulders. He took over. He gently greeted Jackie and took charge of getting our luggage to the rooms and settling in.

After getting Jackie into bed, we talked, and his pain at the new developments was clearly deep and tragic. With his health in such jeopardy, I feared for his future as well as Jackie's. The next day we took Jackie to McClenny. She was obviously at home at once, and she felt relieved to be safe. Here she would be protected from herself, and those around her would understand her illness. That a mental hospital was such a welcomed refuge was both distressing and comforting. That such facilities had become a way of life for her was distressing, but the fact that there was a place for her to be sheltered in safety was comforting. She was not well enough to come home for Christmas, and all of us missed her terribly.

Jack and I went to Virginia for a short summer visit in 1970, especially so that he could see his family. He had not been with them for a fairly long time.

We had been there only a few days when a call came from a doctor who had happened to be in the hospital when Jyl had come to the emergency room complaining of abdominal pains. The doctor, Creighton Pruitt, was a friend, and he simply wanted to let Jack know that he had seen her and found no reason for her complaints. The doctor felt she was agitated, however, and he was very concerned. We left for home almost immediately after calling and talking to Jyl. We thought we needed to see about her as soon as possible because when we had spoken to her on the phone, she did not sound well. Her voice was too shrill, and she talked too fast.

Before we left Staunton we investigated the possibility of bringing her to DeJarnette's Hospital near Fishersville. We had learned that they were having remarkable successes in helping mentally ill people recover. When we got home it was not surprising to find Jyl somewhat disorientated and obviously in need of help. I flew back to Virginia with her and helped her get admitted to DeJarnette's. It was not the usual mental health facility atmosphere, and she settled in quite happily. It seemed more like a small friendly campus. Before I returned home, I talked with her psychiatrist, who was familiar with the community. Upon my expression of dismay at having two mentally troubled children, he asked me if I was unaware that mental illness had been a cross to bear for Jack's family for generations. He stated that luckily, for unknown reasons, most family members then living had escaped the grim tortures of severe illness. Since my only knowledge had concerned one brother-in-law, I was taken aback, and I felt shocked, saddened, and defeated as to the future of Jackie and Jyl, our two mentally ill daughters.

I never, however, prior to Jyl's murder by Jackie, imagined the ultimate toll that mental illness would eventually take on our family. Jyl was not ill enough to be confined after her orientation. She was soon able to go out and visit relatives, go shopping, and pursue other activities that more fortunate people take for granted as everyday pleasures. For her it was exciting to be cheerfully functioning again. She seemed to be carefree when she arrived home for Christmas. We were certainly relieved that she had apparently benefited greatly from her stay at DeJarnette's Hospital.

Once again Jyl enrolled at the junior college. In March 1971 she wrote to Jackie:

Dear Jackie,

It certainly was nice hearing from you. I hope that you will write us
again. In your letter you mentioned not being able to control your
situation. I know exactly how you feel because I went through the
same thing. I had delusions, but when I realized that they weren't
real, I quit fantasizing. Your delusions aren't real. This program that
you are imagining is purely fantasy. I know how hard it is to accept
the fact that these delusions aren't real because it is easier to accept
these delusions as fact, easier to escape reality than to face it, easier
to hide behind them because it is more comfortable, although sometimes painful. I am able to have control over my situation now and
hope that you, too, soon will have control over your situation. To
completely give up is the coward's way, so don't give up and consider
your situation as totally hopeless. I am in school now and doing well,
although sometimes I am lazy about it. I'm still not sure about what
occupation to go into. I haven't made a failing grade yet. Jan is fine
and Mom and Dad are, too. We're with you in this battle.

Love, Jyl.

After Jyl's murder, after Jackie was assigned to Florida State Hospital as a
ward of the State in the forensic ward, I found her letter to Jackie. Jackie had
saved it along with some other things she must have treasured. At the time it
was written, Jyl was living at home with me. Jan was living in her apartment
on the property while attending SPJC. Jack was public health director of Hernando County and was home only for weekends and holidays.

Things for Jyl seemed to be going well. She seemed so well that I was able
to consider going to be with Jack in Brooksville. I applied for a position to
teach science in Hernando County, and I was awarded a contract. Since the
house was vacant we rented it. We felt better about my moving to Brooksville
with the house rented because Jan and Jyl would not be the only people living
on the property. I moved to Brooksville in August 1971. The decision to move
to Brooksville was made with trepidation. Since Jack had been working there,
my feelings were torn between responsibility for my ill children and my loyalty
to my husband with his health problems. I needed to be in two places at once.

My decision was soon brought into question by events and my own heart.
Jan called late one night in November to tell us that she felt somewhat appre-

hensive because Jyl seemed extremely upset. Jan could hear her pacing the floor upstairs, but Jan did not think she should go up to see about her. We had told Jan to be wary and to avoid putting herself in place for any kind of verbal abuse that we knew to be possible if Jyl became frustrated, impatient, or angry within the framework of her frustrations and mental difficulties. We knew that she rightfully believed her life to be very restrictive and difficult. Jack and I told Jan we thought it best for her to go out to spend the night. She did, but she rode by the apartments once during the early morning hours to call and say that the lights were on in the upstairs apartment, and she thought Jyl had not gone out anywhere. It was a long night. Very early the next morning, I drove the seventy miles home to see exactly what was going on.

When I showed up at the apartment, Jyl was surprised to see me, but I fluffed that off by pretending I had come to pick up some items needed in Brooksville. As I talked with her she became more and more agitated and began to pace the floor. I said, "Jyl, how about going to see the doctor. Maybe you need some medication to help you simmer down. She did not resist the idea, and we drove into Saint Petersburg to the doctor's office. She went into the doctor's inner office while I waited in the reception room. I informed the nurse about her behavior the night before and her continued hyperactivity.

Soon, the doctor came out with Jyl to tell me he had called Bayfront Medical Center and made arrangements for Jyl to be admitted. Jyl was very disturbed, and her body language acted out anxiety to an extreme degree. Her fists were clenched, and she looked almost like she was gritting her teeth. It was a tough time for her, and the hospital suggestion was a sentence away from freedom for her. I asked the doctor in an aside if one of his nurses might possibly ride down to the hospital with me because I was not comfortable about being in the car with Jyl if she became more and more opposed to being admitted into the hospital. The doctor looked at me and said, with the most sadistic look in his eyes I have ever seen from anyone, "You can take her without fear. I have given her medication." He surely had to know that I knew that the medicine had not yet taken affect. This doctor was the one to whom Jyl had told stories about me. The look on his face assured me that he believed any malicious things she may have said, and I felt, with some bitterness, that he was having satisfaction in seeing me get my just dues.

I went back to Jyl and said, "Jyl, let's go to the hospital so you can get some rest. You look tired, and your father and I want you to have extra care and attention just now. OK?" She seemed to relax and slowly walked with me to the car. We were in city traffic, which made me feel more secure than if we had been away from people. Jyl never said a word as we rode to Bayfront. I attempted some light general conversation, but understandably she did not respond. She was controlling her anxiety admirably. When I pulled into the parking lot, she laid her hand gently on my arm and said, "Please, Mom, don't make me go in there." I put my hand over hers, looked into her eyes, and said, "Jyl, sometimes we have to do what seems temporarily best even though we don't wish to. I don't want to take you into the hospital, but, Jyl, I think it's best for now, please." She gave me a wan little smile and said, "OK."

I wanted to stand in the parking lot and scream and scream and scream. I would have come back home from Brooksville. I would have come back to the apartment to live with her, had there been any hope that she could continue school and be contented, but, from many such past experiences, I knew that being home for Jyl in her present mental state was not possible. For the first time since the 1965 onset of mental illness for my daughters, I wondered whether I had made a dreadful, wrong decision. Should I have stayed at home with her? If I had, perhaps she could have stayed in school and gotten past her melancholia.

Now, many years later, tears stream from my eyes as I remember that day when I took Jyl to the hospital. I have managed through the years to repress this reel. Unsealing it makes me cringe with grief. I wonder whether I should have left Jyl in favor of her father. I have to think I acted wisely, and I have to store the reel away again. That scene caused another crack in a mirror that I once expected to reflect a charmed life. Jyl was twenty-two years old. She had been dating, she was in school, and the doctor had advised us that he believed that she could manage an independent life. I would advise any parent to do exactly what I did because the test for her had to happen sometime. I know the common sense decision to go live with Jack was correct, but my conscience does not free me easily.

Jyl and I went into the hospital and through the admitting process. As I had done so many times, I walked through a locked door. Then I exited back through it to my world of reality, and I left a child in the midst of madness. Jan, Jack, and I were all once again challenged to go about our daily lives with gratitude that we were able to somehow function in spite of mental illnesses that put chasms of impossible, unfathomable hallucinations and delusions between us and Jackie and Jyl.

I drove back to Brooksville and was back in my classroom the next morning. Jack went to his office. I taught school. Jan went to classes. We three somehow continued our "normal," daily routine lives. Jackie was safe at the state hospital. Jyl was safe at Bayfront Hospital. We did not share our burdens with Jack's fellow workers, the faculty where I taught, or with Jan's classmates. There was nothing to tell. There was no way to make others understand our traumatic lives.

People then, as now, do not usually try to absorb facts about mental illness. They give no credence to the actuality that severely mentally ill people are not capable of being accountable for their actions. They somehow seem unable to comprehend total loss of abilities to control one's behavior. That some human beings may not possess their own mentalities is difficult to comprehend. For a severely mentally ill individual, nothing takes precedence over delusion beliefs or commands given by silent command or by "the voices." Nothing except proper medication decreases "program" tortures. The untreated severely mentally ill, ruled by mysteriously created programs in their brains, are unable to stop their delusions and tortures. There is no escape from taunting voices. Citizens see hapless people, homeless people, in unexpected and undesirable living spaces, and they look away, heartlessly. They choose not to admit that unabated voices and/or delusions are haunting the human beings that they are ignoring. Intentional neglect fosters homelessness.

When Jack and I came home a few days later to check on Jyl, the doctor recommended that she be hospitalized long term, so she was sent to McClenny. We were going to be visiting with a second daughter in McClenny.

During the previous summer, after a stay of eight months, Jackie had moved from McClenny to a halfway house in Gainesville. Dr. Arthur Wells, a psychologist at Northeast Hospital in McClenny, who lived in Gainesville, was helpful with Jackie's transfer to the halfway house. He introduced her to his family, and he gave her a feeling of belonging to a community. She worked in a library in Gainesville until volunteers found that she was mentally ill and requested that she not be allowed to work there. Unfortunately Jackie was made aware of their requests for her removal, which was not conducive to her well being, but she pulled through that fairly well. Her next job was as a maid at a motel, and since she needed to work through the holidays, she could not come home for Christmas. At Christmas 1971, neither Jackie nor Jyl were home for Christmas.

At the end of the 1971–1972 school year, Jyl was allowed to leave McClenny. I drove to McClenny, picked her up at Northeast Florida State Hospital, and then picked up Jackie in Gainesville. We drove over to Neptune

Beach, had dinner, and spent the night in celebration of the return home again for all of us.

The next day it was wonderful to drive into our home driveway, unload everyone's possessions, and put everything away in rightful places. Life soon began to move along smoothly. Jack enjoyed his weekends at home with us.

During Jyl's hospital stay she had heard about a facility in Winter Park that resembled a commune. All of the residents had responsibilities in managing the house. The group did fun things together as they worked their way back to independent community living. The idea sounded good to Jyl, and it sounded good to us. She moved to Winter Park shortly after her return home. She called home frequently with good reports, and she wrote about her life there with enthusiasm.

I went over to the annual Winter Park Sidewalk Art Festival, which is a magnificent sophisticated show. I stayed at the old Interlachen Inn. Winter Park itself is one of the most beautiful cities in Florida, and the environment is uplifting. Jyl and I had a great time going to the show, having dinner at the Inn, and generally living it up. She was getting ready to go to Mexico with her "family" group. She was busy planning what to take and reading about Mexico. The trip to Mexico, from her descriptions when she returned, sounded like it was interesting and educational. She managed to bring home a clay statue of a shepherd with a lamb over his shoulder and a unique pottery vase. That she cared enough to worry herself with such perishable, difficult items to carry and bring them home was touching and typical of Jyl's thoughtfulness for others. She bought an inexpensive pewter poison ring with a fake amethyst stone for herself. The stone lifts open to hide a poison pill or any other pill one may wish to carry. Jyl was intrigued with it. I sometimes wear it with loving feelings for Jyl.

Jyl seemed to settle in and make herself quite at home at the commune house after the trip. I had been over to see her several times, had met the manager before she left, and felt impressed with their seeming sincerity and patience with their house members. They were encouraging Jyl to look around and decide what she wanted to do when she left the house. She was most undecided about her move out of the house as to where to go and what to do.

Jack and I never understood the next climatic thing that happened to Jyl. We thought the managers exhibited maximum poor judgment and indolent failure to understand Jyl's inherent impractical side to have done such a wanton thing to her. Once a friend said to me, "I wonder what Jyl will finally end up doing? I think you have an Elizabeth Browning on your hands." Jyl loved to paint and write. That was all she wanted to do and had always done both since she was old enough to hold painting brushes or writing instruments in her hands.

Jyl telephoned one afternoon to say that she was using the last of her money to make the phone call. She told me that she was in the lobby of the Interlachen Inn with her belongings stacked around a chair. "What in the world happened, Jyl?" I asked. She said, "Mom, they told me it was time for me to hit the road, and they put me out. They said I have to learn to fend for myself." I said, "Go sit down in the chair by your things, and I will be there as soon as I can drive over there to pick you up." A friend of mine who loved Jyl went with me.

Once again I met a dejected woman child who felt rejected by those she had hoped to befriend. She felt deserted by those who she believed had come to love her and be her friends. I drove by the house on the pretext of checking to see whether she had inadvertently left anything behind. When I went in and asked them why they had put Jyl out, they told me exactly what they had told her. When I looked into the managers' cold and alienating faces, I knew any further discussion would be redundant and nonproductive for Jyl. An exhausted Jyl stretched out on the back seat of the car and slowly seemed to chant to herself as we rode back to Redington Beach. Jyl was coming home to join Jackie and me. The tenants were gone from the house, so we reclaimed the extra space with relief. I did not teach in Brooksville again. Jack adamantly believed that it was best for me to stay in Pinellas County, and he would come home on weekends as he had ever since his political ouster in 1970.

I taught the year of 1972–1973 at Tyrone Junior High School. My school year went along without any new alarms. Jyl fooled around happily with her painting and writing. She attended some college classes. Jackie worked as a caseworker for a few weeks, determining whether welfare applicants were eligible for benefits. She hated that. She got too upset over the terrible plights of the people she talked with, so she took a job in our professor friend Tom Howze's office in Clearwater's Saint Petersburg Junior College as a clerk. That was too overwhelming also. In the fall she enrolled at the Pinellas University of South Florida extension in Saint Petersburg but soon gave it up. Through all of this, however, Jackie was calm and simply seemed to accept her limitations with courage, without displaying excessive concern. She seemed to be relieved to have no outside activities, and she was most helpful with the household. I gave her the grocery money. She made grocery lists and did the grocery shopping. Sometimes Jyl helped her. Jackie had a car, and she drove around town on errands all the time. Jyl had never shown any interest in learning to drive, so Jackie was a happy willing chauffeur for her. My mother lived only a few blocks away in the winter, and sometimes Jackie would drive her places she wished to go.

In the spring of 1972, Jan got married and went to live in Babson Park. Jack and I were not pleased that she chose to discontinue college, but we felt that she really needed to get away from our unfortunate home situation. Jan expressed no desire for the usual wedding activities, and she went off and got married in Georgia with our blessing. A traditional wedding under our circumstances simply could not be planned.

Attentions that Jan should have had were not possible because the kind of family life Jack and I had worked toward so hard for so many years was impossible. It was a sad time for Jack and me because we had wanted so much to have our children's lives as perfect as possible. Jan never had questioned—and even then did not question—that her life was not as smooth running as lives of other young people. Jan was an exemplary sister through all trials and tribulations. This is not to say that Jan was always perfect plus. She had a few minor teenage flights from best behavior, as one would expect. Whether we succeeded, I do not know, but Jack and I tried very hard to make her realize that we did not expect her to be three times as great as she was to make up for her less fortunate sisters. Jan made such a difference for us in being able to cope with the illnesses of Jackie and Jyl. Jack deeply loved and appreciated Jan. He told me, "She is my salvation through it all." The mention of her name always brought a gentle loving look to his face.

Jack was wonderful with Jackie and Jyl. He bought a small boat, and he took Jackie fishing almost every Saturday when he was home on weekends. Before he was forced to leave the county to work, he had enrolled himself, Jackie, and Jyl in a crafts class and attended it with them. I have a painted female head that he painted while a fellow craft student with the girls.

In the fall of 1972, Tyrone Middle School ninth grade classes were transferred to Dixie Hollins High School, and I began teaching science in a fourth Pinellas County school assignment. I was beginning to think of discontinuing teaching school. New freedoms for students in the classrooms seemed to bring with them a lack of disciplined thinking patterns. I always had found it necessary to teach some study habits, but one could not teach all of them. It was exasperating to try to teach science when students found it so difficult to put a few facts together and draw obvious conclusions.

I took the Florida real estate tests, and my real estate certificate came on December thirteenth. When I got home from school that day, Jan and her mother-in-law were there. Jan seemed happy in Babson Park, and her mother-in-law was a sweet, kind person. I was surprised and glad to see them. As soon as I walked through the door, Jyl said, "Mother, go look at your mail." There had been discussion and many jokes about whether I might fail the real estate tests, and so I had awaited the nix or the certificate rather eagerly. I opened the mail and found a certificate. I exclaimed with delight, "OK, everybody, it's out to dinner anywhere you wish to go. It's anything anywhere. We are going to celebrate." We went to Tiki Gardens, had appetizers, salads, dinner, desserts, the works. Jyl confessed that she had opened the letter from the Real Estate Commission and resealed it. She said, "Mom, I decided that we should know so that if you had failed, we could plan how to rebuild your ego if that was necessary." She was as excited as I that I had passed. That gala evening at Tiki Gardens is a favorite reel. It was too bad Jack was not there, but he was as pleased as I when I told him how great it was to have all three girls together around a dinner table, enjoying the occasion just like other people celebrating special times.

Forgotten was the fact that Jyl had asked me a few weeks before whether I thought there was any danger that Jackie could be dangerous. That evening Jackie was a pleasing member of a successful, memorable dinner party. She was in high good humor, and all of us enjoyed being with her. She was the central conversationalist, and she displayed original humor.

On Saturday night, December fifteenth, I was lying on the sofa in the living room reading when Jackie came running down the steps with a pillow in her arms. She moved toward me playfully like she was going to smother me. She laughed, as she turned away and said, "I could kill you. I was watching a terrible show upstairs, and people were being killed by smothering."

Jack had stayed in Brooksville because he had things he wanted to do there to prepare for being home more days than usual during the upcoming holidays. I gave a passing thought to calling him to come home because Jackie's comment was momentarily troubling. I felt wary, but I dismissed it. Then I silently chastised myself for always thinking of Jackie as sick. Any person might have made such a jest, I thought. She sat down beside me, and we chatted casually until we went upstairs to bed.

Jyl's Murder

Christmas seasons are especially poignant for me. Christmas reels, a cherished treasury of mirrored reflections, bring to mind crossroads and turning points in my life, whether for elaborately celebrated or less ceremoniously observed holidays. Some seasons are free from care. Some seasons are fraught with sadness. Best loved are those that reflect brightly hued joy.

Other times than Christmas are just as soulfully recorded. I have stored and played back memory reels for as long as I can remember. Though some seem sealed, all of them wait in place, ever ready and willing to play. Sagas from my heart, mysteriously and firmly stashed within my brain, usually play only when consciously requested, but sometimes a willful reel momentarily shoves aside a choice I make and appears unexpectedly with no respect for time or place. Regulated or unruly, my wonderful reels pictorially mirror the joys, traumas, sorrows, ecstasies, fantasies, and foolishness of my life with pathos and humor. Some are haunting, some difficult to share, some painful to remember. But always, like a reference library, they are there. They concisely reflect, detail, and clarify my eighty-six years of life.

My 1973 Christmas reel plays back more vividly and painfully than all others. To be able to write this book, I am deliberately breaking the seal of my saddest Christmas reel. Sometimes this reel is willful, but through the years I have been able to keep it suppressed most of the time. There have been more than fourscore Christmas seasons for me, but the 1973 Christmas reel makes all other Christmas memories more precious. Living through the night of December 18, 1973, taught me that, like survival of stormy nights to see sunlit dawns, the darkness of traumas sharply contrasted with the joys of living heightens appreciation for a multitude of pleasures that are always waiting to be found if one chooses to look for them. I am fortunate that I am able to see the beauty of nature, am appreciative of the arts, and recognize lights of joy shining forth from many people. Finding joys everyday almost everywhere is responsible for my self-survival.

On December 18, 1973, I wakened to find Jyl sound asleep beside me. We had sat up the night before talking with Anne, a friend of mine, and we had gone to sleep still chatting and laughing. It pleased me when this entertaining twenty-four year old daughter crawled into my bed. Since her father was working out of town, there was a void there beside me.

That morning, December eighteenth, because there was a chill in the Florida air, and because Christmas was coming, I put on a red and green plaid wool suit. I thought my students might find pleasure in seeing their teacher festively dressed. As I left the room I impulsively stopped and smiled as I looked down at Jyl. She was sound asleep, face down with arms overhead. Her beautiful, long golden hair streamed across her shoulders. "She looks like an angel," I thought.

I hurried to Jackie's room to remind her that a bed would be delivered sometime during the day. I asked her to please have the deliverymen set up the new furniture in the upstairs front bedroom. She looked sleepy, but she smiled and assured me that she would take care of it. She did. When questioned by detectives, one of the deliverymen so stated. He described Jackie, who was wearing a dark green housecoat, as the person who had answered the door around one o'clock and told him where to set up the bed. He added that there was nothing unusual in her behavior.

I hurried out of the house to get to school on time, cheerfully looking forward to Christmas vacation. I left the house feeling more carefree than I had most of the time since 1965 when Jackie told me that she is a paranoid schizophrenic.

I often went to the teacher's lounge in the afternoon during my period freed for planning. That day as I sat and talked with another teacher, I suddenly felt my body shiver. A chilling sensation seemed to turn my entire body to quivering Jell-O. Shaken, I hesitated in the middle of a sentence. The sensation was fleeting, eerie. I remarked to the teacher, "I have just had the weirdest feeling." When she looked at me questioningly, I shrugged to put her at ease, and we continued our conversation.

Later I would realize that at that time Jackie was either planning to murder Jyl or was killing Jyl. In moments of reviewing those torturing memories, I wonder if Jyl's urgent need for help was being communicated to me as she frenziedly ran from one house exit to another and around the dining room table. Was Jyl at that moment desperately fleeing from the knife that Jackie wielded so persistently? Jyl was viciously stabbed again and again, according to the autopsy, to cause more than thirty wounds.

Driving north on Gulf Boulevard in Redington Beach that fateful evening, I considered going a few blocks past my home to speak to my mother before going home for the evening. I decided to call Mother later. I thought Jackie and Jyl were probably waiting to do something about dinner. Jackie, Jyl, and I planned to finish readying Christmas CARE cards, a family tradition, for mailing after dinner. There were still a few packages to wrap and some house decorations to be put in place. This year Christmas was going to be gloriously and traditionally celebrated.

I marveled that Jackie, Jyl, and Jan would be together at Christmas. Jack and I felt tremendously grateful that all five members of the family were going to be home for Christmas. He would be home in a few days. The Christmas spirit seemed to have invigorated all of us.

Jyl was taking some college classes. Jackie was planning to start her third-year college classes at South Florida University's Saint Petersburg Bayshore campus in January. It would be Jackie's sixth college. She did not wish to leave home for college, so it was fortunate that this campus was close enough for her to drive back and forth. It would be a situation making it possible for Jack and me to monitor her mental health closely.

We struggled to do it, but we somehow managed to maintain high hopes that all three of our daughters would graduate from college. We strongly believed education to be an important factor in an individual's ability to value and appreciate life.

I dashed jubilantly up the front steps of the house to the outer entrance door. I was almost delirious from happy thoughts of spending the evening near our trimmed Christmas tree where presents waited for Christmas Day. The future looked more promising for the family than it had since 1965. Once again, it all seemed too good to be true.

After unlocking the front door and after walking across the foyer, I saw Jyl's upturned bare feet just inside the windowed French doors between the foyer and living room. As I opened the doors, I broke into laughter. Jyl was lying face down on the floor, arms over her head with her beautiful golden hair streaming across her shoulders just as it had been in the morning when I last saw her. She was lying in exactly the same position as I had seen her in the morning. I had looked at her in the morning and thought she looked like an angel.

I looked at her now in the dusk and saw her as the lovable jokester she often was. In the dusk, the ever-etched mirror of that reel still shows Jyl wearing a tie-dyed shirt. I wondered where that tie-dyed shirt came from. I did not remember her having a tie-dyed shirt. Still laughing, I stooped over, tapped her sides, and said, "Hey, this is not funny."

The world seemed to shudder. The world crashed thunderously around me. Jyl's body, still warm, was deathly still. Turning frantically to a nearby dimmer light switch, I turned it up. Jyl's shirt was not tie-dyed; it was blood soaked. Her body was in a pool of blood. "She is dead! She is dead! She is dead!" The words screamed in my brain like shrill blaring sirens. I heard myself scream "Jackie." There was no answer.

I ran to the kitchen to call for help. My hands trembled so much that I could not dial the old-fashioned phone. Then I saw more blood everywhere. Sheer fear for my own life took possession of my thoughts. Jackie's apparent death, since she did not answer when I called out her name, and no spark of life from Jyl, combined to produce sudden terror of being murdered myself. I rushed back toward the front doors to leave the house.

Even though I was starkly fearful, even after the soul-searing horror of finding Jyl's bloody body, even though I believed there was an urgent need to flee for my own safety, I stopped to kneel beside Jyl's body. I did it involuntarily, knowing that a murderer could be lurking in the stairwell of the nearby steps going upstairs. I did it without a second thought. Completely abandoning my fear for the moment, I knelt beside her. In that gesture, there is testament to a mother's instinct to care for her young without regard for her own peril. I am not a brave person, and that act, as look back, seems inconceivable. I truly believed Jyl was dead, but I could not leave her there alone in the pool of her blood until I felt absolutely certain.

Stunned, in shock, with a distraught, grief-battered mind, I drove a few blocks to Redington Beach City Building. As I struggled to drive fast and carefully to get help, it became horrifyingly clear to me that Jackie might have killed Jyl and then committed suicide. Thoughts with voices screamed through my head and rebounded from all sides of the car. Jyl is dead! Jyl is dead! Jyl is dead!

Throughout this sorrowful, deeply wrenching drive, I struggled, fighting helplessness, to collect my brain, calm my heart, and gather enough fortitude to endure and survive this incomprehensible ordeal.

When I got to the City Building, I jumped out of the car and banged on the door until someone came. I implored, "Please, please, call the police.

Please ask the them to hurry and bring an ambulance." The man looked at me wide-eyed, but calmly, and asked the address. He quickly made the call.

Jyl was killed in the main house of our property on the Gulf of Mexico beach. Facing Gulf Boulevard, running behind the property, was a guesthouse. When I arrived home from school, I had parked between the house and guesthouse. When I returned, I parked between the street and guesthouse. Feeling fearful and all alone in the world, I waited and waited and waited and waited for what seemed an eternity for help to come.

I forced myself to consider all possible things that might be known before this night ended. When a young policeman arrived, I said to him, "You need to know that I think my daughter Jyl is dead. I think that another daughter, Jackie, who is mentally ill, is in the house. I do not know whether Jackie is dead or alive. Perhaps you will need to be prepared." Since Jackie had not answered when I called her, I believed that she must be dead also, but I had, with cruel clarity, begun to fear that she might have murdered Jyl.

I knew that Jackie must be in the house because her car was parked between the house and guesthouse. As the officer and I walked up the driveway, I was extremely confused, frightfully wondering what could have happened. It was now dark. As we walked up the driveway, a light suddenly came on upstairs in the house. I cannot find words to describe the absolutely despairing internal trembling that I suffered when that menacing light shone forth. A beam seemed to flash through my eyes like searing lightning into the core of my being. I knew Jackie was alive. I felt more certain that Jackie might have killed Jyl. I was so emotionally battered and physically weakened that I could barely muster enough strength to continue walking.

I don't think I spoke again until after the officer and I stepped cautiously around Jyl's lifeless, bloody, mutilated body as we entered the house. Though careful, we were unable to avoid walking through puddles of blood. The young officer knelt by Jyl's body to examine it. I continued to walk toward the kitchen. In the kitchen, I sank down into a large rocking chair between an antique pine drop leaf breakfast table and the telephone.

Soon the officer came into the room and asked to use the phone. There were no cell phones or beepers in 1973 for instant communication. He spoke to someone and requested that they come to our address. He said that it was a Code 5, which was a local code number in 1973.

I knew the call number must identify a murder scene. I knew the house would soon be overrun with people. It was difficult to resist strong, irrational impulses to run out of the house and flee screaming down the driveway as fast as possible to get as far away as possible.

Sitting there in the kitchen, encircled by the blood that had spurted from Jyl's severed arteries onto the antique pine breakfast table, ceiling, walls, and counters, I thought Jackie and I should go over to the guesthouse right away. I did not think either of us should have to endure another moment in such shocking, sad surroundings. I told the officer that I was going and would take Jackie with me. He quietly, kindly, and firmly told me that Jackie apparently had been in the house when the murder occurred and that she could not leave. I asked if he would take care of her if I left, and he assured me that he would.

As I reentered the living room to leave the house, I was surprised to see Jackie sitting in a wing chair no more than six feet from Jyl's body. She was not crying. She did not appear upset. When I walked over and put my hand gently against her face and told her that I was going to the apartments, she looked up dazedly and innocently at me. No emotion was evident. Sitting there amidst the mayhem seemed of no concern to her. I told her that she had to stay in the house since she had been there in the afternoon. Again, no emotion was evident. I cautioned her not to talk with anyone about anything that had happened that day. Again, blank, dazed eyes looked up at me. I hesitated to leave her, but, even as emotionally torn as I was, I was beginning to realize that in addition to her not talking with others about what had happened, I should not give her an opportunity to talk to me about what had happened in our home that day. I left her where she apparently wished to be.

The officer later told me that as he went up the steps when he first arrived, Jackie was coming downstairs. She said, "I think you may be looking for me." "Instead of retreating back upstairs as would be expected, she calmly and deliberately continued down the steps with him into the living room. She just as calmly and deliberately sat down in a wing chair near her dead sister's body.

Jackie has since told me, "When I sat down and looked at Jyl's still body, I thought, "My God, what have I done? Could I really have hurt her?" Recently she told me that the officer came up the steps with gun drawn. He heeded my earlier warning words spoken to him in the parking area between Gulf Boulevard and the apartments. He was prepared for any eventuality.

Once again I forced myself to step carefully around Jyl's dead body. I felt frozen in time, but I managed to keep moving. I struggled to think clearly. Sternly disciplined reactions were very studied and unnatural for me. I summoned every possible vestige of mental and physical strength to maintain my composure because I knew many necessary tasks were going to be required of me. This memory reel plays back as an "out-of-body" experience.

As I was walking across the driveway to the guesthouse apartments, the thought came to me that this entire situation, as bad as it was, could be much worse. I did not have to stay in the house in the midst of blood and gore. I did not have to stay where so much necessary, unpleasant activity was about to take place.

From the 1945 trauma of three-hour-old Jon's death during World II, when Jack was thousands of miles away in Pacific combat, came a message learned for survival during intense throes of sorrow. When Jon died I had learned that if pause is taken to look back and then to look beyond immediate moments, comforts are found. There would be a future beyond the horrors being experienced. There was a past to offer soothing comfort.

The downstairs guest apartment had only one bedroom, but I entered it because it was more accessible. It was too small for the accommodations I would later need for friends and family during that long night. Inside, I stood alone wishing that somehow, just one week before Christmas, I could spare everyone I knew the telling of Jyl's murder. I stood there lonely, again frozen in time, seeking strength, garnering stamina. There was no choice but to absorb and act upon these new, unwelcome, overpowering facts of fate.

Questions, "What next? What to do? What next? What to do?" tumbled confusingly through my mind. I forced myself to first consider, "What now?"

Our lives beside the serene and beautiful white sandy beach of the Gulf of Mexico had sometimes been less than tranquil as we valiantly tried to live as normally as possible. We seemed to our neighbors to live just like any normal family; but we struggled to understand and to endure with patience the mental illnesses of our two oldest daughters. In 1973 the stigma of mental illness in the family of a public official could be very detrimental. Now tragedy had brutally wiped away all semblance of normalcy and all privacy. Now stark shock had to be managed and shared.

I knew it was up to me to handle things. I considered that I had known since 1968 that Jack had brittle diabetes and could not be expected to live long. I thought of Jan who was seventy miles away in Babson Park. I thought of Jyl's grandmother, an elderly Virginia lady, only a few blocks away in her wintertime condominium. These three vulnerable people would soon have to hear unanticipated, heart-wrenching news. I would have to tell them the news, and tell them soon. One thing I almost immediately determined was to prevent other family members from seeing Jyl as I had last seen her. It was important to make sure that Jyl, as she deserved, would be remembered clearly as the vibrant, creative, living person she had been. When detectives came to talk with me, I told them that I wished to spare others from remembering Jyl as I had found her. They responded with compassion and promised to work with the body as quickly as possible so that it could be moved out of the house before other family members arrived.

I stood in the middle of the apartment living room feeling total disquiet while struggling to make up my mind about what to do next. I realized that I could not manage everything alone. I knew that I had to summon help even though I was finding it difficult to decide to burden others with such sorrow. Reluctantly, I called our friends, Joella and Gerry Hall. Joella answered the phone. I said, "Joella, can you and Gerry come out here? Jyl has been killed." After a short, stunned silence, she said, "We'll be there in a few minutes."

By the time, Gerry and Joella arrived, I had gone upstairs to the larger two-bedroom guest apartment. When they got there I told them all I knew. All of us were in shock. It was amazing that each of us retained enough equanimity to think about notifying family and friends. From Jack's public relationships with the media, I knew that requests would have to be made for patience about putting this sensational news on the air. Family members and friends should not hear such crushing news before being personally notified.

Joella said, "Whom have you called?" "No one," I said, "Our friends are busy getting ready for Christmas. Carol and Dave Pedley have small children. I am not going to call them no matter what. Virginia and Tom Howze are planning to leave for Washington in the morning for Christmas. Henny and Jim Walsh have guests tonight, I think." Joella said, "Maxene, you should call all of these people. I think they can help, and they will want to help. I am sure they would want to be here." I continued to resist calling the Pedleys, but Joella insisted, and she did finally call them. It was a great relief when friends came to share the sorrow and unexpected responsibilities that were so overwhelming me.

I continued to be emphatic that members of the media be contacted first. Tom Howze took care of that. He explained to radio and television stations personnel that I did not want to call any family members home before Jyl's body was moved away and the house was cleaned. The media responded with great consideration, and Jyl's murder was not announced on television or radio before eleven o'clock.

Tom suggested that he call Larry Black, an attorney friend, to come and stay with Jackie. Larry came and sat with her. I was relieved when Larry came.

I felt better knowing that Jackie was not alone and that Larry would protect her privacy and the family's privacy. He was a stalwart friend and a necessary support that night and for many weeks thereafter.

When I worried and wondered aloud if I would be able to find a janitorial service to come immediately to clean the house, Tom, Virginia, Gerry, and Jim nobly volunteered to wash away Jyl's blood. I know that for each of them it must have provided ongoing nightmares for a long time. The nearby Christmas tree, scattered Christmas cards, and gaily wrapped presents heightened the tragedy and incongruity of the bloody house. Working so intimately, in shock, in sorrow, under such difficult conditions near the dead and disfigured body of someone they had known and loved surely was beyond all calls of grim duty. I stayed at the apartment. I could not summon the courage to return to the house until it was cleaned. It would have been impossible for me to help clean the house.

One of the detectives knocked on the door of the apartment to say, "I'm sorry to bother you, but the little poodle is extremely distressed, snarling, and trying to keep us away from your daughter's body. He actually seems vicious. Do you mind coming to get him?"

I had not thought of Fluffy, a little gray toy poodle that loved Jyl devotedly, or of our two Siamese cats. One cat belonged to Jackie; one cat belonged to Jyl. A friend had given Fluffy to Jack, but Fluffy had become whole-heartedly loyal to Jyl. Later Jackie told me that she had put the animals in her bedroom, so that was why I had not seen them when I had been in the house earlier. She also told me that she was in another upstairs room listening to music until I returned home with the policeman.

Fluff was not going to desert Jyl under any circumstances. Muddled as my thoughts were, I thought about how attached Jack was to Fluffy. He had always taken him to Brooksville with him until the summer of 1972, when Jyl had returned home from her therapeutic trip to Mexico. When Jack got ready to go back to Brooksville on Sundays, he always called, "Come on Fluff Wuff, it's time to go." Fluffy always came running with tail wagging ecstatically to jump onto the front seat of the car. Then he would put his tiny front paws onto the dashboard so he could look around the countryside as they rode along. He was good company for Jack. I hoped that his company was some compensation for my absence from Brooksville; an absence necessitated by the illnesses of Jackie and Jyl.

It was Jyl's first Sunday home when Fluff did not come running when he heard the familiar call to travel. We all looked for him until we found him crouching under Jyl's bed. Fluff wanted to stay with Jyl. I felt deep empathy for Jack as he sadly smiled and said, "If he loves Jyl that much, he needs to stay here." After that Fluff was never far from Jyl when she was in or near the house. Now he could never be near her again.

I walked over to the front of the house, stood at the bottom of the entrance steps where Jyl's body was not visible, and softly called through the open doors, "Fluff, Fluff, come here." He came slowly, crouched in despondency. I picked up the precious little trembling animal and carried him over to the apartment. His small drooping body in my arms was like a burden of grief pressed into my own devastated heart.

When I was told that the house would soon be freed of evidence from the gruesome murder, and Jyl's body could be taken to the morgue before Jack or Jan could get home, I called the family. I knew that Jack and Jan had to be called first because it would take some time for them to travel home. I put off going to tell Mother as long as I could. I remember thinking that I should call Jack's administrative assistant to go and tell Jack so that Jack would not be alone when told that Jyl was dead.

I almost froze in my tracks as I walked toward the phone. I noticed a coffeepot that I had seen earlier on the kitchen counter in the house with its ON red light shining. It had been carried over to the apartment and plugged in. During the evening I had a flashing thought that Jyl might have been getting a cup of coffee when she was first stabbed. The pot containing coffee that she must have made loomed oversize; Jackie never drank coffee. The ON light seemed magnified, and I was mesmerized by its presence. I could not concentrate on anything else. I don't know how long I stood transfixed. I could see nothing in the room other than the coffee pot with its glaring ON light. As soon as I could, I went to the phone.

Jackie has told me recently that Jyl was standing by the coffeepot near the knife rack in the kitchen when she was first stabbed. Jackie has said, "As I went into the kitchen to stab Jyl, I thought what a terrible thing this is that I have to do." But she never wavered. She took a large butcher knife from the rack and plunged it deep into Jyl's abdomen. She has told me that she stabbed Jyl in the abdomen intentionally. When talking about it, she paused a moment as she remembered, and then mused, "I had read somewhere that someone stabbed in the abdomen would die, but Jyl didn't die, she ran."

When I finally got to the telephone, I could not remember Jack's assistant's name. Joella took the phone and called another person in Brooksville whose name and phone number I was able to recall to get the information we needed.

Harold Bolesta was the administrative assistant's name. When he answered his phone, I said, "Harold, will you please take a doctor or nurse with you and go over to tell Jack that Jyl is dead." I do not remember how much detail I told him. I do remember saying, "Try not to tell him more than you must. Also, will you please drive him home? Under no circumstances let him drive, please." I knew that Jack's diabetic condition would make the dire news doubly damaging, and I wanted to be sure he was well enough to come home before he left Brooksville. Harold did get a nurse, and he did drive Jack home. I never knew who followed Harold to take him back to Brooksville. In fact, I never wondered about that until just now. In all the appreciation that I expressed to people who were helpful that night and the following weeks, I failed to thank someone who so generously made an unexpected, long, depressing, late-hour one-hundred-forty-mile drive.

Before leaving Brooksville, Jack called and said, "Maxene, what happened?" I said, "Jack, there has been an accident." He took for granted that Jackie was driving and that Jyl had been killed in a car wreck. He knew that Jackie often drove Mother and Jyl to places when they needed a ride. He asked, "Is Jackie all right?" "Yes," I replied. Was your Mother hurt?" "No," I replied. "Jack, it was not a car accident. Please come home. I need you here. I really don't want to talk about it now. Please just come home." Jack replied, "I will drive down right away." I said, "Fine. I'll see you soon."

I put the phone down, confidant that Harold would not let him drive. It might have been truly disastrous had Jack driven, because his blood sugar level soared. Harold said that he did not speak on the way from Brooksville during the first forty miles of the seventy-mile trip. Then he seemed to rouse enough from shock to ask, "Harold, do you know where Jackie was?" By that time Jack, in his grievously befuddled mind, must have been trying to figure out exactly what had happened. He probably had begun to fear the worst.

When I called Jan, much to my surprise, she answered the phone. I had hoped her father in-law would answer the phone in the main house. She and her husband Ed lived in a guesthouse on his parent's property in Babson Park. I asked to speak to Ed; that was unusual, and that surprised Jan. She said, "Please, let's not get silly with the Christmas spirit. You can talk to me about my Christmas presents." She absolutely refused to hand Ed the phone and continued to tease. I said, "Jan, are you sitting down?" She laughed. In a moment, still with laughter in her voice, she said, "OK. Now I am sitting down." I said, "Jan, I have very bad news" I paused, waiting and hoping that thought would register, and then I said, "Jan, Jyl is dead." Jan's scream, as she threw or dropped the phone, shrieks clearly in my mind as I write. It was an agonizing scream that sounded exactly as I felt. Her piercing cry still reverberates with my own inner scream, two screams still felt from that memory reel. I still recoil from thinking of Jyl's murder. It is very difficult now as I write to allow, as I must, ghastly parts of the reel to surface. Ed picked up the phone. I asked, "Please, Ed, will you bring Jan home? Jyl has been killed." He gasped, and then quietly replied, "Of course."

After the ambulance rolled down the driveway carrying Jyl's body to the morgue, Joella and Gerry drove me the few blocks to Mother's apartment. Woofie, as I affectionately called her because her maiden name was Bare, was very pleased to see us and surprised to find us at her door unannounced after nine o'clock. We went into the den. Then I told her. She literally collapsed sobbing onto the sofa and rested there for a short time. She was a young eighty years old, and she soon rallied. I told her that I had opened the apartments, and no one would be sleeping in the house. I asked her to get ready, please, because I wanted her to be with us. She quickly got her things together, and we left for a home happily prepared for Christmas in the morning, but deeply enmeshed in unholy horror this night.

When Gerry, Joella, Mother, and I drove into the driveway, I saw a house still decorated for Christmas. Once again the events surrounding our family were surreal. Lids were being put on trashcans on the apartment patio. I knew those cans contained blood soaked rags and CARE cards almost ready for mailing that were now blood spattered. Now they were trashed and gone. It was not obvious that Jyl's body had been taken away. It was not obvious that our home had been scrubbed clean of blood and evidence cleared from a murder scene. But official cars everywhere, lights on everywhere, illuminating people moving around the place in deathly quiet, signified that something most untoward had happened. Seeing this invasion of our lives and privacy caused by death from a devastating deed done by someone determined to kill Jyl is as real on my memory reel as it was surreal that night. There is no closure. For survival of those left living, there must be only acceptance. Acceptance without the worrisome and useless question, "Why?" Why ask when there are no known answers. "Why?" "Why me?" only exhausts, frustrates, and delays finding joy again.

When Jack arrived, he walked into the apartment, his arms filled with Christmas presents that he had gotten and wrapped in Brooksville. Someone took them from him, but he kept one in his hand. After greeting everyone in a rather detached, dazed, and distanced way, he sat down in the silent room and began opening the package in his hand.

As he untied the ribbons, he remarked, "This is one of Jyl's presents. I guess she won't need it now." I almost gasped aloud when I saw the small box, a joke gift. He lighted a cigarette and stuck it into a slit in the box. Then he took a key, wound it up, and placed the gimmick on the floor. A skeleton hand appeared grotesquely waving the smoking cigarette, as the box seemed to crawl across the floor. Shrill ghostly laughter came from a person imagined trapped within the grotesque box. Jyl would have enjoyed the silly present bought as a powerful hint to discourage her from smoking. To everyone's horrified, hushed and sorrowful shock, the insidious thing crawled around and laughed for a few seconds until I picked it up and shut it off. To see this handsome intelligent man reduced to a splintered, grief-stricken person was not easy for anyone in the room. Within the hour, though, Jack pulled himself together and asked for facts about what had happened. I told him how Jyl had been murdered. He heard it without emotional reaction at that time. He was obviously in shock, but he managed to keep himself under control publicly thereafter.

Once again time moved slowly; it seemed another eternity before official cars started driving away. After most of them were gone, and the bright lights were removed, late that night, the Redington Beach Police Chief knocked on the apartment door and asked Jack and me to come outside and speak with the officials that were still there. Concerned, caring faces could be seen clearly in the harshly bright moonlight. The chief said, "I have told these men that you are good people and can be trusted. We have decided to release your daughter from the house to you now."

Jack and I turned and looked at one another in consternation. We had not even thought about what would happen to Jackie now. Immediately we decided Jackie should be hospitalized. We, deeply grief stricken, were not qualified to help her deal with anything that might be considered to have happened in our home that day. Jack explained our feelings to the kind and understanding Chief of Police.

I went into the apartment, phoned, and wakened the psychiatrist who had been treating Jackie and Jyl. This was the doctor whom they had seen a few weeks before Jyl's murder. This was the doctor who had been very reassuring about Jackie's medical treatment and had been firm in his belief that she lacked tendencies toward violence. I explained my call and requested that he contact the hospital to arrange for Jackie's admittance. He was obviously dumbfounded. He expressed astonished, total concern. He, as we, must have immediately wondered and worried that Jackie had succumbed to compelling, controlling commands unknown and unreal to anyone but herself. He agreed that it was essential that she be hospitalized.

As the doctor responded, I recalled that Jyl had asked me one day when we were riding in the car, "Mom, do you think Jackie could be dangerous?" "All I can tell you, Jyl, is what all of the doctors she has seen have told me. They have said that she has never seemed dangerous to others, and there is no reason to suspect that she would hurt anyone." Jyl replied, "Sometimes when we are home alone, I look up and see her looking at me very strangely." "Jyl," I said, "both of you are seeing the doctor in a few days. Be sure you tell him exactly what you have just told me. Get out of the house immediately if ever, if ever, you have the slightest reason to fear her. Run to the boulevard, stay out of the house; go where there are people, call me, and wait for me to pick you up."

Jyl did tell the doctor. He reassured her. I called him. He reassured me. I told him that Jackie seemed hyperactive. I also suggested that her medical dosage might need adjustment. The doctor replied. "I think she is getting along so well that I do not wish to take a chance by altering her medical treatment."

I wish my wisdom had been as advanced when I talked with Jyl that day as we rode in the car as it is now. I am now aware of a number of factors that I did not know then. Through the years since then, I have learned from experts, many families of the severely mentally ill, consumers of social services, service providers, elected and appointed executive and administrative governing officials and their staffs. I learned from them during tenures of my professional volunteer positions. Experts on violence, assembled by Governor Graham's staff, stated some facts very clearly. Unfortunately, they explained, with mentally well and mentally ill people, extreme violence is frequently unexpected and shocking in its nature.

Murder prompted by madness can happen on the streets, in church, at home, or wherever there are human beings. Many murders prompted by madness can be prevented if common sense and common decency are used to develop humane policies and procedures. Terror from untreated, seriously ill homeless individuals must be examined; it is a serious matter. Irresponsible roles played by politicians, attorneys, and judges daily endanger lives. Failure to change laws, misuse of public funds, and refusal to grant rights to assure everyone safety, keeps us from being safe at home, at school, at church, shopping, everywhere.

There are many cases where individuals have sought safety from violent persons, whether mentally ill, alcoholic, or otherwise, and have been denied help. Many tragedies result from the apparent inability of our legal and judicial systems to protect those at the mercy of such people. Safety is a right that needs urgently to be addressed. Freedom from terror created by untreated ill individuals should be available to all. Safety should be a right established for untreated, seriously mentally ill people to prevent damage to themselves or others.

I testified before the US Senate Judiciary Subcommittee in July 1982 regarding the insanity plea. In my testimony requesting consideration for a national standard for judging insanity, I strongly recommended that the sentence should use, "Guilty, but Insane." To imply lack of guilt with sentencing language, "Not Guilty by Reason of Insanity," I said, "credits innocence to the sick person, and it is in fact inaccurate language." I advocated that any sentencing language should absolutely state that the perpetrator of the crime is "Guilty." Just as strongly I advocated for recognition of the perpetrator's mental illness within sentencing language. I also explained, "It is only reasonable to assume that any suicidal person is capable of committing homicide. It is only reasonable to suspect that persons driven by delusions to harm or kill themselves could also be driven by delusions to harm or kill others." By inclusion of this belief, I implied that a suicide attempt by the perpetuator should serve as evidence of tendencies toward violence. I believe that to strengthen an insanity plea, it is necessary that all historical factors of violent deviant behavior demonstrated by the perpetuator be publicly presented.

When preparing the testimony, I recalled Dr. Elefthery's admonition to me in 1966 that I should never pretend to Jackie that something was OK when it wasn't. This admonishment is repeated here to emphasize that unless one wishes to further confuse a mentally ill individual, truth should always be told. Dr. Eleftery believed that his patients instinctively knew deep within themselves when they were not behaving normally. He believed that if it seemed to Jackie that I found her abnormal behavior acceptable, it would be detrimental and confusing to her already chaotic state of mind. He advised, "Be honest with her and be true to yourself."

Judgments I made from 1965, when Jackie first identified her illness, through all of those harrowing struggles the family had with her illness until December 1973, when she murdered Jyl, are not the same judgments I would make today, given the same circumstances. That is why I am literally forcing myself to write this book. It would have been much easier to just leave everything dormant on memory reels, but I cannot in good conscience do that. I do not pretend to have answers for others, but I feel obliged to share insights that I have unexpectedly learned from the unusual happenings in my life. My hopes are that some things that I write about may lighten burdens for others. I am writing to you, the reader, in an effort to make you aware of things I wish I had known forty years ago.

Today there are improved drugs. Delivery of care today, however, is still fragmented and just as discriminatory as it has ever been. Some social services are stupidly dehumanized by the use of automated telephone answering services. Imagine being mentally ill, dirty, hungry, or homeless. Imagine being confused and desperately needing help. Imagine standing on a street corner and listening to a tape offering directions when the phone cuts off because telephone time is up. Imagine craving to hear the sound of a live humane voice offering comfort. Imagine being rebuffed by multiple swiftly spoken recorded messages. Imagine being that lonely and deserted.

The increasing crescendo of automated voices in our new millennium is difficult enough when one is sanely seated in a comfortable chair with coffee nearby. Long waits and complex communication processes bedevil all consumers of services and products these days. Imagine the bedevilment for those mired in madness. Automated answering processes, unfortunately, are an introduction to many policies, procedures, and processes of bureaucratic care and treatment that may be just as numbing and confusing. The severely mentally ill are simply unable to negotiate the maze of these processes alone. Their voices may tell them to run from the very institutions that might help; they often lack the abilities to have the concentration, judgment, and desire to find the help they need.

Jackie was carefully put on a stretcher and carried out of the house to the ambulance. Neither Jack nor I could make ourselves go outside to watch her leave home that night. We had experienced many excruciating separations from Jackie and Jyl when they were hospitalized. This time a depth of hopelessness existed that we had not known before. It was dreadful for us. We knew it must be doubly dreadful for her. We knew that for her to see us so absolutely devastated would surely increase her dismay, so we requested that Larry ride with her to the hospital. We did not want her to feel alone. Larry climbed into the ambulance with her to ride along on that frightful trip. Again the ambulance could be heard rolling slowly down the driveway, then onto

Gulf Boulevard, and away into the darkness of the night. Darkness of the despair in our hearts rode with Jackie in that ambulance. The dissolution of our family was complete. Although we could not know it that night, both Jackie and Jyl had left home forever.

I fear that Jan, from what Jackie and others have told me, will always carry deep scars from watching Jackie leave. I was told later that Jan cried out to Jackie as Jackie was carried out of the house on a stretcher and placed in the ambulance, "Jackie! Jackie!" I was told that Jan was crying almost uncontrollably. Jan, who through the years was always lovingly loyal and helpful to her ill sisters, could no longer help them. Jackie has told me of her torment when she looked back through the entry door of the ambulance after she had been placed inside and saw Jan's grief stricken face. When she heard her crying, she told me that she wished with all her heart that she had not had to kill Jyl. Jackie and Jyl were now fatally beyond the reach of everyone. As a mother I will always know the anguish of those two departing stretchers in ambulances. To lose two sisters in one night has to be equally as anguishing for Jan.

In the years since Jyl's murder, a sorrow for me has been to know that some people believe that Jackie is by nature a malicious, evil person. At least once a week, the media reports others as ill as Jackie performing heinous acts for which they, with justice fairly and ethically practiced, cannot be held accountable.

Unfortunately, thanks to voter apathy and ignorance, some lawyers and accommodating friends who sit in legislative bodies write laws favoring the interests of attorneys rather than those of our severely mentally ill citizens. Ludicrous, expensive courtroom scenarios freely advertise the prowess of prosecutors and attorneys who actually misrepresent hapless defendants. With zeal the courts and uninformed juries, by their cruel deliberations, publicly proclaim their ignorance of what severe mental illness is all about. Some participants in the proceedings, with no apologies, pocket money generated by the misuse and abuse of something professed to be justice.

A friend of Jackie's, who drowned her children in a bathtub many years ago, sometimes comes to the phone and talks to me when Jackie calls. This woman has said to me more than once, "Why do you think God insisted that I send my children back to him? I loved them so much. I miss them so much. It was terrible to have to drown those precious little ones that were more important to me than anything else in my life. I cry for them almost every day." I just hear her out and then say something like, "I know that you miss your children, and I am so sorry that they are no longer with you." Her illness has created a web of falsehoods in her brain that nothing can erase. Her tragedy is multiplied everyday by deaths of other innocent victims by actions crazily taken by untreated or inappropriately treated severely mentally ill people.

Someday voters will go to town meetings from necessity to ask the right questions and demand the right answers. Safety for voters and safety for homeless, untreated, severely mentally ill citizens will someday be recognized as a necessary, legitimate, enforceable right for everyone. Safety is a primary need, a right, for everyone. Safety for all of us is a right that someday will have to be sought by politicians and judicial systems. Safety should not have to be demanded by voters. As the population explosion continues, with severe mental illness increasing in direct ratio to it, politicians may be cornered by the accompanying increase of preventable crimes and violence in the streets.

Jack broke down into bitter weeping that night when only he, Jan, and I remained in the apartment living room after Mother and Ed had gone to their rooms. He moaned, "How can this have happened to Jyl? She never did anything unkind to anyone in her life." I started to get up to go across the room to comfort him, but Jan said, "No. Don't. Let him get it out." We sat with him until he calmed down. Then he stood up slowly and limped away to a bedroom.

Jan's presence was the greatest comfort that Jack and I had. That she existed had always lessened the agony we felt because of her sisters' illnesses. We tried in many ways to make her realize that we did not expect her to make up in any way for her their inability to bring us the same pleasures that she did. We did everything we could to make her life as "normal" as possible, but there was no way that her home life could be anything but difficult.

Jan never once mentioned that she felt imposed upon by having to share a home with two people who made all of our lives troublesome many times. Jan had to feel less carefree than she might have if the home environment had been "normal." She must have sometimes felt what would be natural teenage resentment, but she spared us from any spoken complaints. Still today, I feel a wonderful respect and appreciation for the fact that Jan was truly there for her parents and her sisters through thick and thin, as it might be tritely said. The old admonition often humorously added to the loyalty statement, "If things get too thick, I will thin out." never seemed to apply to the relationship that the rest of the family had with Jan during the time she lived at home enduring the hellish illnesses of her two older sisters.

But, who knows what Jan's perceptions really were during those trying years? We told her as soon as we had a diagnosis for Jyl's illness about the vitamin shots I had been given before she was born. Jack believed that the illness would one day be found to be a biological phenomenon. We knew that to tell Jan these things might cause her some personal fear that she too might some-day find that she had inherited the unwanted genes. However, we emphasized her birth weight and the fact that she had been the only truly strong and healthy baby born to us. We believed Jan to be free of the genes that had ruined the lives of her sisters.

We wondered if, in feeling naturally defensive for her sisters, Jan might think we had just sent them off to mental facilities for our own convenience. Who knows what deep, subconscious feelings she may have today, or may have consciously felt years ago? Both Jack and I often spoke about the how unfortunate it was for Jan to be denied teenage years free of strife because of the unwelcome presence of mental illness in our home. We felt grief for that.

Paranoia, when symptomatic of an illness, creates attitudes that are some-times encouraged or enhanced by psychiatrists. Parents may not be portrayed as good people or nice people to patients by psychiatrists. There were instances when the psychiatrists seemed to accept paranoid delusions as facts. Jack and I knew what kind of malarkey was probably on medical records as they related to us as people and as parents, but we chose not to fret about falla-cious records. We did worry and wonder whether Jan recognized her sisters' negative feelings as being part of their illness. We realized that she was unusu-ally intelligent, so we had to take for granted that she would not be gullible about perceptions caused by mental illness. We could do nothing except hope that she would have the best understanding that a teenager could have.

As Jack left the apartment living room after his heart-rending outburst, a heavy cloud of gloom replaced his presence. His shortened leg from back sur-gery in 1962, his diabetes, his lupus brought home from World War II, his weariness from resisting past pressures from unethical Pinellas County elected officials, now capped with Jyl's murder, made his life seem more threatened than it had been only one day earlier. Jan and I sat quietly for a few minutes before she, too, went off to bed.

Once again I was alone to wonder, "What next?" I paced the floor until dawn. I worried and wondered who could have wanted to murder Jyl. I knew that Jackie would not have wanted to kill her sister. Fear that her delusions had compelled her to kill rolled again and again through my thoughts.

Jyl's murder was worse than a horrendous nightmare. As I paced back and forth, again and again, all through the night, I silently lamented a mantra, "This is real. This is real. This is real. This is real." I had to keep my mind focused to enable me to comprehend everything that had happened and to accept what it would be like without Jyl for days, weeks, and years in the future. It was hours before I could accept the unavoidable challenge to face the grim truth and acknowledge that Jyl's companionship was gone forever. I would never hear her wondrous contagious laughter again. I would never enjoy serious or humorous conversations with her again. She was dead. She was dead. She was dead.

Though my life and person seemed hopelessly crushed, I knew that when dawn came my family and the city would waken. I knew that I had no option but to decide how to behave when daybreak came. Daybreak would solidify somber new realities that would forever seem cast in stone. Whatever approach I took the next day, whether Jackie was guilty or not guilty, would endure. My approach might influence attitudes about mental illness in the minds of the public. My world was crumbled, but for those who did not know our family the world would be unchanged. I, too, for my own sake and for the comfort of others, had to go on living and seem unchanged.

I made some unwavering and lasting decisions during those early morning hours. What we said and how we handled ourselves now would affect reactions of others to Jyl's murder. My reactions to Jyl's murder would affect my future interactions with Jackie and with the rest of the family, relationships within the community, and my world at large. I had to decide how I would appear in public, what to say, what not to say, how to look, to enable, and to act according to the decisions I was making. Once again I recognized that there were no easy options. I knew that, no matter how difficult, I had to choose to display studied, steady, stoic composure. I had to make a resolution to try to lighten this appalling burden for others. The kindest thing I could do in memory of Jyl was to avoid dejection, while sharing anguish with others. This was a difficult decision, but I had to follow through with it in tribute to Jyl. I believed that I could avoid hurt for others if I managed to keep these promises to myself. As Jyl had lived, I, too, wanted to avoid intentionally making others feel unhappy or hurt. I felt that my wholesome acceptance of our tragedy was essential to help Jack enjoy the years he had left to live.

After that long, sleepless night, I began the day at dawn by thinking of my students whose day at school should not be disturbed by a calamity in my life. Before anyone was stirring in the apartments I drove to Dixie Hollins High School, only a few miles away. I placed a note on the assistant principal's desk telling him what had happened so he would call a substitute teacher. Then I went to my classroom and checked my prepared lesson plans. I put them on my desk for the substitute teacher. My accountability to others had not changed, even though my life would never be the same again and would have to change direction.

Once again, more strongly than within the trauma of our tiny three-hour-old Jon's death in 1945 during World War II when Jack was in combat in the Pacific, I felt my place in time and my minuscule presence in the universe. All people, mere blimps in the context of life on Earth, are offered by birth certain responsibilities that their lives may or may not reflect. What responsibilities to honor or demean are choices afforded those competent enough to choose.

Darkest depths of grief were mine when Jon died, but I never saw him. I never knew him. I knew Jyl for twenty-four years and nine months. The trauma suffered when our newborn son died will never be less than traumatic, but Jyl's death brought pain more deeply felt. This agony was compounded by many years of knowing, nurturing, and loving Jyl.

When I returned to the apartments from Dixie Hollins, everyone was awake and getting dressed. It was customary when Jack was home on week-ends for me to walk down the beach to The Little House Restaurant at John's Pass in Madeira Beach to meet him for breakfast. Jack's foot drop prevented him from walking easily, so he always drove to meet me. After breakfast, we would sit and talk. It was our time to have privacy away from our house, so beset with illness. That morning, with Jyl not yet dead for a day, Mother, Jack, Jan, Ed, and I decided to go to our familiar breakfast place. Getting away from our place, now so saturated with sadness, was a relief for all of us. The restaurant was filled with tourists, and our waitress was unusually considerate. It helped us to step for some time into a neutral place where our privacy was respected. We needed to be removed from the setting of our ordeal for a while. We needed to be reminded that a world awaited our return.

After breakfast I went over to the house. I went alone. No one else mentioned going, but I believed and hoped that there might be some clues to help identify Jyl's murderer. I had to go. There were dried, bloody footprints on the entrance steps. Bloody prints on the driveway marked the entrances and exits of those present the night before. Later I found encrusted blood on the sides of the soles of my shoes.

I forced myself to go in. I could not avoid walking on the bloodstains just inside the foyer doors. We were never able to completely clear those dark, patchy stains. I made it into the living room, where I paused to look around. There was a small green book lying opened on the coffee table. I picked it up and read two pages where some reader must have stopped reading and put the book aside. These lines from Shakespeare's *Othello* jumped out at me from the page: "My blood begins my safer guides to rule, And passion, having my best judgment collided, Assays to lead the way." This book, shelved with us for many years, came from my childhood home. I was puzzled to find it on the table. Later I asked Jackie, "Who was reading *Othello* the day Jyl was killed?" She replied, "I was."

I went upstairs to my desk, where I often spent hours writing and watching the gentle tides of the Gulf as they washed ashore or flowed away. There in that room more drama unfolded.

The Door, a poem written by Jyl, was lying on my desk. She would never know when it brought her national recognition. She had submitted it to a national contest, but she did not live to see the letter that came a few weeks after her death, recognizing her talent and praising her poem. Jyl wrote from internal passion. Rejection slips had never discouraged her. Ironically, *The Door* was published a few months later.

The Door offers comfort to me. The essence of the poem helps me to accept Jyl's door to the universe being slammed shut by a sharp, seven-inch butcher knife ruthlessly guided by the fiendish hallucinations running riot in Jackie's brain. Though Jyl's door to this universe may be firmly closed forever, my door is open. I cannot do other than step through my open door.

The Door

The grains of sand grinding.
The caw of the gull harsh.
The roar of the sea deafening.
All mingling with calling voices of "Peace."
To walk away from a crowd.
To be Alone,
To hope for something fresh.
To stop your pounding ears is bliss.
For a world of your own
Closes the door
On the Universe.
And opens a door for you.

I read *The Door* with steeled heart and determined courage. I could not let myself begin to cry. I thought that, if I cried, it would be like opening a floodgate of tears. I was not sure that I could ever stop them. Today I feel compelled to step through a horrifically opened door to write this book for Jyl. I cannot believe that she has died for naught. I believe, and I think, she would wish her death to be a knell for awakening compassionate understanding of mental illness.

As I looked around the room, searching for any clues that might help me fathom Jyl's untimely and undeserved death, I saw earphones lying on the floor in front of my desk. As mentioned before, Jackie told me later that she was sitting there on the floor, looking toward the Gulf, and listening to music when I called out to her after I found Jyl's body.

Beside my telephone I found a sheet torn from a notepad. It seemed to me at that monstrous time and still today a magnificent, soothing message from Jyl. She wrote:

A SIMPLE PRAYER

Lord, make me an instrument of your peace. Where there is hatred, let me sow love. Where there is injury, pardon. Where there is doubt, faith. Where there is despair, joy. O Divine Master, grant that I may not so much seek to be consoled: as to console. To be understood, as to understand. To be loved, as to love. It is in giving that we receive. It is in pardoning that we are pardoned. It is in dying that we are born to eternal life.

There were no books nearby. Jyl must have sat at my desk the day of her death, watching peaceful Gulf of Mexico waters lapping the broad, white, sandy beach. These words of St. Francis of Assisi must have come into her mind. All her life she jotted down her original poems wherever she happened to be on whatever paper was nearby. Finding something written by someone else and quoted from memory was unusual. It was as though Jyl had come into the room and said, "Do not grieve. I am fine. Whatever has happened is to be pardoned. Do not despair. Find joy."

I sat there gripping the simple prayer in my hand for what seemed to be a very long time. Like Jyl the day before, I watched the waves soothingly lap the shoreline, speaking from time immemorial and for infinity. Then, rousing from my reverie, I got up, picked up the earphones from the floor, put them in their proper place, and carried Jyl's simple prayer with me as a memoir to save.

I left the room. It was as it had been the morning before when I so cheerfully went off to school. The room remained the same. Jack, Jan, and I remained, but we could never be the same as before Jyl was murdered, or before Jackie became ill

Next I checked the bathroom medicine closet to count Jackie's Melarill tablets. The number of pills I found told me that there were too many left in the bottle from the date when the prescription was filled for her to have been consistently taking her medicine as the doctor had prescribed. Jackie admits she took the pills for only about two weeks within that time frame.

I now know that people living with severely mentally ill individuals need to vigilantly monitor their prescribed intake of drugs. I now know that it is often symptomatic for severely mentally ill persons to believe that drugs are not essential when they begin to feel "normal" after taking medication. I now know that discontinuing medication when patients say they feel "normal" is not uncommon. I also know how dangerously unwise that decision is. Some innocent, unsuspecting people, some known and some unknown to their killers, have died when a severely mentally ill individual stopped taking prescribed medication. Improperly or untreated mentally ill people can be driven by merciless, persuasive forces that have penetrated their minds and misdirected their thinking processes. Seriously mentally ill people are involved every day in heinous or petty crimes. These desperately ill people do not own their minds. They follow the dictates of invasive thoughts within their brains that demonstrate no rhyme or reason. Their brains may be possessed and obsessed by these thinking processes every day and night, every hour, and every minute. Every day and night, every hour, and every minute, on our wonderful planet, there are ongoing countless crimes committed, caused by unknown forces in brains possessed by demons.

All over the world people look away in denial as their paths cross those of untreated, severely mentally ill individuals in almost any public setting you choose to visit. The scandalous performance of officials in the United States and in all other countries who encourage, by their indifference, the untreated seriously mentally ill to roam however and wherever they wish, with no official concern, compassion, or caution taken for their state of mind or their physical well-being is scandalous and fearsome folly. Grievous suffering by perpetrators and victims alike are simply reflections of erroneous decisions callously made.

Those in positions to make changes to benefit both the concerned and the unconcerned don't do their homework. They repeatedly fail to consider the cost to society and to individuals of allowing severely mentally ill persons to remain untreated. They fail to provide funds for mental health care, and they do not create laws that actually relate to the needs of the mentally ill or to the protection of society, but instead perpetuate ancient misunderstandings. They refuse to educate themselves or the public about severe mental illnesses. They waste millions of dollars that could provide care for severely mentally ill people. They waste millions of dollars that should be used to prevent street crimes. It is very unwise to spend millions of dollars every day and night, every hour, and every minute for punitive, ineffective policies and practices.

I went into Jackie's room to look around. I opened drawers to see if there was anything unusual to be found. My hand touched a small envelope as my hand explored under clothing in a drawer. I pulled a small envelope out and opened it to find a bank box key. I dropped the key into my pocket with the St. Francis of Assisi prayer. I returned downstairs, picked up the little green book, turned down the corners of the opened pages, and took it with me to the apartment. I carried three items with me; one that I felt may have fed into Jackie's delusions if she had killed Jyl, a key that might lead me to something unknown, and a comforting prayer.

A close friend who had gone to dinner with me the night of December seventeenth, the night before Jyl's murder, came by to see how she could help. I asked her if she would take Fluffy. His presence was so unnerving to Jack that it was troublesome. When I said to Jack, "Anne is downstairs offering to take Fluffy home with her, get him bathed, and take care of him for a while," he said, "Just give him to her."

Fluffy's coat, matted in some places with Jyl's lifeblood, was a reminder we all wished out of sight, but no one had the time or had even thought of taking him to be groomed. All of us were totally engrossed in our grief and in the management of more difficult, immediate tasks. At that point, I think Jack thought he would never be able to look at Fluffy again without feeling the misery of Jyl's death. When I made Jack's offer, Anne stated firmly, "No. I will just take him now and take care of him. He will be there for you anytime if you wish to have him back."

Anne also knew that I had received my real estate license the week before. She told me that she had spoken to her former husband, Kenneth Kleier, president of a Saint Petersburg real estate office, who suggested she bring the license to hang in his office. The license had to be put somewhere to keep it active. So Anne took Fluffy and the real estate license with her when she left. By doing these two things, Anne helped us over two small but important hurdles that our benumbed states of mind had kept us from considering. She had been very fond of Jyl. I think that, of all my friends, she may have been most affected by Jyl's unmerciful, untimely death. Anne was the last person outside the family to laugh and talk with Jyl.

Joella went with me to the John S. Rhodes funeral home to make arrangements for a private funeral on Saturday, the twenty-second of December. Jack and I had never considered any thing other than a closed casket and a short private graveside ceremony. Every casket viewed reflected Jyl's sleeping face to me. There was no casket that seemed to be a place for her. With Jyl not yet dead twenty-four hours, in spite of resolutions made during the night, choosing her casket demanded a level of acceptance of reality that was almost impossible. Somehow, finally, we chose a casket. I cannot tell you today what it looked like. I ordered a vault. Gravesites, caskets, and vaults should be chosen long before they are needed. Like wills, selection of these things should be taken care of when everyone involved with the activities is healthy, happy, and not under duress.

Mr. Rhodes asked whether we owned a gravesite. Cremation with shipment of remains to Virginia never occurred to Jack and me. We had planned ahead for burial spaces, and we owned lots in Augusta Memorial Park near Fishersville in the Shenandoah Valley. Jack is buried there. There are spaces there for my remains and for Jackie's remains to be buried. Those lots are on the highest hill in the cemetery, where the famous Blue Ridge Mountains that Jack and I remembered from childhood can easily be seen. Those sites were far away and frozen solid. I remembered how Jyl thanked us many times for bringing her to the land of sunshine and beaches, so it seemed right that she be buried in her favored state.

Some frivolous thoughts flew through my head when Mr. Rhodes asked about the cemetery lot. One of my memory reels unrolled without proper provocation or request. When a salesperson from Augusta Memorial Cemetery had contacted us years ago while we still lived in Waynesboro, we asked him to stop by the office after it closed one evening. When he arrived, we asked him to please skip the sales pitch. We told him that we wanted lots if the price seemed right and there was a location that we liked. We closed the deal in fairly fast time. Then the young man asked if we had friends that might be interested. Jack looked at me with the merry twinkle in his eye that I loved so much. We proceeded to give the salesman a long list of our friends' names with the provision that he would not disclose the source of his referrals. Just to show what kind of reputation we had, I tell you that in a few days we started getting calls from friends: some were angry, some were laughing. It was easy to characterize our friends by the way they responded to our silliness. That intrusion from a willful reel about silliness, quickly flashed into my thoughts at that time, only heightened the tragedy of the moment.

Mr. Rhodes kindly called the office of Memorial Park Cemetery and made arrangements for someone to talk with us. Joella and I drove there to choose a burial site. I said to the saleslady, "Do you have space away from city noise where it is quiet and peaceful?" She suggested a specific area, and we went there to look. We chose two lots by a small lake where ducks swim. There also is a tree where birds sit on branches to sing. The chimes of the cemetery are not far away. When I am in the area, I sometimes go by, feed the ducks, leave a daisy on Jyl's grave, and enjoy memory reels of Jyl's poetry as I remember her hearty wonderful laughter when she was alive.

The extra lot there is for Jan if she ever wishes to use it. There is also an extra lot in Virginia if she wishes to use that. Jan prefers quiet places, too. She practiced yoga for many years, probably still does. I think she, like Jyl, considers Florida her home state. She moved from Virginia to Florida when she was only eight years old. I don't think roots put down in Virginia by her paternal and maternal ancestors for generations are deep within Jan's heart.

When Joella and I returned to the apartment, someone had called requesting that Jack and I come down town to the State Attorney General's office that afternoon for routine questioning. I later read in the paper that Jimmy Russell, the state attorney, was on vacation, but returned because of Jyl's murder. When we entered the office, he was sitting at a desk in the reception area. When we went in to talk with members of his staff, we entered a room that seemed crowded with people. I vaguely remember a few faces and names. I do not recall whether the state attorney was in the room. The room may not have been as crowded as it seemed, but the idea of being questioned and having to talk personally and intimately about Jyl and our family in such a stressful public atmosphere gave Jack and me a sense of being cornered and confined. We seemed encircled by questioning, puzzled, unsmiling faces. The feeling of again becoming smothered by surreal circumstances became almost intolerable in that room.

We understood the necessity for our being there, but understanding did not make the questions and suggestions less harrowing. We were asked for names of Jyl's friends and names of persons she had dated. We were asked where each family member was at the time of the murder. The memory reel reflects no answer as to how long we stayed there. There are blank spaces on that reel as it rolls through that scenario. It does display the face of one officer who looked kindly at me as we left the room, and softly said, "I wish I could have known you under different circumstances." Here was someone who felt our pain and eased some of our discomfort and misery. I still appreciate his compassion. His remark made that histrionic afternoon less hurtful then and now in memory.

On December twenty-first, the newspaper reported the interview had taken place. One paragraph read as follows: "After a lengthy investigative interview yesterday, Pinellas-Pasco State Attorney James Russell would not comment on the case. When asked if he would interview the two sisters, Russell said, "It is very difficult to interview potential defendants." After a short pause, he added, "It is difficult even if they are not potential defendants." When Jack and I read those quotes, we appreciated that he left no doubt in readers' minds that we were not considered potential defendants. Jan was never called to come in which increased our gratitude to the state attorney.

In Virginia, there was deep snow and ice on December eighteenth. When we contacted family members and friends there, they told us that airports were having trouble and roads were closed in some places. Jack and I told all family members and friends that we would prefer and appreciate their coming later, rather than coming into the middle of our baffling stress and strain.

When sorrowful news is relayed, it is much easier if it can be done early in the day because sad news at night guarantees sleepless nights. It is much kinder to give the recipient of bad news a chance to be as rested as possible. Morning bad news, at least, finds more energy available than a restless night provides. We would have waited until the morning of December nineteenth to call anyone, but we were afraid news might be relayed from other sources if we did not make contacts the night of the murder. Before we went to bed that first night, we made calls to family members, and some of them were asked to get in touch with our friends.

I remember one call we received that night as the news spread in Virginia. When I came to the phone, a friend, unable to speak, blurted out, "Maxene, I cannot talk, but I had to call." I thanked her and put the phone down. Tears sting my eyes as I sit here working at my computer today and hear that loving consoling voice from more than thirty years ago.

When people say that they have not responded to some sad event because they don't know what to do or what to say, I tell them, "Always do something, even if it seems clumsy. What you do is not what matters. That you cared enough to try to help is what makes the difference to those enduring trouble or grief." Ramona and Ambrose Updegraff called immediately to offer help, even though they had to be very busy with his medical practice and plans for a family Christmas celebration. During those first hours of our sorrow, their call helped us to realize that there were caring people out there who were concerned for us.

Only one Virginia friend that I expected to hear from never called. When I saw her more than a year later, she just stood speechless in front of me and said, "I am so sorry. I just couldn't bring myself to call you. All of it was so awful." In a social setting during a brunch that a friend and I were hosting at Waynesboro Country Club, I was hideously reminded of something that I was trying hard to keep reeled deep within my brain. As my timid friend spoke I managed not to burst into tears. She did me no favor by waiting to express her condolences.

That friend is dead. The friend with whom I was entertaining is dead. I have pictures of family and friends on my desk, walls, chests, and all around me as I sit writing in my upstairs hall, my writer's attic, in our Bloomfield, Kentucky, 1831 antebellum house. Digressing thoughts distress and distract me from my writing and sometimes bemuse. A great deal of soul searching and reminiscing take place when one is writing a book that includes anecdotes from one's life. Writing of death and rereading the Assisi prayer reminds me of family and friends no longer on this planet. I look around and count more than seventy faces pictured nearby. Forty of those pictured are physically dead. My memory reels depict the wealth of fun and love I shared with each of them during their lifetimes. I remember begging my father to take exercise when he was eighty years old. He said with his usual levity, "Please, Maxene, I get enough exercise going to my friend's funerals."

I rarely attend funerals. I prefer giving time to the living. I am not trying to avoid exercise. I am, in truth, avoiding the selfish grief I feel for the absence of the person being buried. Funerals are never easy for me. When I attend a funeral, a willful reel insists on coming forth to remind me of the dreary, cold, inexorably sad day of December twenty-second in 1973.

Another friend, very near death with cancer in Maryland, called to say, "Mac, I just have to tell you how sorry I am that you and Jack are having such a tough time." I replied, "Lewis, I think you are having the toughest time." He replied, "Oh no. Losing a child is tougher than what is happening to me." This man and I had a special rapport, and when we finished talking I felt so comforted that I had heard his voice once again before he died. I greatly admire his ability to sincerely love all people all during his lifetime. As wealthy and as busy as Lewis Funkhouser was, he never forgot the plight of others less fortunate. He visited jails, prisons, and mental institutions, never being judgmental, just to convey concern from the outside world to incarcerated inmates.

Lewis's wife is a lifelong friend from Keister school days. It was she who took me by her house for a treat after my first day of school in Harrisonburg. She writes to Jackie every year at Christmas. Another friend, Lillian, did the same thing until she died. Her daughter continued doing that as requested by Lillian before she died. Good friends like these are hard to find. I am so fortunate to have known so many. Just as traumas in my life have heightened joys, deaths of some of my friends has heightened my pleasure with those friends still living. It is remarkably true and unfortunate that it sometimes takes deprivation to develop appreciation; it is noteworthy, I think, that we may never fully feel appreciation until we have suffered deprivation.

Jack and I knew many people, and the outpouring of their distress and caring eased our spirits, both immediately and long afterward. Because we had a private funeral, because the weather was miserable in Virginia, because we had asked friends to wait to visit, our travail was much easier. How many times there is the rush of food, flowers, and visits when crises occur. Within a short time, though, friends become busy with other things, and grief stricken individuals may feel deserted. That silent heartbreak sometimes causes the bereaved to experience excessive late-onset grieving. A large church was filled to overflowing at my father's funeral. One couple, Percy and Kay Sowers, asked my mother to go to dinner every Sunday for a year thereafter. Dr. Bill Thomas, the son of one of my mother's late friends, also escorted Mother to various local activities. They and a few others, who still remembered later on some of Mother's lonely days, brought good cheer and consolation to her.

It was difficult to read the *St. Petersburg Times* on the morning of December nineteenth. I made myself read a front-page headlined article about Jyl's murder. I cringed when I read that her father had "headed the Pinellas County Health Department from June 1964 until June 1970 when he was fired." The newspaper editors and writers, whom we had always found friendly and compassionate, knew what kind of political chicaneries we had endured as a few county commissioners twisted, turned, and invented reasons to drive away an honest public servant who would not grant their unethical requests. Jack met many times with newspaper editors or writers for discussions about it. I had worked with them also. It was distressing to sense unkindness in an article that was already so agonizing to read, from a newspaper that we had considered reasonable and supportive of Jack's efforts to do a good job as Health Director of Pinellas and Pasco counties. I suppose it was an early touch of the tabloid reporting that has today become ordinary reporting. Friends exclaimed their outrage that a respected newspaper had demonstrated yellow tabloid characteristics. One friend wrote the paper immediately of her concern for such callousness, and the paper did publish her letter.

In 1973, sordid scandals and tawdry, overly dramatized personal stories were not the media meat they are today. The general public was not into the feeding frenzy now apparently relished at gossip troughs created by media that were once more respected and dignified. The evening newspaper used the article, but it eliminated the sentence about Jack's firing. He had been fired because he had refused to resign when asked to—because he had done no wrong. I later went downtown to personally thank Bob Stiff, editor of The Evening Independent, for his well-known vigilance for honesty and professional management of news.

Jack's nephew Sam Obenschain and his wife Nancy came from Atlanta. They were not iced in, and they gave up their Christmas holidays to come stay with us. Sam's presence was particularly important to Jack. Nancy and Sam were important mainstays for Jack and me during those long, disheartening days and nights.

The first night of their arrival, December twenty-first, they went over to the house to sleep. Soon the apartment phone rang. Sam said, "Maxene, please look outside to see if there is anyone at the front door of the house." It was after midnight. I looked and saw no one. I said, "Why do you ask, Sam?" He replied, "There has been extremely loud beating on the door. We thought one of you might have come to get help with some unexpected development. It was scary." "We will watch from our windows. Turn on all outside lights and quickly come over here to sleep," I replied.

Needless to say they were in our apartment within a few minutes. We still did not know who had killed Jyl. We had no way of knowing whether a crime perpetuator might return to the scene of the crime. Jack went back to bed. I opened a bottle of Four Roses eggnog that someone had brought to us. Nancy does not drink alcoholic beverages, so Sam and I drank some Yuletide eggnog. It was a good, relaxing sleep potion.

I found the eggnog soothing enough to purchase more quarts and to consume some every evening. I recall someone suggesting that family members should take something to make existence less stressful and more tolerable. Jack had given me some medication for Mother, but I doubt that she ever took it. I never asked whether he was medicating himself. I settled for something from traditional Virginia Christmas customs, perhaps because I felt I was tapping my supportive Virginia roots by drinking that soothing concoction. It surely provided some comfort, and it helped me to relax.

I knew sleep was vital for supplying energy to meet each unpredictable day. After the first sleepless night of December eighteenth, I determined that I would teach myself to go to sleep, free from daily concerns. I necessarily began a sleep exercise the night of December nineteenth. I had not been to bed for more than forty hours when I went to bed that night. I was unaware of whether I was tired or not. The adrenaline had kept pumping all those previous hours, but I managed to gear down my energy level by sheer determination to get the rest I knew I had to have. I knew that I had to continue to function with as much accountability and reliability as possible. I succeeded. I went to sleep quickly. Of course because of not having gone to bed the night before, I was exhausted, but I had no awareness of fatigue.

Since that night, when I inducted new sleeping habits, I go to bed, close my eyes, and close the door on the universe. I envision emptying my mind by simply saying over and over again internally, "Nothing. Nothing. Nothing. Think nothing. Go to sleep." It works for me. The habit that I put into place the first night that I went to bed after Jyl was killed continues because I wish to function as capably as possible every waking hour. Memory reels, past and present, are silenced every night so that I can fall soundly asleep.

I confess that one must first be willing to think and visualize with dimmed intelligence to go to sleep in moments with such a simplistic mantra. All brain drains must be seen as opened wide so that the sandman can move in. I rarely waken during the night but, if I do, I glance at the clock to see whether I have had enough time resting. When the clock says I have had at least six hours of sleep, if I feel rested, and if the day has dawned, I get up. If the hours are too short, even if there is daylight, I immediately go back to sleep.

Some rare times when I feel restless, I get out of bed and read or find some simple household chore. I usually manage to prevent my mind from straying toward those ever-waiting, sorrowful memory reels stashed within my brain. I never lie in bed when unable to sleep. I use physical activity, combined with some pleasant mental activity to take my attention and uplift my spirits for a short time and then return to bed and go back to sleep. I own my mind.

During the days after Jyl's murder, I felt refreshed and alert. Looking back, I wonder whether others around me thought that to be true. All things seemed clearly identified to me, and my attention seemed tightly focused on matters immediately at hand while I was functioning in shock. I think that state of mind dulled some horrors of those days, saturated with sorrow and horror and enabled me to have the reactions I had resolved to maintain. At some moments I seemed to be floating outside myself, watching myself as I carried on some difficult task. Deep down inside myself, I wanted to be separated from the things that were happening that I found almost impossible to believe or endure. At the risk of sounding trite, even frivolous, I think I sometimes just pretended that I was acting out in some drama unrelated to me. Scarlet in *Gone With the Wind* learned how to turn off her brain. I remember her saying, "I'll think about that tomorrow." Everyone has to learn that skill to some extent, I think, just to stay in touch with current realities.

Today, thirty-two years later, I rarely notice those 1973 Christmas reels wanting to roll. When they do forcefully appear, I feel those same sensations that I felt during that time of indescribable suffering. It is not easy to write this book. Friends have asked why I am reliving those days. "Why can't you leave it alone?" "Why are you doing this to yourself? "Why write a book?" I don't think I know how to explain to them the depth of my sense of duty to share things so dearly learned. I must try to help others, who may suffer such devastating events as I have, to somehow survive joyfully. I have no choice but to write this book. It would be irresponsible for me to ignore issues that I think I see more clearly now than before the traumas in my life. With this book, the most I hope for is to stimulate inquisitive thought. Perhaps the book will help to generate new approaches with charitable, nonjudgmental hearts to domestic and public challenges that need to be addressed with intelligent common sense. Common sense needs to be used to promote betterment of our homes, our communities, our state, our nation, and our world.

All of the family, by sheer tenacity, managed enough sustained strength to persevere through each day as it came. The nightmare that we were living through demanded unflinching, unswerving attention to duties never before experienced. Over and over we rehashed what might have happened. We discussed names of young men whom Jyl had dated, but there was never any suggestion that one of them might have killed her. I don't remember anyone ever wondering aloud whether Jackie had killed Jyl. We just kept trying to rationalize that it had to be someone we did not know. The detectives gave us no information. They did telephone to request permission to come out to the house to remove the kitchen knife rack. They came and got it and left without stating any reason for wanting it.

Jan returned to Babson Park. Mother went back to her Gulf Harbor apartment. Jack usually went to bed early. Every night while Nancy and Sam were there, we sat and talked. Every night we wondered when we would hear something from the State Attorney's office about who they believed had murdered Jyl. We were eager for charges to be made for the murder of Jyl.

Investigators were as accommodating as possible with the questions we asked. We noticed a place that seemed to have recently been dug near our seawall. We called it to their attention, and they obliged us by digging up debris that some beach walker had likely chosen to bury rather than trash the beach in front of our house. We thought a hidden weapon might be buried there. We were looking everywhere for clues.

I telephoned the manager of our bank, and I told him about the key I had found in Jackie's drawer. I told him I wanted to enter the box and asked how I could do that. He said he would have to witness the opening. The manager asked me what I expected to find when I got to the bank. I said, "Papers. Jackie is a prolific writer, and I think she has put some of her writings in safe keeping." Sure enough, the box was stuffed with papers. The box had been rented on December fifteenth. In this book's chapter, Jackie Writes in 2002, much of the material found in the bank box papers is restated. The themes of her madness have not changed.

In June 2002 Jackie asked me to come to Florida State Hospital, Chattahoochee, Florida, where she lives to talk about her delusions and "my crime" as she refers to Jyl's murder. "I know that if you are writing a book to try to make people understand severe mental illness that you will be writing about my crime," she said. "Mom, I want to tell you about my delusions, and I want to explain why I killed Jyl," she insisted. Jackie says that she is as eager as I for people to understand her illness. She knows that she would probably be homeless now if it were not for my vigilance to keep her safe. She tells me that sometimes patients deny their delusions so that they will be released from the hospital. Jackie has asked to contribute to this book. Chapter Six is dedicated to her thoughts and beliefs from within her world.

Jackie seems as concerned as I about the indifference of those who have the power, but not the courage, to bring fair justice to those who suffer as she does. She courageously speaks out in this book. Both of us speak, irrespective of what others may think of our thoughts and actions. Our primary purpose is to simply try to help as many people as possible to understand what severe mental illness does to those who unwittingly and unwillingly harbor its demonic delusions, programs, and voices. Jackie and I feel driven to try to promote understanding. Motivation for practical legal reforms for proper treatment, decent housing, and safety for the severely mentally ill can never happen without understanding. We know why Jyl is dead. We are determined to promote prevention of more undeserved irrational killings. As you read, we ask you to open your heart to feel our pain and open your ears to hear our pleas.

My files here in my "attic" writer's retreat are on the floor, on shelves, and in chests of drawers. Framed on the walls and on the tops of furnishings are pictures and writings as tributes to all three daughters. I have many poems and one essay that Jyl wrote that was published when she was eighteen. Jan has had books published, and she also authored a syndicated column answering questions about computers in the mid-eighties. Jackie had a letter published just a few years ago in *Brill's Content,* a nationally known magazine at that time. Jackie has her own laptop computer and a copier at Florida State Hospital. She writes incessantly. As already stated, she writes to you in a later chapter.

Redington Beach is wide with beautiful, well-packed white sand. It is a favored place to walk, for both local people and tourists. For days after the murder, it was more heavily traveled than usual. People actually stopped and stared toward the house. People actually halted to point fingers and have discussions in full view of whoever might be watching from inside the house. The curious walkers were amazingly thoughtless.

The main thoroughfare for the beaches, Gulf Boulevard, is on the east boundary of the property. Some cars came slowly by with peering passengers. Some almost stopped to see where the newsworthy murder had taken place. Privacy became a sought-after but difficult-to-find relief.

Writing this book has necessarily brought forth many memory reels of scenes long repressed. It is not easy to go through them, to pick over the contents, to live again the horror and fear. This book is written for neither fame nor fortune. After the murder, and during Jack's political skirmishes with some county officials, I experienced what it is to be the object of public attention for whatever reason, whether pity, blame, disbelief, or even misguided sympathy. Whatever feeling or judgment is out there, one somehow becomes public property to be whispered about, pointed at, spoken to inappropriately. It was difficult. After handing service people credit cards, to see those people walk away to speak softly to someone who turned to stare was not pleasant. Relatively speaking, fame has been minimal for me, but I have had all I wish for the rest of my life. This does not diminish my desire to have this book published. I want it to be read by a large audience. I cannot hesitate to share beliefs that have evolved from lessons taught from welcome and unwelcome events in my life. By sharing, I hope to relay interesting, helpful information and educational ideas that will provoke responsive, objective emotions.

No matter what my loss of privacy may cost, it will be welcomed if this book finds readers who try to understand the tenacious grip of mental illness. My words are meant to challenge improper attitudes about severely mentally ill people, and to foster changes in the way that callous bureaucracies deal with people. The greatest reward for having bared my soul will be if systems of care for severely mentally ill people are impacted and transformed.

Understanding can happen. Reforms can be economically put in place to provide monitored treatment for severely mentally ill people. But first the greed and political goals of many politicians will have to mellow and blend with sincere concern for constituents. The priority concern by many politicians for campaign fund raising and personal power cannot be considered as compassion for constituents.

A reporter from the St. Petersburg Times called one morning and asked if she could come out to the house. She said she wanted to apologize to Jack for the remark made about his being fired in the first St. Petersburg Times article written about Jyl's murder. I asked Jack if he minded. Shrugging his shoulders as he grimaced, he said, "Why not? The paper has never before been unkind. Why not?" When the reporter arrived, I did not go into the living room with her to where Jack was sitting. She stayed only moments and came out visibly shaken. I never asked and never knew what they said to one another. Jack had an unusual ability to speak pithily, so I expect she got the best of that talent with chastisement and forgiveness delivered in a single sentence.

Nancy was doing some tidying up around the apartment when the reporter sat down uninvited on the glassed in porch to talk with me. I noticed that she watched Nancy closely. For the first time since 1966, and until 1969, when arrhythmia had caused my heart to flutter during the early days of Jackie's illness and during the first rumblings of the unsavory political atmosphere around Jack, I felt my heart beating irregularly. I did not want the reporter to ask about Jackie, and she did not. I managed to partake in a rambling conversation fashioned to distract her from speaking to Nancy. I was feeling frantically anxious because I did not want the reporter to ask where Jackie was. I rattled on in spite of my fear and weariness until the woman left.

She apparently believed Nancy to be Jackie because she referred to Nancy as Jackie in an article she treacherously wrote when she returned to her office. Never would we have given anyone an interview opportunity under the umbrella of our tragedy. The next morning the paper renewed its tabloid trend with an article, which included my aimless, troubled conversation provided to the reporter under duress. For a second time, we felt media chill from a newspaper we had always found friendly toward Jack during his ludicrous political skirmishes.

Experience with the young, ambitious St. Petersburg Times reporter taught me a lesson that I always remember when I lobby. Whenever speaking with someone from the media, for protection, I ask, "Is this conversation off the record?" Then I wait for an eyeball-to-eyeball reply. I learned in that unfortunate situation that reporters consider all remarks fair game unless confidentiality has been established. Any representative from the media who responds negatively to such a request needs to be credited with honesty and most likely future trust. Any representative from the media responding with "yes," who respects the commitment can be a friend. A "yes" not honored sounds alarms for future avoidance. I run for safety from such unprofessional reporters.

There were other articles in the paper with large black headlines. The public read titles like: Obenschain's Daughter Slain, Obenschain Death: Police Tight Lipped, 'Life Goes On' for the Obenschains, No Warrants Yet in Murder Case, Psychiatric Tests Ordered in Obenschain Death Case, Sister Charged in Obenschain Murder Case, Girl Pleads Innocent to Sister's Murder, Jacquelyn Obenschain Competent, Incompetent. Finally on May 19, 1974: Insanity Ruled in Obenschain Murder Case. Those blistering public titles wounded us deeply, but we understood the newsworthiness of reporting crimes.

It was extremely cold on December 22. The funeral director's chairs beside the gravesite seemed as hard and cold as stone. It was a bleak day. The gaping hole in the ground beside fake grass over a symbolic dirt mound accentuated the day's bleakness. Lacy Harwell, friend of the family and our Presbyterian minister, as well as counselor for Jyl, must have said comforting things, but I cannot remember them. Sitting there by Jyl's casket and hearing Lacy's voice just kept reminding me how much Lacy had tried to help Jyl when she was depressed. While she lived, he made her life more endurable. Now she was dead, and everyone there had come to hear Lacy say good-bye to Jyl.

When Lacy finished the service, he stepped over to where Jack and I sat to press our clasped hands. That said more than spoken words. Since it was a private funeral, no reporters lurked nearby. We were granted privacy. We had prevailed that no public announcements be made about the funeral before or after its occurrence. We did not stay to see the complete descent of the casket into the ground. The murder was still too fresh a memory for us to be able to witness one more wrenching farewell.

With the crime unsolved, the funeral was rife with an exceptional conflict of emotions. There could be no celebration of life triumphantly ended; instead there remained a raw hole. Grief seemed exaggerated. A life was ended, not yet complete. There were no more than fifteen people at the funeral. We never considered bringing Jackie to the funeral, and there was no indication from her that she wished to attend. We went home afterward without opening our home to welcome our weary friends. Everyone needed repose, quiet, and relief from the stressful days we had somehow survived.

When we went to the hospital to see Jackie, she was always glad to see us. Conversation was not stilted. We always came away in bewildered wonderment that she seemed so unemotional about Jyl's death. Once when Jan and I left the hospital after Jackie had been charged with murder, Jan said to me, "Mother, I can't believe you go into that room and don't make certain that you sit between Jackie and a door for exit." It still seemed impossible for me to be suspicious or afraid of my own child.

Christmas 1973 holidays, with red and green colors swirling everywhere for the festivities that other people were enjoying, contrasted sharply with our days of angst-ridden struggles with suspicions. Could it be that one child was dead because of another child's madness? Again and again we went over and over names of Jyl's friends who might have visited the house that day. I think that all the time that we were speculating, we all silently feared that the police would not find a suspect other than Jackie.

I have trouble recalling anything about Christmas Day. There are spotty or blank places and, perhaps, some erroneous images on my reels from that heinous holiday season. Jyl's shirt, first seen when I entered the house and found her, still looks tie-dyed, not blood-soaked.

On Christmas Day we brought wrapped presents from under the gaily-decorated tree in the house over to the apartment. Jyl had wrapped some presents. Jackie had wrapped some presents. They had done some of the wrapping working side by side at the dining table that Jyl had circled in her unsuccessful effort to run away from Jackie. There were presents there from Jackie to Jyl and from Jyl to Jackie. I remember only two presents. One was the crass walking hand that Jack put down on the floor when he got home the night of the murder. The other was a small vanity mirror Jyl had chosen for me.

On December twenty-eighth Mother and I went to meet Jan's in-laws in Tampa for lunch. Charlie, Ed's father, had experience in law enforcement. We were meeting with him and his wife to ask him to try to decipher for us what was going on behind the scenes in the investigation of Jyl's death. Unexpectedly I was called to the phone in the midst of some speculative discussion when lunch was only half finished.

Jan said, "The State Attorney's office just called to tell us that Jackie is being charged with murder." Jan was again on the front line, facing the harsh realities of her sister's death. One sister was being accused of murdering another sister. Suspicions we had all kept from expressing had been replaced by factual, harsh realities. Harsh realities had become daily intruders into our lives. These new harsh realities were more difficult than those experienced before the murder when we had tried to live normally, with mental illnesses permeating every corner of our home and every fiber of our beings. These new harsh realities cast our past challenges as memories of better days. Only now have I wondered what they said to Jan when they called. At the time no one wanted to discuss details. They were too painfully cruel.

When Jan told me on the phone that Jackie was being charged for Jyl's murder, I numbly responded to the best of my recollection by telling her that we would be home as soon as possible. One does not scream in the middle of a restaurant for any reason if born and bred to be a lady as my mother, a genuine lady, tried to teach me to be. Reasons for the Tampa trip became null and void. Before we quickly left the restaurant, we asked, "What can we expect now?" Charlie gave us a fast-forward rundown that lessened shocks later on.

Mother and I drove back over the Howard Franklin causeway to Pinellas County in silent mourning. She, a gentle refined person, was still having trouble just as I was accepting that these two young women that we loved so much had come to such fateful endings of lives that had once held such wonderful promises. Her grandchildren, my children, had come to be involved with things that happened only to strangers about whom one reads in newspapers or about whom one hears on the evening news with horror, sorrow, even revulsion.

And so we drove home, numb to that beautiful ride from Hillsborough County to the peninsular Pinellas County. All the way we were surrounded by blue waters on both sides of a highway that had somehow been dredged up from the bottoms of the surrounding bodies of water. During that ride I almost broke into tears. As I listened to the wheels of the car taking us back to the scene of the crime, I recalled the trip crossing the bay when I had taken Jackie for her first hospitalization in Tampa on the night of May 9, 1966. That night I had ridden with hope in my heart. This day I rode knowing that hope had to be cruelly abandoned. Now Jackie was in another hospital, charged with murder, and I was riding along with her broken-hearted grand-mother by my side.

Jackie's arrest charged her with second-degree murder punishable by up to thirty years in prison. Second-degree murder is defined as "the killing of a human being by doing an act imminently dangerous to others, evincing a wanton and depraved mind." The sheriff then publicly confirmed that no evidence had found indicating that the slayer had broken into the family's home. He also indicated that the suspected weapon was a large knife, which he described as "a butcher knife."

After Jackie was booked in Pinellas County Jail in Clearwater, Jack and I bailed her out on the condition that she would be returned to Bayfront Medical Center in Saint Petersburg. We had been notified that the booking was to take place, and we made arrangements for bail before going to Clearwater.

After the booking, Jackie begged us to take her back to the hospital in our car. We were totally nonplused when an officer encouraged and insisted on this. He said it was permissible. It had been very hard for Jack and me to come to the courthouse to hear the charges read. I was feeling very concerned about the stress that it had caused for both of us, particularly Jack. Neither of us felt emotionally up to taking Jackie back to the hospital. Once again we felt that her mental condition might be such that we might have real difficulty with her in the car. She had attempted suicide twice when provocation was much less than she had now. What if she should attempt to jump out of the car?

I exchanged some rather curt words with the officer, making it clear that we would not take Jackie to the hospital. When we made it clear that we would gladly pay ambulance charges for her transportation to the hospital, he relaxed, and an ambulance was called. The officer had made our decision to not give Jackie a ride back to the hospital seem hard-hearted and cold to everyone standing around. He displayed his own indifference to our obvious discomfort, apparently because he did not wish the sheriff's department to pay an ambulance fee.

Sam went with us to the booking. Nancy stayed at the apartment with Mother. I had brought Mother there so she would not be alone when the evening TV news reported the booking. Nancy later told me that Mother broke down when the news talked about Jackie murdering Jyl. Mother never broke down in my presence after December eighteenth when I told her Jyl had been murdered. Sam has since told me that she told him that she felt she had to remain composed for my sake. I am glad she was able to keep from weeping when I was around because it would have been very difficult for me to see her visibly shaken. Seeing Jack cry had almost flipped me into the bottomless pit of the screaming grief I felt.

There are those who advocate strong physical reactions and loud proclamations to relieve the pressure that grieving places upon a person. I do not happen to find that avenue of expression suitable for me. I thought, as I paced the floor the night of Jyl's murder, what such reactions would mean to the rest of the family who were trying to sleep and trying to be brave. I had to keep myself as calm as possible. I think letting go and letting down the bars of composure does not help one in management of urgent things that become so important when grievous situations are at hand. Everyone is different chemically, biologically, intellectually, emotionally, and in any other way that might come to mind. What reactions serve me best in times of crises may not necessarily serve others well. I understand that I may seem "cold" to others sometimes. I suggest that outer surfaces may never, in any case with anyone, actually or truly represent inner turmoil or true feelings. All I can do is to be true to my own self. I happen not to believe that obvious presentations of emotions always reflect sincere emotions felt by individuals reacting to circumstances to the best of their ability.

To digress while speaking of emotional expressions, I wonder how many readers remember the discovery of strange-looking little puffs of soft stuff with feelers on their heads and big eyes made to represent warm fuzzy and cold prickly feelings. I laughed out loud when I first saw them. That adults needed or that children were being taught that these silly little items could be used to convey their feelings upset me as I realized that some degree of genuine self-expression was being sacrificed. I teased some of my friends who were enthusiastically embracing and giving out these pesky little freaky things by asking if they were meant to be sexual. I still have a few of them that were foisted on me in the mid-nineteen-eighties when they were found sticking around everywhere one turned. I've kept them as humorous reminders of the incongruities that can be devised to save face when the ability is lacking to articulate feelings, or the person wishes to avoid taking the time to do something really meaningful for the recipient of a warm fuzzy or a cold prickly. Sick humor, perhaps, but a warm fuzzy or a cold prickly still makes me wryly smile when I come across one, saved for posterity, on one of my desks.

Sam and Nancy made our behavior more calm and collected than might have been possible had we not had them there during the events that happened during those first days after the murder. That is when we felt our deepest agonies as we tried to adjust with revulsion to what had happened to Jyl.

Sam and Nancy helped to lessen the pain of looking beyond the truth-defying event to a whole new prospective future for those Jyl left behind. Their presence was as comforting s it was stabilizing. Jack and I did not need to be alone with our misery. Distraction was important to help us maintain our composure and to provide a better sense of realism. Sam and Nancy's mature demeanor during the entire time belied their respective ages of less than thirty years. Mother and Jan were at their own homes much of the time. We were glad that they were not there with us in the middle of all of the depressing activities that had to be taken care of there.

The morning after the booking there was a large picture of Jackie being wheeled away from the jail. It was front-page news. There was a long, detailed article accompanying the ghastly picture, showing a young woman stretched out on a gurney. There, in misery, was a young woman who would become a felon if found guilty. She could have been taken out of the building from another entrance, but there she was stretched out on the gurney, staring fearfully upward as she left the place where she had been booked. Jackie, the oldest of our beloved daughters, who might possibly live out the rest of her life as a felon, did not seem to elicit concern for her privacy or dignity. I wondered what it would have been like for her had we not been there. An officer did kindly say to us, "There are many reporters out there waiting for you. Come with me through a private entrance." He led the way out, and he walked with us to the car so the reporters would be unable to question us. Once again I wondered. I wondered what it would have been like had Jack not formerly been one of the county's top officials.

The 1974 New Year holiday approached. Jan, Nancy, and I had to remember that we were schoolteachers. Sam also needed to get back to work in his law office. Schools would be opening soon. Nancy and Sam went back to Atlanta. Jan went back to Babson Park. Jack went back to Brooksville on January second. I was alone in the apartment.

I went back to the classroom and an environment apart from tragedy. Before going, I called the school principal to tell him that it occurred to me that parents of children I taught, due to lack of understanding of mental illness, might think I came to school from a home dominated by violence. Perhaps, I told him, I should resign. If I thought some teacher lived and sanctioned violence at home or anywhere else, I would not want that teacher in a position to influence attitudes of my child. He was quick to tell me that if any parents were ignorant enough to believe that to be true and complained, he could easily calm their false fears. It was touching and reassuring later in the day when a call came from the county school board office to tell me how much they wanted and needed me in the classroom.

My aversion to violence in any form anywhere made Jyl's murder even more incomprehensible. How could such violence have erupted in our house? Madness had destroyed dreams and hopes at our house. When I was a teenager, I usually found other things to do on Saturday afternoons when friends went to cowboy movies and stuffed away popcorn for a couple of hours. The father of one of my best friends owned the theater, so I sometimes had to go for the preservation of our friendship. I would sit there hating the wild shotgun confrontations in dusty, dirty towns preceded by, or followed by, grown men chasing one another on horseback like a bunch of unruly kids. All of that was make believe.

Recognizing real violence in my own family was difficult; it was impossible to completely fathom. It was sometimes necessary to repeat the mantra; this is real, this is real, this is real.

There were about ninety teachers on the Dixie Hollins High School faculty, and though it was not spoken, I felt their support for me like unseen vapor whenever I was with them. I knew that few of them, if any, understood the circumstances of the murder, and I never discussed it with them. One teacher did happen to come into the ladies restroom when I was there. No one else was in the room, and she said in her discomfiture, "Maxene, my daughter has told me that she has been angry enough with her sister sometimes to kill her. I understand." It was better that she said something than nothing. Her remark clearly illustrated what I already knew. No one really understood. I smiled and replied, "Jackie was not angry with Jyl. Jackie is mentally ill. We think if she is guilty that she would have killed whoever happened to be there. Jyl happened to be there." I smiled again and left the room. I think similar scenes will occur as long as I live. It is not wise to express understanding of a situation when one is not intimately involved. It is not possible for an "outsider" to understand.

Over and over again during the years since Jyl's murder, I have had to say, when asked what my children do, where my children live, or how many children do I have, "I have two children. One lives in Pinellas County; the other is a ward of the state and lives in Chattahoochee because she killed her sister in 1973." Usually, in shocked tones, the questioner says something like, "Oh I am so sorry. Why did your daughter kill her sister?" When I reply, "Jackie is mentally ill," almost without exception, I am then asked, "But what reason did she have for killing her sister?" I usually say again, "Jackie is mentally ill." The look in the eyes of the questioner often makes it obvious that I still have not given a satisfactory answer. Then I change the subject. Defining mental illness is not fitting nor is it welcomed in social settings. In fact there simply seems to be little caring or interest in the plight of mentally ill individuals. Sometimes if one is lucky, the "kids" questions stop after, "How many children do you have?" and I say, "two," and then I ask to hear about the questioner's offspring. Sometimes when listening to idle conversations of others, I find that people simply are not willing to let go of finding culprits punishable by prison or execution for every crime committed, irrespective of the perpetrator's mental health.

I am not ashamed of mental illness within my family. I am always dismayed to find family members who deny the existence of those family members unfortunate enough to be mentally ill. Parents in this kind of denial increase the difficulty of educating the public about mental illness. During the eighties, when I first started speaking publicly to groups about mental illness, I would lean forward and say quietly, looking like I was about to whisper a secret into their ears, "Guess what? I am going to come out of the closet. The gays have left, and it is lonely in here." After laughter subsided, I would add, "I have had two mentally ill daughters, and I am going to talk about them and their illness."

According to the paper there was a brief arraignment before a circuit judge in Saint Petersburg on January 18, 1974, one month from the date of Jyl's murder. We were not notified. The paper explained that "After the arraignment, escorted by sheriff's deputies, Jackie, was returned quickly to Bayfront Medical Center where she had been a patient since the night her sister, Jyl, 24, was found stabbed to death in the dining room of the family home on Gulf Boulevard." Jackie pleaded innocent. No trial date was set. Felony hearings were usually held in Clearwater, but the hearing was apparently transferred to Saint Petersburg since Jackie was hospitalized there.

After the arraignment I took the papers I had found in Jackie's bank box to the judge assigned to her case. We never knew his feelings about the papers, but we knew they were a testament to her madness. We wanted the judge to be as knowledgeable as possible because we could not imagine anything other than acceptance of an insanity plea. We wanted to do everything possible to prevent her from being imprisoned in an environment much worse than a mental institution. In a mental institution there would be treatment and understanding, which we knew were sorely lacking within the prison system.

In 1973, the horror of jails and prisons being used as replacements for mental health hospitals had not happened.

Jackie's demeanor did not change after she was charged and arraigned. There was still no comment about Jyl's death, no mention of sorrow that Jyl was dead. Her attorney was having problems. She was not cooperative. Jack and I discussed what to do. We discussed what to do with her doctor. Jail seemed to be the only answer. Something had to happen to try to create a sense of reality for her. We reluctantly decided to request that she be sent from the hospital to the jail.

After arrangements were made, I telephoned the sheriff to tell him that she was being sent to his jail. He was surprised and said, "Oh no." I explained the reasons for transfer to him and told him that Jack and I felt concerned for her welfare within the jail. He assured me that she would be well taken care of. When I put the phone down, I folded my arms on the desk and wearily put my head down on my arms, thinking how ludicrous it seemed to suggest protection for an alleged murderer. How? How could it be my daughter that I was talking about?

I had never been inside a jail. Jack said he simply could not go. I understood. I knew he was having more trouble than usual with his diabetes, and I did not want him to go. After Jack left for Brooksville around lunchtime on the first Sunday that Jackie was in jail, I went to see her. There was a locked entrance door. A line of people waited on the steps and on the sidewalk for admittance. I stood with much trepidation on the first step up from the sidewalk. A noisy young woman was standing two steps above me. Suddenly she wheeled around and flipped a switchblade so that its blade tip touched the center of my chest. She stood holding it in place leering down at me. I froze looking straight into her eyes and did not move one muscle. I knew I should not do anything to further aggravate whatever was upsetting her. Another girl who must have been with her and knew her name called down to her. To distract her she very quietly said, "Hey, look at this." When the knife owner turned to look, I quickly and quietly stepped down to the sidewalk and went swiftly to the back of the jail. All during this episode, there was total silence. No one screamed. No one moved. A scream or rapid movement might have been enough to startle a knife-thrust to my heart.

The irony of it was that a person coming to see someone alleged to have stabbed another to death found a stranger's knife prepared to stab on the jail-house steps. That unknown young girl did more than flip a switchblade. She could not have known the thoughts and terror in my heart as I connected with Jyl, who might have known much greater fear for a much longer time.

When I found an officer, I explained what had happened. I waited until he went through the jail and came from inside to arrest the girl. I wanted to be sure that she did not associate me with her arrest, so I gave him plenty of time to do his duty. Then I went back, took my place in line, and waited until the entrance door was unlocked, opened, and everyone was admitted.

Each person was examined to see whether they carried anything not permitted within the jail. After passing the checkpoint, I was sent through a door that rolled and clanged shut. The clanging closed door locked me inside. The clanging of the door was blood curdling. I had been through so many doors that were then locked behind me in mental facilities that I felt like leaving immediately to find a place to retch. I didn't leave. I stayed, I followed directions, and I sat down on an uncomfortable seat opposite Jackie, who was waiting dry eyed and solemn behind a thick glass window. There was a phone apparatus for her and one for me. We picked up the phones and talked about inanities for our allotted time, and then I left. I left Jackie there with her jail companions. When exiting through that clanging door, I felt as though I were escaping from hell. This place I was leaving represented imprisonment, whereas a mental hospital represented a place of caring, not punishment. I had managed to live through the visit without transmitting negative feelings to Jackie. She needed to see someone who cared about her; I knew I would have to return again and again. I too was serving a sentence.

That first visit was in January. I went back to visit on the remaining Sundays in January and every Sunday in February, March, April, as well as on the first three Sundays in May. The clanging door was always as nerve racking as the very first clanging at my first visit. The glass shield between Jackie and me became colder and colder. The visits became more and more difficult as the trial date of May twentieth came closer and closer. One thing was different from my first visit. There was always an officer present near the line of waiting visitors.

After a few of those Sunday visits, some young girls began to come near the window. I asked about them and, since they never had visitors, I talked to them. I discovered that they were there on minor charges involving drugs. I also discovered that some of them were runaways. When I learned that, I began asking them about letting me call their mothers to tell them where they were. Some gave me names and phone numbers. I called the parents of those who decided to let me get in touch with their families. It was wonderful to bring relief to parents who did not know where their young daughters were. Even jail is better than not knowing. I wondered whether anyone from any church or any organization in the community ever came to see these young jail inmates. A matron was put on duty in Jackie's area, and Jackie talked about how kind she was. Her presence was extremely comforting to Jack and to me. Once when I visited, Jackie told me that she and her cellmates could hear others being molested during the night, but in her area there was no activity like that.

On the last Thursday before the Monday when Jackie's trial was to begin, we received word that Jackie's fate was going to be determined in the judge's chambers. On Friday we were present to hear the judge declare Jackie, "Not guilty by reason of insanity." After she heard the verdict and was taken from the room, the judge told us that she would never go to trial. It was such a relief to know that I would never be questioned publicly on a witness stand about our family and Jyl's murder. But now I find myself seeking public attention to our tragedy for reasons that I must honor for the sake of my own integrity. Now I know how rare it is that others as ill as Jackie find justice in the courts. She received appropriate justice, justice that should be there for all severely mentally ill defendants. It was fortunate for Jackie that a wise judge handled her case.

Justice can prevail for all severely mentally ill defendants. How? Another book. Another day. This book suggests challenges begging solutions. If this book is thought provoking enough to motivate more voters to insist on being better informed so that politicians can be influenced to bring about the needed reforms and changes, Jyl's death will not have been in vain. Jyl believed in activism. So do I. So must voters.

We were spared the ordeal of seeing Jackie sent to a mental facility to be drugged into a condition for court room appearance in order to find her competent to stand trial, and then likely sentenced to prison or death. We were not going to see on trial a different person in the courtroom, a person drugged into temporary competency, a person different from the one who chased Jyl with an insane killer mentality. For months we had dreaded my turn on the stand to testify about a crime in which our child of ill fate could not honestly be held accountable.

We doubted that a jury could be found, when reacting within a punitive courtroom, to demonstrate the integrity of courageous wisdom, as it should be for cases like Jackie's. We knew there were no laws to adequately protect the severely mentally ill perpetrator or the public from expensive, erroneous, and poorly conceived judgments. Our relief that there would be no trial knew no bounds.

From December 28, 1973, until May 17, 1974, I lived each day silently dreading May 20, 1974, when the trial had been scheduled to take place. Now no farcical trial would be held. No more newspaper stories were going to be written about a murder by those who did not understand anything about an insane motive to kill. No reporter, no prosecutor, no defending attorney, no judge was going to have moments in the limelight that would push readers farther into ignorance shelters where severe mental illness is not understood.

Now I know how rare it is that others as ill as Jackie find justice in the courts. She received appropriate justice, justice that should be there for all severely mentally ill defendants. It was fortunate for Jackie that a wise judge handled her case. We were spared a flaunting of the McNaughton Rule

I have discussed the McNaughton Rule with Larry Pedley, an attorney friend. He offers the opinion that the McNaughton Rule is a carryover from the dark ages and is still here because the courts, doctors, and the public have not been able to reach consensus on anything else. He added that anything to do with the brain and/or mental illness scares the hell out of Joe Average Guy."

The criterion of the McNaughton Rule is whether or not an individual knows right from wrong when a crime is committed. The McNaughton Rule has no relevance to crimes committed by severely mentally ill individuals. Demons of madness allow no practical application for this archaic rule. As long as the McNaughton Rule exists credence will be given by attorneys and judges to an anachronism formulated from ignorance.

Jackie knew right from wrong. She preconceived the murder according to her delusions. She was the perfect victim for a prosecuting attorney victory. Jackie, in trial, could have put a victory feather in a prosecutor's cap. No one would notice that the feather came at the cost of truth and decency. You read every week of such victories by conscienceless prosecutors. You read every week of sentencing by conscienceless judges. If you read, listen to the radio, or watch television, you can probably find a feather award every day.

On Sunday, after we had appeared in the judge's chambers on Friday, I went to the jail as usual to visit Jackie. When the entrance doors were unlocked, and visitors were admitted, the dreadful clanging doors rolled open. After I was checked to see whether I was trying to bring anything disallowed when visiting with a prisoner, the attendant asked me, as usual, whom I wished to see. I said, "Jackie Obenschain." The attendant said, "She is no longer here." I was dumbfounded. "Where is she?" I asked, and I heard, "I do not know, and I could not tell you if I did know. You will have to call the office tomorrow, and they may tell you." Of course I left.

I drove home in a stultified daze. I could not believe that a person would be moved away with no notice given to the family. I had not yet begun to understand that Jackie, now a ward of the state, was totally under the supervision and guardianship of the state of Florida. I had not fully comprehended exactly what that meant. The silver cord had been severed with a vengeance.

As soon as the sheriff's office opened the next morning, I called for information. I learned that Jackie was now a resident of the forensic ward at Florida State Hospital in Chattahoochee. I was told that she would have limited permission to use a telephone and that we should expect to hear from her.

I did call the hospital for assurance that she was there and to ask whether she was responding to a medication plan. I spoke to someone who very kindly reassured me that all was going as well as could be expected under the circumstances. There was nothing to do but wait until she called. When she did call some weeks later, she immediately asked when we could come to see her. She asked that Jack, Jan, and I please come without Ed because she wanted to talk with us alone.

When we went to see her, she was extremely glad to see us and very pleased that we were there. She was obviously being medicated, and she seemed calm and in control of her emotions. Without any kind of dramatic behavior, she told us that she wanted to tell us what had happened to Jyl. She began by telling us that she had stabbed Jyl. She did not say that she had killed Jyl. She abruptly continued by saying that when she stabbed Jyl in the abdomen, Jyl did not scream, but turned and grabbed her by the hair to try and pull or shove her away. "But," Jackie said, "Jyl almost immediately turned loose of my hair and said, "I'm sorry." Jan said, "That was Jyl."

I, at long last, involuntarily screamed. I envisioned the scene as clearly as if the action were happening in front of us there in that hospital visiting room. For a moment I believed that I was going to lose consciousness. This was more than seemed humanly possible to bear. It was so horrifying to think of Jyl being stabbed. That she apologized for pulling the hair of someone trying to kill her was soul searing. As Jack had said the night of Jyl's murder, "Jyl never did anything to hurt anyone." To the end of her life that was true.

As soon as the exclamation of dismay left my body, Jackie calmly got up out of her chair, came across the room, put her arms around me, and said, "Please don't be upset. Jyl is not dead." Someone, I think it was Jack, said, "Jackie, we have buried Jyl." Jackie replied, "I don't know where Jyl is, but she is not dead." Nothing we said or did made any difference in Jackie's firm contention that Jyl was not really dead.

She expressed no remorse for Jyl or for our misery. She insisted that Jyl was not dead. This assertion has continued through all of the years since Jyl's death. Today she speaks of killing Jyl. Then in the next sentence, she may insist that Jyl is not dead. Today she laments what she did to the family. She blames "them" for everything. "They made me do it" has been drilled into my ears until I hear it without Jackie being anywhere nearby or on the phone.

The general public needs to understand, as I do that "they" are out there on the streets, in the marketplace, and in other places we visit everyday. "They" are alive and unwell in the brains of many homeless, untreated, severely mentally ill individuals. I agree with Jackie that "they" caused Jyl's death. I have never, for one moment, considered Jackie accountable for Jyl's death.

I know you, the reader, must be thinking that none of this is making any sense. You are correct, and I agree with you. However, what we think about it has no reference or meaning for Jackie or for most other severely mentally ill people. She does not own her mind. Homeless, untreated, severely mentally ill people do not own their minds. Human brains are sometimes possessed by demons.

The psychiatrist who had been seeing Jackie before "her crime," as she speaks of it, told me after she was charged that he did not think that she could ever be mentally healthy because the horror of what she, as a decent person, had done would be more than she, as a sane person, could endure.

Jack, Jan, and I finally told her good-bye and drove back to Redington Beach with renewed grief in our hearts. It was a long trip home. It has been more than thirty years since her "my crime," as she refers to it, but it will always seem like yesterday to me. There is no closure for such heinous happenings.

In chapter six, when Jackie explains her illness, she speaks from her perceptions. When she talks about those perceptions and about killing Jyl, you may join me in my bewilderment and sorrow that my highly intelligent daughter is so ill. If you feel empathy, you may then begin to feel that you want a safer world for yourself as well as for the homeless victims of untreated, severe mental illness, especially for those who have been turned away from hospitals or other safe havens and who have no alternative to homelessness.

Safety is essential for the well being of everyone. Please hear the keyword, *safety*. If you listen clearly and without prejudice, when you read or hear about events relevant to possessed mentalities, those events will serve as reminders to warn you of your own perils. Those events will serve to remind you that, if safety is provided, lives will be saved.

Fortunately, before and since Jyl's murder, there have been more pleasant, compensating experiences than traumatic times. I carefully file away all happy rejuvenating reels too. My memory reel reflections serve many purposes, including grief relief.

Jackie Writes

Part One

I am mentally ill. I am a paranoid schizophrenic. Paranoid schizophrenics that I have known in the thirty-eight years that I have been "crazy" do not believe themselves to be mentally ill. They believe their beliefs are true and that their psychiatrists are persecuting them.

I believe the government is persecuting me and that I am a hypnotized slave. I believe the *program* or the government agency in charge of the hypnotized slaves wants me to cooperate with them and help them psychologically torture people. I refuse to cooperate with them, and they have persecuted me for nearly forty years by threatening me with fire, car accidents, heartburn, migraine headaches, being framed for a crime, rape, pain, paralysis, and any other torture that they think will make me be cooperative.

I refuse to cooperate. My mother and father, some fifty years ago, agreed to cooperate with the *program* after the *program* and Americans tortured them by killing my brother as an infant. My mom and dad probably fought them too until the government, so called, killed their infant son by saying he died at birth. He didn't die. He is somewhere living in America and is probably cooperating with the *program* because the *program* tortured him until he agreed to cooperate.

My mother and father tortured me all my life with criticism and refusing to talk to me and confide in me. I can't remember what all they did. You see, they have destroyed my memory with psychotropic drugs, and now I can hardly remember my past. But I fight on. I refuse to torture people with psychological torture like the government wants me to do. I have figured out that they want me to kill my mom. I love my mom, and there is no way that I am going to hurt her.

I feel I have MPD, which is a Multiple Personality Disorder. My other personalities come out and steal from me, delete what I write on my computer, and harass me. I don't *truly* believe I have MPD. I believe the government is giving me a hypnotic suggestion to do all these things, and I feel they would have the so-called other personalities come out and kill my mom. That is not going to happen.

I am going to stay safe and secure in this mental institution where I have been since I killed my sister twenty-nine years ago. The *program* tortured me with TV, radio, conversations, song lyrics, noises, signs, colors, gestures, and anything else you can imagine answering my thoughts and feelings.

I guess you don't understand exactly what went on, and I can't tell you. I feel that evil doctors have deliberately destroyed my memory with drugs so that I would not be able to defend myself. I am alone. Nearly everyone is cooperating with the government and torturing me. But I am brave, and I have fought them for thirty-nine years.

I am known all over the world for my brave fight against the government that I feel tortures its hypnotized slaves with no mercy or compassion. The government is evil. I believe in love, sympathy, and decency and I will refuse to cooperate with them and will refuse to torture my mom, sister, other mental patients, or any other people. I feel that you already know this because you defend America's torture slave democracy by saying that the government we now have gives so many advantages to Americans.

I don't want to write all of this down because it is so difficult. My memory and thinking ability have been destroyed by Mellaril, Navanne, Stellacine, Thorazine, Olanzapine, Respiradal, and all the other drugs that have caused me to lose my memory.

I read the other day that Wuanano, who killed men with whom she had sex while being a prostitute, was tortured to death. Hours before she was executed, she abruptly left a reporter—in all probability he was torturing her psychologically. I don't know why I am writing this. You have probably tortured people psychologically and then lied and said your victim was mentally ill. Wuanano turned to religion for support and tried to defend herself before they injected drugs into her. She was trying to ease her suffering by accusing the witnesses who watched her die. She admitted that she killed her victims in order to help her friend who was tortured by the police. To get Wuanano to confess, the police cleverly used this friend to get information.

I just heard laughter outside my door. People are always showing disdain for me, and they have for my entire life. I don't even want to write anymore because you already know what I have been through, and you don't care one bit. You have rejected, disdained, been indifferent, criticized, ridiculed, gossiped about, tortured, and sadistically enjoyed my suffering all of my life. You tortured the black slaves, and now you are torturing hypnotized slaves. You had no sympathy for the blacks, and now white people have no sympathy for the hypnotized slaves. I am all alone.

But, you know something? I am not all alone. I have myself as a friend who has loved me all my life and now never rejects me. I used to reject myself. After you rejected and treated me with disdain, I criticized myself and thought that I must be inferior with an inferior personality, deserving of constant criticism and torture. Now I love myself. I realize now that I was given drugs to make me unable to think of anything to say, which caused me to be unable to think complexly and logically. You tortured me and criticized me instead of yourselves. Now I criticize you for being evil people. You have been evil toward me all of my life.

I know you are saying, "She's whining. She deserves what she got. You don't kill your own sister. She deserves what she got. Anyone that would kill her sister deserves to suffer." You tortured me for nine years and then stood back and let me kill my sister. You murdered my sister. If you hadn't tortured me, I *never* would have killed Jyl. You know what happened.

This book is unnecessary. You are all ready to treat me like you treated Wuanano. You are just as evil as she was portrayed. She killed people like you because you abused her all of her life. She let her emotions get out of control, and she defensively did what gave her pleasant emotions. She was just trying to be happy and, by getting revenge, she made her emotions feel pleasant. Her emotions caused her to kill. After you tortured me for nine years, my emotions got out of control, and I went berserk and killed my sister.

I know. I know. (More laughter outside my doorway.) You think there is no justification for what I did. I don't think there is any justification for what you did to me.

I am going to stay in a mental institution the rest of my life because I don't want to put up with your rejection, self-righteousness, indifference, criticism, and gossip. I know you know about me. I am all alone. But so are you. Didn't the twin towers teach you anything? Didn't WWI and WWII teach you anything? You tortured people and caused those two wars. Now you are facing terrorism because you insist on torturing people. The terrorists are my friends. They were protesting your brutal torture that you cold-bloodedly inflict on the slaves. When will you learn?

I don't know why I am even bothering to write this in my mom's book. You know what I think and believe because my thoughts go out all over the world. I am famous because I have fought for thirty-nine years against the government. I guess that reasoning will not change the minds of people who think driving a person to murder, degradation, and suicide is funny and interesting. Are you enjoying the torture? (Laughter outside my door again. Someone says, "Who are you talking to?")

I have peace and happiness. I know that I am going to be tortured physically. You are evil, and I know what you have done in the past. You crucified Jesus Christ. And then you burned at the stake anyone that said he wasn't the Son of God. You are very evil, and I am scared of you. I am going to stay inside of my safe, secure, and comfortable mental institution even though the aides and other mental patients torture me and cold-bloodedly feel disdain, snobbery, and self-righteousness towards me.

I have done everything I can do to stop the torture. But I can't touch the ridicule, criticism, ruthlessness, and scorn. You try to be superior by making other people suffer. You sadistically gloat over my suffering. What is wrong with you? I guess that the tabloid writers are going to read this book that my mom is writing and will torture me in the apparent world where I am mentally ill and the government isn't persecuting anyone. I am tired of this whole thing. I will continue to think and figure out how you, God, and I are motivated.

I know how I am motivated. But I don't know how you are motivated. I just don't understand why you crucified Jesus when he had done nothing wrong. And then you let a murderer go free and chose Jesus to be the one that was tortured to death. I don't understand you. I would have been a friend to Jesus and would have tried to convince him that people are motivated by trying to feel superior. Their evil is because they feel inferior. People can't help having emotions that are evil. Even though you rejected and ridiculed me all my life, I don't dislike anyone. People can't help the way they were created. They did not create their evil emotions.

Now I've got the Christians trying to torture me. I have to hide my religious beliefs because the Christians will be self-righteous about my beliefs. I would not put it past them to want to torture me to death for my Unitarian beliefs. I thought we had put bigotry in the past. But in all of the TV shows, the movies, and books, there is brainwashing of people to cause them to have negative emotions. Why do Americans just sit back and let the global rich get away with making their children into criminals? Why don't they protest and insist on a change in the literature and in the laws?

(Outside my door someone is singing, "Na-nana," disdainfully.) Now, someone says, "It is time to go out." That means that the *program* is saying to me that it is time for me to leave the mental institution. I am going nowhere. I will commit suicide if they make me go. I am not going to take the risk that the other "personalities" will come out and kill my mom. (Someone just said, "It is almost time for supper." That means that I shouldn't complain because I have food, and many people in the world are poor and suffer by starving to death. Therefore, since America is more prosperous due to its torture-type government, it is all right to torture its hypnotized slaves.)

The tabloids, I guess, are going to torture me. I don't want to be famous. The purpose of my life is to find out life's truths. I want to know how lives are motivated. (Outside my door someone is saying, "Wu-wu-wu!" with disdain in the voice. They are always trying to torture me.) Well, I guess I am going to be famous in my apparent world as well as in the *program* world when this book is published. I don't like fame. People are crazy to think fame makes them superior. Every single thing you say may wind up in the tabloids, and the tabloids will lie about you.

My mom wants me to write something for her book, and I love her, so I told her I would write about so-called mental illness for the book. I don't want to be famous in the apparent world. In the *program* world, I am fighting a brave struggle against the government and exposure of what its *program* is doing to me. Literature has been deliberately created to cause people to have negative emotions, be emotionally disturbed, and be unable to think. (Someone just clapped real loudly outside my door about what I just wrote.)

Even though I am bravely struggling to try to stop all of the torture, no one appreciates my struggle except my supporters and some charities. Some charities write me, praising me as a leader and saying such things as, "You get the connection. Bush doesn't." (Now there is loud, sadistic laughter outside my door.) They love torturing me, and I don't know why. I will know one day though. I am going to continue to think and analyze to figure out the laws that all emotions and thoughts obey. The type of people that crucified Christ are going to crucify me. Mom, I am tired of all this, and I am going to bed and listen to some soothing music. I love you, Mom, and I am sorry that you cooperated because you feared the cruelty of people around you.

Part Two

I am not going to cooperate with the *program*. When you have a courageous conscience, you have pleasant emotions. If you are a conscience coward, you will have unpleasant emotions. I want pleasant emotions, so I am going to continue to believe in love, sympathy, and decency, even though I do not feel those emotions. When you are tortured you have negative emotions such as indifference, sadism, conceit, snobbery, disdain, self-righteousness, and all the other negative emotions, which is the mind's way of making you feel superior as you battle your feelings of inferiority. People are evil because they feel inferior.

There are so many ways to feel inferior or superior. There is being *status superior*, which is being superior in ways the community respects, such as being intelligent, good looking, wealthy, knowing the right people, being educated, having a professional job, going to an Ivy League college, being in the upper class, dressing well, being thin, having talent, and having expensive possessions such as cars, pools, and mansions. All of these things are shown in positive ways.

The *welfare superior* is portrayed as having no considerable problems. *Social superiority* is portrayed as having many friends. *Moral superiority* traits are portrayed as being good and helping others. *Superior traits* presented are being mature, courageous, responsible, honest, and hardworking. *Emotional superiority* is illustrated as having pleasant emotions, being happy, and having inner peace. *Victim superiority* is shown as ability to accept unjust suffering. *Treatment superiority* is being treated with love, affection, sympathy, and other positive treatments.

Pos (meaning positive) *superiority* is treating people positively like Christ wanted us to treat one another. *Treneg* (meaning treating negatively) is treating people negatively to give yourself sadistic happiness. *Love superiority* is being loved. *Compassionate superiority* is treating others with compassion. *Ability superiority* is having ability in business, administration, and leadership, being talented, and having common sense. *Family superiority* is having a spouse and having children.

I am figuring out the psychological laws that all emotions and thoughts obey so I can know how to maintain pleasant emotions for myself. Yes, I am selfish. When you are ridiculed, rejected, and disdained all of your life, you are going to feel inferior and have negative emotions like selfishness, which helps you to feel superior. I just wish the literature I obsessively read to be superior (reading is considered to be *intellectually superior*) had been written in such a way that it taught me the psychological laws, how people are motivated, and how to relate to others with love.

Fiction ought to teach everyone how people think and feel, and clever ways to relate to people in such a way that they will be respected, loved, liked, and approved of. The literature that I read is what caused me to have negative emotions, feel inferior, and be ignorant of how people really think and feel. The literature caused me to be unable to think and analyze. It has taken me thirty-nine years to learn to think and analyze well. When I watch TV, it causes me to be unable to think for a whole half-hour after I come away from the television screen.

Well, Mom, I have done the best I can to write about myself. I can't do better because of the drugs that have largely destroyed my memory and ability to think. You insist that I take these drugs. I feel that you have no sympathy for the trouble that these drugs are causing me. I feel that you are cooperating with the government, who wants to destroy my mind so that I can't defend myself from cooperating with them. But I will never cooperate with them, despite all the psychological, mental, social, and chemical torture. I believe in love, and I will never cooperate in such a brutal and corrupt system.

Last night I finally figured out how you readers are motivated. You like to try to make people feel and be inferior. That makes you feel superior. Everyone is motivated the same way. Everyone wants to feel and be superior. I never deliberately, cruelly try to make someone feel inferior by ridiculing, rejecting, or insulting. I admit I ridiculed, rejected, insulted, and was cruel in the past. It was because I was trying to feel superior instead of trying to make other people feel and be inferior. I didn't realize until last night that you enjoy making other people feel inferior and be inferior because you sadistically enjoy that.

I never realized that Jyl was suffering. I brutally negged her. *Negged* means that from having negative thoughts and feelings toward someone, you treat them negatively because of those thoughts and feelings. I feel that both Jyl and I had been trenegged, which is different from being negged. *Trenegging* means to treat someone negatively because you want him or her to feel and be inferior so you can feel superior. I didn't want Jyl to feel inferior or be inferior, I just had negative feelings toward her and didn't realize that my negging would make her suffer and feel inferior. I never trenegged anyone, although I was constantly negging others with criticism, ridicule, scorn, and conceit for status inferiority; indifference, and sadism for welfare inferiority; and self-righteousness for moral inferiority. I call all of that *fineg*, which is neg for inferiority. I finegged everyone. People couldn't stand me because they could hear my thoughts and feelings. My finegging alienated everyone.

But it wasn't my fault that I finegged everyone. When you are negged all of your life, you are going to feel inferior. When you feel inferior, you will feel neg emotions. If you feel neg emotions, it means you are feeling inferior. Neg emotions are the mind's way of making you feel superior. Everyone wants to feel superior.

I used to read all of the time to escape my loneliness. Superior characters in fiction would fineg inferior characters, causing me to imitate their finegging of people if they were inferior. Superior characters would give friendliness and praise to the superior characters that were negging the inferior characters. The literature would fineg inferiority and pos superiority. *Pos* means to treat positively with friendliness, sympathy, liking, love, respect, praise, and understanding. I wanted to be superior, so I imitated the superior characters.

After reading this insidious literature as a child and teenager, I developed a neg personality. The *program* told everyone that I was evil because I negged everyone. What they didn't explain was that they had deliberately brainwashed me to have neg emotions and thoughts. They made my mom encourage me to read so that I would imitate the neg of superior characters.

I was also negged and trenegged by everyone. That caused me to feel inferior with neg emotions and thoughts. The *program* deliberately brainwashed, isolated, drugged, and trenegged me so that I would have a neg personality. They deliberately alienated everyone from me saying that I was evil and deserved to be trenegged because I was neg. It has taken years to figure out all of this. I realized a long time ago that I have to stay away from literature because I cannot help imitating the neg of characters.

The characters also suved me. *Suv* means to be superior to others. The characters would be compassionate, beautiful, loved and loving, respected, wealthy, educated, happy, intelligent, and helpful to others, and they never complained. They never felt inferior, never suffered emotionally, and never attempted suicide. If you have read a child's fairy tale, you can see what I mean. Fairy tales will make a child feel inferior because the characters suv the reader who then feels neg emotions.

I was trying to feel superior all of the time. I took piano lessons and read novels all the time because I wanted to be superior. I thought that if I were superior, I would be posed because in the literature characters were posed when they were superior and negged when they were inferior.

I never thought and analyzed because the literature I read caused me to be unable to do so. I have figured out that I should have been encouraged to study my own and other people's emotions and thoughts to find out how people are motivated. Literature does not teach how people are motivated. Literature has false motivation. It shows people being superior and being posed for the superiority. Not only did fiction cause me to feel inferior; it caused me to neg everyone. The first thing I would do when I met someone would be to look for his or her inferior traits so that I could neg the person to myself. That was all the fault of those stupid fairy tales and other literature. Live happily ever after. Ha! That idea suved me, and I thought my life was like the characters in the fairy tales, and I would live happily ever after.

I finally realized that literature was messing up my mind. After twenty years of staying away from literature, I am finally feeling normal emotions of sympathy and wishing to help others. It has taken years of thinking and analyzing to overcome the brutal effects of all the literature that I have read.

I watch Oprah Winfrey when they are talking about their thoughts and emotions in order to help figure out how people are motivated. Oprah and her guests are always trying to treneg and suv me. Another word I have made up is *caplun*. *Caplun* means truing to make a person feel unpleasant emotions. Oprah and her guests are always capluning me. But they cannot caplun me anymore because I have figured out the psychological laws. I just sit and watch them trying to caplun me while I am learning more about the program's strategy in capluning.

The other day Oprah and her guests were suving the hell out of me. First Oprah showed the smartest boy in the world. He status suved me by talking about all the doctorates he wants to get. Oprah said he graduated from college at the age of eleven. Then she said he had graduated magna cum laude. Next, he morally suved me by saying he wanted to help others and wanted to start a school in an African country to teach people how to live in peace.

Then Oprah showed other children who status suved me. There was a child who was a genius at painting pictures, who sold one for $25,000. Another child was a genius at playing the piano. There was a child who was a genius at figuring out how to invest in the stock market. They showed him teaching a class of students. Their status suved me. After all of the suving, a commercial came on showing a piece of steak being cooked on a grill with fire all over it. They were threatening me with setting me on fire. I don't get upset with all their capluning anymore. I just watch them deliberately suving me, and then after the suv, trenegging me. They are now following a pattern that I have, after twenty-nine years, figured out.

On an Oprah show they showed a wedding dress costing $7,000, expensive flowers, and expensive cakes. They showed the future bride saying that she had always wanted a beautiful wedding, and Oprah said that she was going to give her that beautiful wedding that she had always wanted so badly. The *program* was at work again. They wanted me to have a positive attitude about an expensive wedding. They thought they could brainwash me into having an expensive wedding after I pretend to die and go to live somewhere in America. They said they were going to give me a husband that I would love and that he would love me. My last name means beautiful evening, which means that I will have a beautiful life at the end of my life. They want me to have an expensive wedding because they know it will alienate the poor all over the world.

I don't know why Oprah's program, shown in countries all over the world, including where people are poor and suffering from their poverty, would boast about a dress that costs over $7,000. Oprah's program alienates foreigners from America by boasting and bragging about our country's wealth, but the programming is smart to counteract that by showing Americans helping others and working to create peace.

I get mail all of the time from charities who are trying to help the starving, the refugees, the handicapped, and the people at war. They tell about all the different kinds of suffering and all the different ways that they are trying to help others. I am known all over the world, so I read all of my mail from the charities to try to give them the publicity they need so that people will send them money. I finally figured out that the *program* wants to show the world how Americans are helping others and how others with a different type of government are suffering because they don't have a torture democracy. They don't want me to contribute to charities because they want to alienate foreigners from me. They are always trying to treneg me in the letters by doing such things as emphasizing the word *sister* or in other ways reminding me of my crime and other evils I have done. One charity spelled my name *Obeschain* because I didn't give any money to them. They were saying that my saying I was sympathetic to them was BS. Another charity spelled my name *Obesehain*. They were saying that they saw me in a mental institution and that they were glad I am here and are laughing because I am here. My name is really spelled *Obenschain*. I now think that they meant that I would open the chains that the hypnotized slaves are in.

I write to politicians all the time. I tell them that the schools are a mess. They keep forcing children to memorize trivia instead of teaching them to think. I know. The education that I got destroyed my ability to think. I memorized instead of learning how to think. History should be written so that it shows how people thought and felt in the past, instead of emphasizing names, dates, places, battles, and actions. On TV a woman said that she didn't understand how the people in Iraq allowed Saddam Hussein to stay in power. What was wrong with her? I tell you what: She has a lousy education. History should have taught her how people get into power, how leaders manipulate people, why people have made mistakes throughout history, and how people thought and have felt in the past. Why wars are fought because of thoughts and feelings, and why people think and feel the way they do, should be taught instead of asking students to memorize dates, names, and places. We, the people, are smart. Why are school administrators so stupid?

The literature is also stupid. The literature is making our children into criminals. Two nights before I murdered Jyl, I watched a show about Frankenstein. He cold-bloodedly murdered his creator's pregnant wife and killed a lot of other people violently and brutally. At the end of the show, his creator hugs him as they die together. What is wrong with people who show this mess?

That show caused me to think that I wouldn't be punished for a violent crime. The show seemed to tell me that people wouldn't hold a violent crime against me. If that show had shown violence as being shameful and disgusting, and that it alienates loving people, I feel I would never have gone ahead and killed my sister. But the *program* wanted me to kill Jyl, and they knew the show would encourage me to go ahead and stab her to death. (Someone is scornfully laughing outside my door. I don't know why they laugh at my remorse for my crime. Why?)

I wish that my mom and dad had shown me affection when I came home from school, and they asked, "Did you learn about people today? What do you think they were feeling and thinking? How did they try to be superior? How do you think they are motivated?" That would have encouraged me to think about my motivations and would have prevented me from committing my crime. Now that I have figured out the psychological laws, I don't get upset by psychological torture, and I am going to do only what gives me pleasant emotions.

I am not going to smoke, drink, take illegal drugs, be violent, or abuse others. That is because I want only pleasant emotions in my life. Anything that harms your body or harms others is not going to give you pleasant emotions. If children are taught how to think and analyze about motivation, they won't get into trouble doing illegal and harmful activities. I feel that parents ought to ask their children motivation questions and have conversations with their children about their motivations, about their parents' motivations, and about everyone's motivations—including those of their friends, political leaders, and foreigners. Why do people insist on talking about football, shopping, the weather, and other trivia when conversations about motivations would stop their children from rebelling and getting into trouble?

I don't understand why the news refuses to discuss how foreign leaders and foreign groups are motivated and why they are motivated in those ways. The news talks about what, how, which, when, and where, and never discusses why. Why do Americans sit back and let the global rich get away with controlling the literature and the media? If Americans want to know the political truth from different viewpoints, there are magazines that tell the truth as they see it. Some of them are *The Progressive Populist, The Progressive, In These Times, Dissent, The Nation, Mother Jones, The National Monitor, World Watch, The American Prospect, Fair, Extra, The Hightower, Lowdown,* and *Earth News.*

But I want to know more than what is going on. I want to know about the motivation of the people who make the news and solutions. I want to learn about creative solutions like having kids in high school attend motivation groups to discuss their problems and their motivations. I want to learn about requiring students to visit hospitals, prisons, mental institutions, nursing homes, and other places to discuss motivations with the people they are visiting and going back to school the next day to discuss what they learned in motivation groups or individual discussions. There should be clubs called the *Friends of Love* where people discuss thoughts and feelings, how to relate to one another, and what are good solutions to the world's problems. Let the *Friends of Love* have a *Love Journal* discussing the motivations of leaders and their followers, discussing good political solutions and how to write literature that helps instead of harms.

I think Americans ought to get involved and be politically active. Literature is destroying our country. Now it is time to think and analyze and teach our children how to think and analyze.

I guess you think that I sound like I have good sense. But I still believe that the government has hypnotized slaves who are torturing me for not being cooperative by refusing to psychologically torture people. I have figured out that when you are conscience courageous, you are going to have pleasant emotions. When you are a conscience coward, you are going to feel inferior and have all kinds of unpleasant emotions causing you to try to be status, social, and welfare superior to compensate for your moral inferiority.

I believe the Christians are good people because they believe in love, sympathy, and decency. I believe in turning the other cheek, forgiving seventy-seven times seven, loving my neighbor, and loving my enemy. But I don't believe that Christ was a god. I am a Unitarian. I believe there is a god, but that he had no business creating this universe with all its suffering and cruelty. He had no business creating the need to eat dead animal bodies; creating brutal diseases, like cancer, guinea worm disease, leprosy, and Alzheimer's disease, and creating ignorance of the psychological laws at birth and afterwards. He created cruelty, suffering, evil emotions, and death. I believe that it is not our fault that we sin. It is God's fault. If he hadn't created evil emotions, we wouldn't be sinning. It is our evil emotions that cause us to sin. It is God's fault that we sin.

I believe that everyone goes to paradise when they die. When people die, they lose their thoughts, emotions, and awareness that are just the chemical reactions of their bodies. When our bodies are destroyed, those chemical reactions are destroyed. We go back to where we were before we were conceived—a state of being of pure peace and unfeeling happiness. Death does not punish us for our evil during life. I believe that everyone goes to paradise when they die—both the evil and the good. I don't believe there is a heaven or hell. I believe that death is the end of life. If God could create a heaven, he never would have needed to create this universe. He probably created it in order to alleviate his own suffering. He was alone and decided he wanted entertainment. I don't blame him for his evil. He didn't create himself and couldn't help his need to create this cruel and evil universe. No one deserves to go to hell for the evils that God created.

I would never have confided my religious beliefs to you in the past because you burned people at the stake in the past. My voices tell me that a Christian is going to kill me for my beliefs. I don't care. I feel my beliefs would help people to be unafraid of death. I worship love instead of a god who created this hell of life. I don't believe in after life hell. Why should we be punished for God's evil? I believe in love; I know that being morally superior by believing in love will give you pleasant emotions. I have to admit that if I am ever in a situation of extreme poverty, war, starvation, or pain, I am going to commit pleasant suicide. I don't want to suffer in order to live. It is life that has problems that can't be solved—not death. Death has no problems whatsoever. Death has no need, suffering, or vulnerability to any problem. Death is peace and paradise. God probably wishes he could die. He must be unhappy. I would hate to have on my conscience what He has on his. He has created an evil and cruel universe. He is the one who has sinned, not man.

I guess I shouldn't be telling you about my religious beliefs because they used to burn people like me at the stake. But the *program* world protects me, and, when they pretend to kill me, I am going to live a beautiful life until I die. I am going to live somewhere in America and be given a husband who will love me very much. But I am not going to marry him. I am going to protect the *program's* cruelty by refusing to marry anyone and refusing to cooperate with them and refusing to torture people. I don't want to feel morally inferior and have unpleasant emotions because of feeling morally inferior. I am going to have pleasant emotions that are caused by being morally superior. Moral superiority is the only superiority that will give true happiness. I want to be emotion superior, and that is found only when you believe in love, sympathy, and decency.

HAPPY MOTHER'S DAY 2005

BEAUTIFUL BLOOMING BLUE SILVER

If my mother was a flower,
She would be a Sterling Blue Rose
Growing in a garden of love she would compose
Strong beautiful blue colors of love
She would bloom to me all above
Petals of humor, honor, and honesty
Would interweave her life filigree
Thorns of independence and bravery
offer me a calm canopy
Same but very different she was to me
Others were copper, iron, or steel but to me she was silvery
To me she was a rare precious heart
Giving me confidence, calm, and courage she did impart
My mother bloomed rare but so faire to me
As faire as a romantic fairy

My mom to me
Was a garden fantasy
A flower rare
That loved me as if I was rare
My love for my mom blooms without compare
I can be anywhere and she is there
My mom means love to me
As her love gives me tranquility
Mom, there will never be one to take your place
You give me grace despite my disgrace
I love you always and forever
You gave me my sense of worth forever

I LOVE YOU,
JACKIE

Jackie and Maxene in 1997 at Florida State Hospital in Chattahoochee.

Jackie in 2002

EPILOGUE

I am writing another book. I call it *Springtime at Sixty*. After thirty-eight years of marriage to Jack and after four years as a widow, I married Kenneth Kleier on the first day of spring in 1980 when I was only sixty years old.

The appendix of Possessed Mentalities lists the Kleier volunteer efforts.

Our work efforts include developing a thoroughbred horse business on forty acres of pastureland near Dunnellon, Florida. At this place, Cotton Top Farm, we had the excitement of seeing every horse we foaled win at least one race. We owned and Kenneth managed Beaver Lake Campground west of Tallahassee. We have built and sold condominiums and invested in other real estate. Our twenty-five-year marriage has been filled with interesting activities. Kenneth laughed one day and said to me, "Aren't we lucky that we have not tried to do some of the things that we have considered?" Both of us are inclined to be risk takers.

Kenneth and I fortunately own our minds. Education from life experiences has taught us to accept with equanimity doors that close. We have been enabled to live in the real world contentedly, but we are ever watchful and eager for new doors to open.

Jackie perceives our real world as an "apparent" world. Since Jackie is unable to own her mind, her life goes on in her perceived "program" world that is her world of reality. Our lives exist in our world; her life exists in her world. These coexisting worlds do not prevent friendships that are well understood by all three of us.

Jyl wrote that a world of your own closes the door on the universe and opens a door for you. One interpretation of her words for me says that when individuals possess their mentalities, it is possible to welcome closed doors and appreciate new doors when they open.

APPENDIX

Civic activities in Virginia prior to 1960:

Girl Scout leader, Parent Teacher's Association volunteer, Community Hospital Auxiliary president, Community Hospital volunteer director, Garden Club president, president of Lutheran Church Women.

Civic activities in Florida prior to 1977:

Public-relations representative for public school teachers' organization.

Recruited, trained, installed, and managed 100 Candy Stripers in Mound Park Hospital in Saint Petersburg, Florida.

Resigned from First Vice Presidency of Saint Petersburg League of Women Voters in 1978 to devote full time as an advocate for appropriate expenditure of public funds utilized for delivery of social services to severely mentally ill individuals.

Independent volunteer advocate activities February 1978 to the present:

Organized and oversaw incorporation of Association for Mending Minds, Inc. in 1978.

Loaned purchase money to AMM for house on First Avenue North in Saint Petersburg. Volunteers staffed the house that was a drop-in center for mentally ill individuals, their families, and support system members. Later, lobbying for Open-Door Center funding was successful for locating drop-in centers in other areas.

AMM placed collection jars in stores for "change" funds to disprove the belief that citizens will not support mentally ill individuals. Jars were successful fund collectors.

AMM community center staff was made up of volunteers who did not have mentally ill family members. This disproved once again that community citizens are indifferent to the needs of severely mentally ill people.

Met Senator Bob Graham in 1977 during his first campaign for Florida governor. Senator Graham was responsive to concerns regarding fragmented unfriendly delivery of human services in the state of Florida.

When Governor Graham was elected, opportunities became available to become a statewide advocate. The National Alliance for Mentally Ill Persons was developing with duplication of some Association for Mending Minds, Inc. goals. AMM was discontinued with hopes to support NAMI efforts by acquiring accountable, direct, personalized case management services for mentally ill Floridians needing to learn community living and marketplace vocational skills.

In 1980, after securing endorsements, Senator Harry Johnston and Representative Marilyn Evans-Jones sponsored passage of Florida Statute 394.4573. Hundreds of case manager positions were funded, and the seeds were sown for creation of a statewide Continuity of Care Management System in communities to be in close conjunction with community entities and families to obtain common sense quality assistance for those willing to strive for better lives.

September 1984—Assembled Florida members of NAMI to organize statewide FL NAMI.

There was refining legislation in 1983, 1984, and 1989 to perfect and enhance a Continuity of Care Management System, CCMS, free of bureaucratic red tape and poor policies for delivery of human services.

The proof in the pudding occurred when Kenneth and Maxene Kleier, as volunteer administrators of a CCMS project from 1992–1996, established neighborhood networks of care managers who worked directly with individuals, using their cars as offices. Challenges were met without useless waiting periods or needless paper shuffling.

In 1996, funds were denied to the CCMS project due to efforts of non-profit service providers who wanted the care manager positions for their entities, politicians who refused to hear the pleas of persons being served, politicians who preferred to fund personal turkeys and/or maintain patronage positions, and some entrenched bureaucrats hidden behind comfortable desks. Many bureaucrats are unwilling to shift work positions to direct in-community contact positions so that people can be helped more effectively.

Other volunteer activities:

Chairman of SHRAC (Statewide Human Rights Committee)

Chairman of Florida Council of Alcohol, Drug Abuse, and Mental Health

Advisor to Florida House of Representatives Subcommittee for Mental Health

Member of Governor's Commission for Persons with Disabilities

Member of Governor's Task Force on Community Mental Health

Advisor to HRS Inspector-General's Task Force on Evaluation of Florida Community Mental Health Centers

Establishment of a statewide network of facilitators to expedite communication between state and district social service offices. Policies and training approved and monitored by office of HRS Secretary.

Various official roles in Florida Alliance for the Mentally Ill.

Testimony in 1982 on the insanity plea before the Subcommittee on Criminal Law, Committee on the Judiciary, United States Senate.

Consistent and ongoing volunteer lobbying to date for:

Accountable appropriation of public funds by legislative bodies,

Monitoring of public funds for accountability, and

Elimination of unseemly and expensive bureaucratic processes by intelligent application of common sense to simplistic methodologies to help people as opposed to creation of fragmented complex convoluted networks of workers busy with minutiae rather than practical applications to serious considerations of human needs.

CCMS Comments and Excerpts from June 1, 1993 CCMS Flyer for Counties Served:

Continuity of Care Management System for Delivery of Human Services

A CCMS neighborhood unit consists of a CCMS Unit Manager and Care Managers. County CCMS Roving Care Managers, CCMS Center Staff, and CCMS Volunteers offer support to neighborhood CCMS units.

CCMS is an uninhibited strong advocate for all individuals and their families. CCMS is designed to offer all citizens someone to turn to for coordination and integration of community supports and resources that are available or resources that can be developed.

CCMS exists to demonstrate that no one should ever feel alone. CCMS proves that helping people does not need to be bureaucratized by offering easy access to personalized assistance.

CCMS Care Managers, who are assigned to specific neighborhood areas to work independently, are free to act as friend and advocate, and make home visits, if desired. Home and automobile offices of CCMS Care Managers make living and working within their own neighborhoods friendly, prompt, comfortable, and convenient.

CCMS
    Facilitates grassroots planning for community service needs and legislative budget requests.
    Provides accountability to individuals served, elected officials, communities served, and taxpayers.
    Maximizes manpower hour productivity.
    Minimizes travel costs for recipients of services, CCMS personnel, and community caregivers
    Creates community consciousness for promotion of public/private partnerships to offer assistance to fellow citizens.
    Prevents crises by early intervention and interdiction.

Provides interfacing with city, county, state, and federal entities to alleviate barriers to care for citizens.

Outreaches as neighbor-to-neighbor; may facilitate neighborhood events to develop communication between neighbors.

Eliminates "caseloads". Populations of neighborhoods develop CCMS Care Manager WORKLOADS.

Offers a vehicle for equitable care statewide. When statewide, CCMS will provide consistent ongoing tracked care management for all registered CCMS individuals and their families wherever they may reside or travel within the state of Florida.

About the Author

Maxine Mardell Shank was born one Saturday afternoon at three o'clock on May 31,1919. She entered this world in the front parlor of her mother's childhood antebellum home near Broadway, Virginia. She lived with her parents in the country until she was seven and then the family moved to Harrisonburg, Virginia. She has had many addresses through the years but has been a resident of Florida since 1960.

Maxine graduated from Harrisonburg High School in 1937 and from Madison College, now named James Madison University, in 1941 with a Batchelor of Science degree. She has continued her academic education through the years and has had fun collecting many extra college credits.

She was secretly married to John (Jack) Teaford Obenschain October 15, 1938. A formal wedding was held on August 26, 1941. Maxine and Jack were married until his death at age sixty-two on February 3, 1976. On April 20, 1980, Maxene married Kenneth Carl Kleier to whom she is still married. She changed the spelling of her first name to Maxene when she became involved with selling in the fall of 1976. She believed sales would be better if clients noted and remembered Maxene. Maxene feels very fortunate to have found two individuals who have been supportive and helpful with her multiple volunteer and work efforts while providing interesting companionship.

Maxene has taught school for fifteen years, has been a real estate salesperson, has owned and managed a restaurant, managed her first husband's medical office for six years, and with Kenneth owned and managed a thoroughbred horse farm for five years. She has been a volunteer lobbyist for twenty-five years. Her life has been a blend of glad and sad times that have offered her many lessons—some happily learned, some reluctantly learned. Some lessons wanted; some lessons unwanted.

978-0-595-34436-9
0-595-34436-4